The Memories Continue

Stories of my youth, tributes to Prisoners of War Local Artist and Prominence of the Woodson Lewis Family.

Leo Wright

authorHOUSE®

AuthorHouse™
1663 Liberty Drive
Bloomington, IN 47403
www.authorhouse.com
Phone: 833-262-8899

Published by AuthorHouse 06/15/2022

ISBN: 978-1-6655-6159-4 (sc)
ISBN: 978-1-6655-6158-7 (e)

Print information available on the last page.

This book is printed on acid-free paper.

To my beautiful wife who is gone from us in body only and forever remains in our thoughts and prayers.

Table of Contents

Section 1:   Dedications 1

Section 2:   Endorsements 3

Section 3:   Special Thanks 7

Section 4:   Short Stories of the 1940's & 1950's 9

Section 5:   Procurement & Awarding of Prisoner of
             War Medal..137

Section 6:   Disclaimer 139

Section 7:   The Story of Willie Orville Paxton
             Prisoner of War Serial Number 35 708 735 141

Section 8:   Background - Omar Lyle Shuffett 207

Section 9:   Prominence 269

Section 10: A Tribute to Greensburg's Talented Artists 307

Section 11: Family Photos of the author and family -
             1940's & 1950's 315

Section 12: One Final Tribute to my beautiful wife
             who is gone from us in body only and
             forever remains in our thoughts and prayers 323

SECTION 1

DEDICATIONS

* * *

-----Although this book will contain numerous stories, I could not in all good conscious omit the two gentlemen in Section 7 & Section 8, **Willie Orville Paxton and Omar Lyle Shuffett** who sacrificed years of their youth, surviving under dire and unacceptable circumstances and living conditions in war time and return home to raise a family, earn a living the ole' fashioned way.

* * *

-----**Willie Orville Paxton** was interned as a prisoner of war under the control of Nazi Germany's Third Reich in Germany for a period of 334 days during World War II. **Omar Lyle Shuffett** was interned as a prisoner of war under the Imperial Japanese Army of Japan for a total of 1,215 days in the Philippines.

-----It is with great pride that I dedicate this book to all **United States Veterans**, whose military service has protected this nation since the day our forefathers landed at Plymouth Rock. Our veterans have given unselfishly of their time, talents and too often their lives in order that that we may live in freedom.

-----Their presence is noted in our everyday lives and in cemeteries around the world filled with white crosses, with and without names signifying that these brave Americans may never come home physically but spiritually they are in our hearts and minds daily.

-----Our hero's, now silent, lie beneath the serene surroundings of God's green earth, yet they seem to say, "Be Stalwart America, we are still here."

-----Thank you Veteran and God Bless!!!!!

*　*　*

------This volume of "Greensburg Memories" is dedicated to my wonderful father and mother, **A.T. "Tom" Wright and Morton Earl Blakeman Wright.** The gifts of life that they gave me will always be remembered and that have hopefully been passed on to my wonderful children.

*　*　*

-----To **Laura Johnson and Lanny Tucker** who have always provided me the answers to my questions and provided research that has enabled me to publish my feeble writings.

*　*　*

-----To my 3rd great grandchild **Koby James Johnson**. He is as of this writing beginning to "cooo" a little, look around and tries to smile. He is, as are all great grandchildren very cute and of course, very smart. To you KJJ, I wish you well as I will probably be gone on to a greater place prior to you becoming old enough to read and comprehend this fugal writing. But you must always know my man, that I loved you "Oh So Much!!!!"

*　*　*

SECTION 2

_❧_

ENDORSEMENTS

* * *

"So much of our history is reduced to textbooks full of dates, events and locations. What we often lack are the first-hand, personal stories and "lessons learned" by those who have lived through- and to a great degree - created our history. With Leo Wright's _"Greensburg Memories"_, we get an intimate look at his close-knit community stat shaped life and the lives of countless residents. Through his vivid memories and colorful storytelling, future generations will have front-row access to a s very special place and time."

Dave Adkinson
Past President Kentucky Chamber of Commerce
Past President - Ky Chamber of Commerce

* * *

At times I laughed. At times, I cried. But every time I picked up Leo Wright's book to read the next story, I knew I had made a good choice.

I've known Leo only for a short time, but I have found him to be a person of deep life awareness and wisdom for living. Reading his short stories of personal life experiences will confirm this for you.

Each story reads like the stroke of an artist's brush. It won't be long in fact before you feel as I do, as if you've known Leo Wright all your life.

Leo's book is an engaging library of stories that you'll find entertaining and enlightening.

Steve McSwain
CEO, Foundation for Excellence in Giving, Inc

* * *

The stories of Leo Wright's growing up in Kentucky will take the reader back in time when small towns were the place to grow and enjoy life. The people and adventures Leo describes made me think back to those (mostly) wonderful times I experience of growing up in the 1950's in Kentucky. Enjoy the tales as you relive leo's experiences in Greensburg, a place just south of heaven!

Robert Boyle,
President, Technology Risk Management LLC
(A friend of the author for over 30 years)

* * *

Leo Wright's collection of memories and stories of his youth is a refreshing time out from the relentless pounding from 24-7 cable news and internet! You can feel the cadence of the cranking ice cream freezer on a Saturday afternoon, feel the heat from the destructive flames as they destroyed the local school and sweat with every poke of the chuck-a-luck! Each story takes the reader back to a different time, a time of community, family and those solid small-town values! I read the stories from a familiar perspective as I've had the honor to know and work with Leo in his professional capacity as a manufacturing executive and as a personal coach and consultant to numerous industries and businesses. For those not having that pleasure, those stories will introduce you to this accomplished, elegant and dignified Kentucky Gentleman! Enjoy this trip back to a gentler time and relish our honorary citizenship of the Greensburg community!

Michael T. Baker
Director, Hancock County Industrial Foundation

*   *   *

Leo's stories invite us to consider the best parts of life together, community, love and family. Reading these stories takes me back to when I heard him tell some of them in the company of his wife, Joyce. Then and now, these stories recall an important truth for me, simple moments are the best moments.

Rev. Darren Brandon
Pastor, St. Paul Methodist Church

*   *   *

On paper, Colonel Leo Wright is polished, articulate, warm and charming. Just like he is in person. I loved reading his stories of a time I did not know - the era, the small town, the lifestyle. His passion for everything he touches - his military service, commitment to our servicemen, his writing and his kindness - flow through the pages of this book.

Sara Shaw
Executive Director
The Forum at Brookside

SECTION 3

---❧---

SPECIAL THANKS

-----To **Martha Howard (Pickett) Bardin,** a special thanks for her invaluable input relative to the story of "Telephone Calls 1950's." Martha Howard's mother, Lynxton Pickett was one revered telephone operators of our time.

----To Willie **Sharon (Paxton) Head**, a special thanks for her openness and sharing of information during this process to properly state the events being discussed in "The Story of Willie O Paxton." Her devotion to her father and the sharing of her conversations with him about his war experience made this section what it is, a stirring epic of trials and tribulations of a young man serving half of his military tenure in a Nazi prison camp.

-----To **Ruthie Brummell (Lewis) Derrick** for her devotion of time to ensure that this most prominent family was properly portrayed. Her editing and corrections were invaluable. Her insight into the presentation was of great benefit and her willingness to assist was most professional.

------- To **Carolyn & Mike McDaniels and Fran & George Stroud** for helping fill in the blanks on Omar Lyle Shuffett's career.

Their input was most informative and helpful and it enabled me to provide the reader with a more deeper insight into the life of SSGT Omar Lyle Shuffett.

----- A very special thanks to my wonderful daughters, **Angela Laposki** and **Susan Bell** who have been a tremendous joy to me, have provided unparalleled support and I will be eternally grateful to them for their love and understanding. Angela read volume one and reminded me that "One thing we leave behind us is Memories." And for that comment I'm keeping Memories in the title.

SHORT STORIES OF THE 1940'S & 1950'S

Chapters

Greensburg's Minnesota Fats
The McVickers
The Maddest I Ever Saw My Father
Burning Of Greensburg School
The Saddest Christmas Ever
Asleep At the Altar
The Only Time I Ever Head My Father Curse
Kozy Korner
Mr. W. B. Owens
Death Fall Into The Rock Quarry
You Killed My Dog
Grandparents
Grandparents - Leo & Kate Blakeman
Grandparents - Mose & Elviria Wright
My Celebrity Friend "A Hero Among Us"
Permastone
The Chuck-A-Luck
Fold Up Desk

Mumblety Peg
Mr. Charles Bloyd - Volume II
Jack Allen Sanders
Cross & Easter Sunday - Buckner's Hill
Construction Of A "GATE" across "A GAP"
Telephone Calls 1950's
A New Car & Death On The "S" Curves
Another Use for Shaving Lotion
Money Made And Lost
The Last Year on Henry Street

Greensburg's Minnesota Fats

I suppose every town, big and small, at least In the 1950's had a pool room. Greensburg was no exception. Our pool room was located on north main street two doors down from the Baptist Church and next door to the dry-cleaning shop.

Now, contrary to many opinions, the pool room was not a dark, sinister evil place. In fact, it was just the opposite. There was always a friendly atmosphere, whether one was playing pool or not. Of all my years spent going to the pool room I can never remember an incident of argument or fighting. This may have happened, but I was not aware of it.

Now, I spent my fair share of time in the pool room, as did a lot of other young lads my age. The pool room would open about nine o'clock in the morning and remain open until about eight or nine o'clock in the evening, six days a week.

The interior of the pool room consisted of a lunch counter with about eight stools on the left side as you entered the establishment. On the right side was a bench where onlookers could watch the pool games. The bench seat was raised to about four feet off the floor for better viewing. It was about ten to fifteen feet long to accommodate the loafers and on lookers. As I remember there were about 10 tables. The table at the front was where most of the watchable action took place. Anyone could play at the table, but mostly pool shooters with greater skill occupied this table.

All the tables were lite by a florescent light fixture about three feet long consisting of two bulbs and hanging on a chain from the ceiling and could be turned on and off by a pull chain. The price for a game of pool is somewhat vague for me now but I believe it was a quarter. The front table was the cleanest and had the best cover of green felt. The second table was clean and well maintained. The third table got a little grimmer and so on down the line until he last table where nobody really wanted to play.

A variety of pool games were played there, rotation, eight ball, nine ball and bank. The game of billiards was not played there as far as I can remember. Almost all the games played at the front two or three tables was the game of bank pool.

The winter months provided this elegant establishment with the most participants especially when the tobacco market was being conducted. Rainy days would ensure that the pool hall was overflowing with participants and and onlookers.

This establishment was owned by Mr. Holland Pickett and Mr. Clayton "Tater" Milby. Mr. Pickett was a quiet respected man sporting a beautiful family consisting of his wife, two sons and one daughter. "Tater" was single as well as I can remember. Between these two gentlemen an orderly business was conducted.

"Tater" was a tall thin person standing a little over six feet and how he got the name "Tater" I never knew, but he did have one most distinguishing trademark in that he had a stutter that was consistent every time he opened his mouth to speak. This did not detract from his being a very likable person. He was also an expert pool player. I understand that he would take trips and engage other pool sharks at varying location for tournaments involving betting and I understand he would come away quite often with some winnings. I am not personally aware of these competitive pool tournaments (if that's the right word), however it was always a conversational piece around the pool hall. All this is background leading up to the story of "Greensburg's Own Minnesota Fats."

Before getting to that, let me introduce you to the real Minnesota Fats, Rudolf Walter Wanderone Jr. was an American professional billiards player, knows also as "New York Fats, "Fatty", "The Bank Shot Bandit", The Fat One", "Triple Smart", "Dean of the Green", "Double Smart Fats", etc. He stood 5',10" tall and is noted to have weighted as much as 300 pounds.

He was born in 1913 in Washington Heights, a section of New York City. Even as a youngster he was a showman while spending many hours playing billiards. After gaining some fame, he would travel country to pool rooms and announce, "Can you believe how many so-in-sos wants to hustle me?" Although never winning a world championship, "Fats" was Pool's top orator, comedian and publicity machine. He once claimed to have won two thousand dollars (when that was big money) on a bet he could make a cue ball stop upon a single strand of human hair. The story goes, he made it on his second of three chances a cross-corner shot. He was immortalized in the movie, "The Hustler", played by Jackie Gleason and released on September 25, 1961. "Fats" died in Nashville, Tennessee on January 15, 1996 always being remember as one great pool shark.

Now that you know about the infamous "Fats", let me tell you about Greensburg's own Minnesota Fats. He was not fat, he was small, even little as some might describe him. He was my school mate and a most likable young man. As a lad, he had sugar diabetes. We were in the same grade in school. When in grammar school, it has been on several occasions, that he would slump over at his desk and almost pass out due to low sugar content in his veins. As a cure, the teacher would dispatch someone to Coffey's Restaurant directly across from school to purchase a Double Cola, bring it back and get our own "Minnesota Fats" to drink. He would slowly drink the beverage which was high in sugar content and as the sugary liquid slowly made its way through his digestive system he would revive, become coherent again and everything would return to normal in the classroom.

Well, that's all well and good Leo, but are you going to let us about "Greensburg's Minnesota Fats?" Yes, I am. His name was William David Blakeman, sometimes known as "Little David". He was born March 21, 1936 in Green County. After graduating high school, he married and became a devoted father of three. David was always gainfully employed and was a respectable member of our fair city.

In the years of say 1948 thru 1954, David held a command presence in Pickett and Milby Pool Room. He was absolutely a natural when it came to handling a pool cue and manipulating the cue ball. A cue ball is usually a white or off-white ball, that is to be struck by the pool cue (stick) and thrust forward so as to hit the designated numbered pool ball. The cue ball can be slightly heavier than the other ten colored balls. David mastered the game of bank, eight ball, nine ball and rotation pool early in life and was as good as most of us had ever seen. He was short of statue and slight of build, but he handled that pool stick like it was magic.

His pool shots were carefully planned and executed. A lot of pool players will shoot the cue ball at a fast rate of speed and when connecting with the appropriate target, it would send the appropriate pool ball on a fast route toward the side or end pockets on the pool table. No so with David. His stroke was smooth and never hurried. His pool shots were always executed at a slow rate of speed. This allowed for the pool ball to take advantage of the appropriate amount of "English" placed on the cue ball. The "English" on a cue ball is what is referred to as sidespin applied to the cue ball, hitting right or left of the vertical centerline which generates the proper amount of side spin. This "English" can and does provide planned movement in the cue ball and then be transferred to the appropriate numbered pool ball being hit. In addition to making the pool shot at hand, positioning the cue ball for the next planned shot was equally as important as making the current shot. David could position the cue ball for the next shot by running the cue past the numbered ball be shot or reverse the cue ball by applied reverse "English" be striking the cue ball very close to the bottom making the cue ball "backup" or striking the cue ball high or low on the side depending on which way one wanted the cue ball to traverse after the shot in preparation for the next shot.

The game of Bank Pool was the favored game at the Pickett & Milby Pool Hall in Greensburg. Bank pool is played using a full rack of pool balls numbered from 1 thru 10 plus a cue ball. Bank shots can be made from one rail, two rails, three rails or four rails (sides of the pool table). In serious pool, which is what David always shot, one must call the shot, i.e. "three ball inside pocket," etc. His approach to all shots would be slow and methodical.

I don't see the need to get into the weight of the pool cue or the professional positioning of the hand and fingers forming a hole for the pool cue to be held. You can rest assured that our "Minnesota Fats" was most definitely aware of these fine points of shooting pool.

"Little David" was always a contender. Gambling was not permitted in our pool hall, but there was some serious pool played there. He was an inspiration to all, young and old for his self-made professionalism. I can tell you that it was amazing to sit and watch him make pool shots that were seemingly impossible to accomplish. When he was playing there was always a crowd, quietly sitting or standing and watching our own "Minnesota Fats" perform.

I, David and all the other pool playing classmates graduated in 1954 and went our separate ways. I saw David play a few times after graduating and although he now was supporting a new job and family, he did not appear to have lost any skills of the pool game.

After graduating and leaving for college I did not see David much and as our lives and careers grew separately, I hardly ever saw him after 1960. Much to my and others sorrow, David died on May 17, 1968 at the youthful age of 36. Even though he lived a short life, he lived it to the fullest. He will always be remembered as a likeable person, friendly to all and the extremely skilled pool player that he was. He may have lost some pool games and I'm sure he did but, in all honestly, I cannot ever remember seeing him lose a game of pool.

Although it never happened, I wonder what have been the outcome if David could have engaged Minnesota Fats is a game of bank pool? What do you think, huh?

The McVicker's

The following is not an exciting story or one that will keep you in suspense, but it's a presentation of myself and a few of my friends and our having the opportunity to meet some lads for their summer visit to their grandparents. I suppose I wrote this to preserve the time and experience more for myself than for the readers of this publication. I hope you won't be disappointed. Maybe, just maybe you might have had a similar experience. Think so?

In the 1940's and 1950's a loveable elderly couple, Mr. and Mrs. Walter Russell lived on Columbia Avenue in the second house from the corner from Riverview Drive on the right side of the street going toward Sardin's Ford Road. Their daughter, Lucille, was married to a Mr. Wesley McVicker from Cincinnati. Each summer Mrs. McVicker would come to Greensburg. She brought with her two boys Norman and Charles. They would come to visit their grandparents every summer and stay for an extended period, some four to eight weeks.

The McVicker boys were first noticed by us one warm summer day as we were playing baseball on the lot on the corner of Columbia Avenue and Riverview Drive, directly opposite by the home of Mr. and Mrs. Ashbrook. They came over to where we were playing, we met each other and from that point on developed a relationship that would last for years to come.

As the seasons of summers would include warm comfortable days, we always look for the McVicker boys to come and visit their grandparents. Mr. and Mrs. Russell were lovable and friendly grandparents and they were always very amenable to our playing with their grandchildren.

Mr. Russell's daily routine, in the spring and summer would be to come out early in the morning, sit in the porch swing and usually read the newspaper. He was a very well-dressed gentleman and most friendly with all of us young lads. Mrs. Russel was equally friendly but didn't have as much interface with us as did Mr. Russell.

The boys Norman and Charles would interface with us in about all out activities, movies, baseball, swimming, etc.

We (Greensburg) boys would often go to the Russell's in the morning and end up getting fed lunch. Mr. Russell would always a cheery greeting for us.

It was interesting to note that Mr. McVicker was the owner and operator of the Play-Doh factory in Cincinnati. Play-Doh is a modeling compound for young children to make arts ad crafts projects at home. The product was first manufactured in Cincinnati, Ohio as a wallpaper cleaner in the 1930's. Play-Doh was then reworded and marketed to Cincinnati schools in the mid 1950's. Play-Doh is composed of flour, water, salt, boric acid, and mineral oil. This combination of ingredients creates a soft, squeezable, non-toxic, and reusable modeling compound. We did not use the Play-Doh, but we were impressed that Norman and Charles's father was the owner of a manufacturing facility.

The years that the McVicker boys visited and interfaced were 1946 thru 1951 when we were ten to fifteen years old. The visits stopped after 1952 as other activities kept the McVicker's in Cincinnati.

After they stopped visiting, we never corresponded. As we would pass the Russell's home, we would always wave to Mr. Russell who was most of the time occupying his usual seat on the front porch swing. As we all grew up, went to college started and to work we would remember Norman and Charles McVicker.

Sadly, on April 19, 1964 Mr. Russell passed away. Norman, Charles and their father came to Greensburg to act as pallbearers for Mr. Russell. I was living in Louisville and was not aware of the passing of our friend for some time. When I found out about the passing, I wrote Norman and Charles a note of condolence. I did not hear back from either of them. In August of 1964 Mr. and Mr. Russell sold their home on Columbia Avenue and moved away. Sometimes one just has to grow up I guess!!

Ah well, don't put the book down yet, the next story is more interesting!!

The Maddest I Ever Saw My Father

This will be a short story and it will not take long to present the core subject and the conclusion which I think you will find most interesting. As I will state in another chapter, I only heard my father curse once, so here I will tell you the story of the maddest I ever saw my father. As the reader progresses through this story, it will become readily apparent that my father was the most honest upstanding gentleman that anyone will ever meet, and the events of this chapter will certainly solidify that fact.

The fall elections for elected officials in Greensburg in Green County, Kentucky and National offices were held the 1st Tuesday after the 1st Monday in November. As this was 1948, election day was November 2nd. This was a big day for the citizens of Greensburg and Green County. Everybody wanted to vote and wanted to vote for a winner and there was a big effort by both political parties to ensure that they could amass every eligible voter to vote for the party and candidate of their persuasion. In those days, we had two political parties in our community, Democratic and Republican. Remember now, this was the 1948 and before all other offspring political parties were apparent to our political scene.

As most everyone was aware, there were political personnel of both parties working hard on election day to see that all eligible voters representing the party or office of their choice were provided an opportunity to cast their ballots. There were cars available to go to residences, pick up selected votes and take them to the polls to vote. Without intention to offend anyone here, the fact was that money was distributed on election for various and sundry reasons.

Some voters would get money or some article of clothing for their effort in supporting the candidate of their party's choice. On this election day, dad had delivered merchandise shipped through The Railway Express to Greensburg customers in the early morning and had gone to the farm late in the morning to complete what chores he deemed necessary.

He returned home a little after one pm, had dinner (lunch) with mother, bathed and redressed in more presentable clothing. It just so happens he had bought a couple of new outfits about a month or so prior and chose to wear one of these outfits on this election day.

After lunch, dad proceeded to drive his truck to downtown Greensburg, parked on the square and engaged in some conversation with some other fellow citizens of Greensburg and Green County. They talked about the election, the crowd, the weather I suppose any other subject that might have arisen.

The group soon broke up, each going their respective way, with dad making his way to his polling place. On his way to vote, he encountered a lady (whom he was acquainted, as Greensburg was a small town) and as they were about to exchange greetings, the lady said, "Well, there's Tom in his election clothes!!!" I do not know his immediate reaction. I would suspect that being the gentleman he was he did not reply to this outlandish accusation, but I can guarantee you he was absolutely astounded at her remark.

Without a reply or further remarks, he immediately returned to his truck and came home. Well, by that time school was out and I had come home. I was sitting in the living room, reading a book as I recall, when dad came home. Without a word, he came into the house, went immediately to the bedroom and as he was changing clothes, he told mother of the incident. He told her he had never been hurt as bad in his life and he was returning to the farm and would be back in time for supper. As our house was quite small, I overheard the conversation and was surprised to say the least.

Dad came home from being at the farm and we sat down for a quiet supper. Nothing was said about the election or the incident. Dad never mentioned it and I did not raise the matter. I did find out who the lady who offended dad was and knowing her as she was, it was not intended as an unkind remark. It just came across that way. Kidding or not, it was a mean nasty remark to make to such a fine man.

Nevertheless, it hurt my father severely and through my mother I would hear of his hurt in years to come.

Burning Of Greensburg School

March 2,1950 was a pleasant day and evening, temperature in the high 60's and low 70's. Windows and doors for most residences were not closed to take advantage of the pleasant evening air and it was quiet on Henry Street, as in the entire city of Greensburg. There was nothing special going on, tonight, it was bargain night the movie at the Franklin Theatre and the movie was "Sarge Goes to College" starring Alan Hale, Freddie Stewart and June Preisser. The movie was over somewhere between 9 p.m. or 10 p.m.

There were no plays or basketball games scheduled at the local high school. The only other two establishments open in Greensburg as best as I remember would be the Pickett and Milby Pool Room and A. Ennis & Son restaurant. The drug stores would have already closed around nine thirty or so as usual. All was quiet in our serene community.

Sometime a little after 2 a.m. on Wednesday morning, March 3, 1950, we were awakened by the fire alarm. When the fire alarm sounded in Greensburg it could be heard all over town. Immediately we got up, Dad got dressed and headed for the firehouse. He, like a lot of other men in town were members of the Greensburg Volunteer Fire Department. The fire house was located on Columbia Avenue just behind the Gulf station on Main Street on a garage facing Columbia Avenue. Just as an aside, the fire house was never locked. Access to the fire station was thru two overhead doors with the fire engine being parked on one side and equipment, firefighting clothes, etc. on the other.

The building was a two-story structure with the second-floor space being used by the fire department for meetings and social gatherings. I remember accompanying my father to some of these gatherings where after a short business meeting a big Rook game would be started and continued until around 10 p.m. or so. The second floor was accessible by a wooden staircase on the right of the building. In later years the upstairs was converted to serve as a rental apartment.

Ah yes, back to the story, the school is on fire! It was discovered when Miss Louie Clark who lived across the street from the school first noticed the fire burning on the first floor and notified Mr. W. B. Owen, the school Superintendent, who resided just down the street. Mr. Owen called the fire into the police department who initiated the fire alarm. Mr. Owen then entered the first floor of the school and found the halls to be filled with smoke and a blazing fire coming from the roof.

By this time, the police department had notified the fire chief Mr. Woodrow Squires, who immediately went to the fire house. The process, upon arrival of the volunteer firemen was to raise the doors, start the fire engine and by that time several other volunteer fire fighters would be arriving and two or three would get on the back of the fire truck to ride to the fire. The firefighters who could not get a ride on the fire engine would drive their private automobiles or trucks to the fire. Equipment was rudimentary in those days. The individual equipment was composed of fire hats, maybe some boots and a coat, the best that I remember. I do not remember any trousers or oxygen tanks, etc. The truck contained two ladders that had to be manually engaged to suit the conditions of the fire that was occurring at that time.

On this day, it was readily determined that the fire in the Greensburg Grade and High School building located on Hodgenville Avenue was going to be a huge undertaking. The fire of undetermined origin started in the south side of the building. As the fire raged, most every resident nearby managed to get a front row seat on surrounding street corners to view this huge blaze. As the intensity of the fire increased the fire departments from Campbellsville and Columbia were called and they responded accordingly by sending full crews and appropriate fire -fighting equipment.

I, like all kids made their way to the school to watch the raging inferno. The fire was so intense that (as some of us did) a rock could be thrown thru the windows and the rock would make a hole in the glass without the glass breaking as the heat had transformed the brittle glass panes into almost molten particles.

Sparks began to fly quite heavily across the surrounding homes and garages. I was standing on the corner of the alley that connected Hodgenville Avenue and Henry Street. My dad came up to me and said, "Son, go home, get the water hose and wet down the roof and the garden, to keep the sparks from igniting the buildings and garden." "Yessir," I replied and off I ran. As I was getting the hose out and hooked up to the hydrant, I could see some big sparks hitting the garden with seemingly a heavy glow. I thought the grass was going to catch fire. I immediately put water all over the garden, giving it a soaking and then sprayed water on the roof of the house and garage.

Greensburg School was originally constructed in 1921. The school burned December 21, 1927, was reconstructed in 1928 and was now burning again on March 2, 1950. This picture is of the school as I remember it prior to the fire. Notice the stone foundation in the lower righthand corner and extending to the left and right almost the length of the building. The corner houses the boys dressing room, joined by the cafeteria on the right and basement, etc. on the left. The rock foundation noted here is said to be the same foundation as originally constructed in 1921. Folklore will tell you that a foundation built on again after a destructive fire will only lead to another fire. This structure was later demolished in 2006 to make way for the current intermediate school. The stone foundation is now gone.

The fire departments from Greensburg, Campbellsville and Columbia worked thru the night controlling the fire from spreading. At approximately 8 a.m. on Wednesday morning the fire was brought under control. Cleanup was started and planning was undertaken by the principal and schoolteachers to determine if school would continue and at what locations. Everybody wanted to help, but only so much could be done. The fire fighters and volunteers were provided coffee by the Rotary Club and the fiscal court fed the group.

Now that the fire was over, the clean-up was to begin. As the massive tasks of cleaning up the burned out building and surrounding grounds, the process of purchasing new equipment, books, etc., loomed ahead. The most immediate and critical task was to determine where would classes be held to continue the education of Greensburg's youth. It was truly a community wide effort and plans were finalized that some classes would be held in the Methodist and Presbyterian churches and the Franklin Theatre among others.

Me and my classmates were in the eighth year of elementary school and we were bussed to Summersville school to complete our school year and afterward completing the eighth grade our graduation ceremony was held in the Franklin Theatre.

The Veteran's buildings (formerly barracks) were brought here in 1947 to house classes for military veterans were to be used for classes. The 1954 graduating class of Greensburg High School started our freshman year of 1951 in these buildings. In addition, several one room schools from the county were utilized to provide addition classroom space.

Plans were developed that the Superintendent and staff would have offices in the basement of the Greensburg Deposit Bank. Other buildings on school grounds such as the cannery would be utilized for classrooms. "It will be a makeshift undertaking, but it's the best we can do right now," stated school officials.

The school building was valued at $200,000 but replacement cost was estimated to be much higher. With insurance coverage of $100, 000, additional funding would need to be procured. Fire damage was estimated to be $200,000 same as the valuation of the building. Plans for a bond issue were developed thru Stein Bros and Boyce and Bankers-Bond of Louisville as the fiscal agencies for contracting the bond sale.

And speaking of replacement costs, most everyone, students, teachers, coaches, school employees, etc. lost personal items in the fire. In the case of the basketball team, we had our "tenny" shoes (yes, excuse the spelling but that's what they were called), socks, maybe some school supplies, etc. in the locker room and probably some paper, writing utensils, etc. in desks upstairs or stored in wall lockers. Arrangements were made with the insurance firm of

Cowherd and Calhoun for replacements of personal items lost in the fire. I remember that mom and dad had just purchased me a new pair of "tenny shoes."

A few days after the fire, Cowherd and Calhoun Insurance Agency asked everyone that needed to submit a claim to come to their offices. So I went to the office, got in line and awaited my turn to inform them of my lost items. Everyone was pleasant and did not question the validity of claimed lost items. My loss was only for my new "tenny shoes" and they issued me a check in a few days for the small amount.

Reconstruction of the school building would be via the sale of revenue bonds. Superintendent W. B. Owen and W. C. Burress procured and delivered the $400,000 in revenue bonds to Pohl & Company of Cincinnati to be available for construction of the new building. The contract for the construction of the new school building was awarded to Derby Construction Company. The new reconstruction began and lasted through September 1951, when an announcement was made that Greensburg school would re-open on October 1, 1951 for an evolving full class schedule.

Everyone in the Greensburg and Green County community helped our community and school officials thru this arduous task in some way. Only the teachers really know how difficult a task was and a gracious debt of gratitude is owed to them.

After the burning, the goal was to get the school reopened again for class and related ceremonies. A partial list of maintaining school activities is as follows:

1950

(1) The Junior-Senior banquet was held April 24th, with the theme, "Hitch Your Wagon to A Star." (There was no such activity known as "Prom" in the 1950's.)

(2) Baccalaureate Service for 74 seniors of Greensburg High School would be held at the Greensburg Presbyterian

Church at 3pm, Sunday, May 11th. William R. Reed, student pastor of the church will deliver the message. Special music is planned by a combined choir made up of choirs of all the local churches.

(3) Commencement exercises for the senior class will be held at The Greensburg Methodist Church on Friday, May 19th. Mr. John Brooker, Secretary of the Kentucky Executive Education Association will be the guest speaker with Mr. W. B. Owen, Superintendent will be presenting the diplomas.

(4) Greensburg High School started Monday, September 4, 1950 with opening exercises for the high school, seventh and eighth grades at the Franklin Theatre. One entire side was filled with the Freshman class, possibly the largest number of students ever enrolled in GHS.

(5) The Home Economics class will use the basement of the Presbyterian Church while quarters for the agricultural boys will be set up in the Farm Shop.

(6) Over 100 children are at the Baptist Church in the 4, 5, and 6th grades while around 90 children enrolled in grades 1 through 3 are at the Methodist Church.

(7) Sixth, seventh and eighth grades are at the Summersville school. New desks have been ordered for these students.

1951

(8) On Sunday, May 20th, the Baccalaureate Services was held for the senior class, parents and friends.

(9) Commencement Exercises were held on Friday, May 25th at the Greensburg Methodist Church. Dr. Huntsman, pastor of the Presbyterian Church in Glasgow, was the guest speaker.

(10) The Senior Banquet was held Saturday, May 12th in the Recreation Room of the Presbyterian Church. Dinner was served by the Sophomore girls.

School Re-opening 1951

(11) The Greensburg School will open Monday, October 1st in the new school building.

(12) Plans are to make up days students have missed so far on holidays and Saturdays so the school term to be out by the last of May as previously scheduled.

(13) Bus routes will be published in the Record-Herald on September 21st. Buses cannot go off main roads and cannot go to every pupil's home, but no pupil will walk any farther than they were walking to their rural school.

(14) Except for the gym and part of the basement all the new building will be completed and ready for the classes to begin October 1st. Photo's courtesy of Lanny Tucker. There is conflicting documentation as the year of construction ranging from 1921 to 1923 and 1924.

Greensbrug School prior to destruction by fire

**Veteran's Buildings used for classrooms after the destruction
of Greensburg school by fire**

The Saddest Christmas Ever

Of all the stories I have written, this is by far the most challenging. I had very few sad times as a boy, but this was the saddest. It is the fault of no one especially my mother and father, but just an event that occurred in what was a very difficult time, not only for me but for my mother and father.

It has often been said, "Christmas is for Children." Every child regardless of race, where you live, economic condition, community status, etc. yearns for a big happy Christmas. And so do adults for that matter.

In 1945, we lived on Henry Street, and it had been a cold miserable winter. Lots of snow, rain, sleet, and just plain cold. Mom always put up the Christmas Tree around the first of December, as she did this year. In preceding years, from the time the tree was put up every few days there would be a new present or two under the tree. No, they weren't all my presents, but I would always look and sometimes there would be a name and sometimes there wasn't. I like most kids got a few things for Christmas and was very happy to get the presents.

Mom had not yet gone to work for the American Needlecraft. However, she would commence work there in the spring of 1946.

Then there's the Santa Claus issue, was he real, and when did he become someone other than the bearded man in a red suit driving a sleigh through the night on Christmas Eve.

Well, we are past that at this point. I remember my father would come home from work and he and mother would be very quiet and always go to bed early. As late November and early December rolled around dad and mom spent a great deal of their time in bed, ill as they might be. I remember that Dr. Simmons came to the house to visit, saw them in their bedroom and left obviously with some needed medicine and instructions. School soon let out for the Christmas holidays and although my memory is somewhat vague, I do remember that leaving school for the scheduled holidays was not a pleasant experience for me knowing that the condition of my mother and father was not exactly the best. Other kids in my class seemed to be very happy for the break in school activities, but this was not shared by me.

Realizing that Christmas Eve was getting closer I remember gathering up some of my toys and making a futile attempt at wrapping them as gifts and putting them under the tree. I distinctly remember talking with mom and dad and showing them the presents I had wrapped for Christmas. Their comments did not resonate with me then and I do not remember them now.

On Christmas Eve, I remember lying in bed in my bedroom in the back of the house and seeing the shadows dancing on the wall in the living being provided by the low burning coals in the fireplace. I thought in my own imagination that maybe it was some things for me that were being projected via the shadows over the walls and ceiling of the living room where the Christmas tree was located.

I guess I finally went to sleep and when I awoke on Christmas morning and soon discovered that the only gifts for me were the item's I had wrapped for myself. Sad, yes it was, but time proved to overcome the illness of mom and dad, school resumed in January as best as I remember with most of the talk being about what presents my fellow classmates had gotten for Christmas.

New Year's came, the tree came down, the winter finally subsided, mom and dad got well, spring had become a new season and the Christmas of 1945 soon became a thing of the past. I don't remember dwelling on it much as a ten-year old as other activities seemed to overcome the reality of the Christmas past.

As I recall, there was never any mention of the Christmas of 1945 in any of the years that followed. As I grew older, I began to remember more and more about that Christmas. All other Christmas's after that were quite pleasant. I got a few toys, food was plentiful, mom and dad both had a job and our family continued to go about the business of living and not remembering.

Now look, I'm not blaming my mother and father. I know it hurt them more than it hurt me. They were the kindest most loving two parents one could ever have. They did without to give to me, and I shall be ever thankful and grateful.

As I grew older, became married and had two beautiful children, I can assure you that no Christmas ever went without gifts for all years to come. In fact, Joyce my beloved wife and mother was a big one for Christmas and we always had a **BIG** Christmas. In later years I do remember that when handing out the gifts on Christmas Eve and Christmas morning I would accumulate my gifts and wait until everyone else had opened theirs.

It was just a thing with me that I wanted to be sure that Joyce, Angela and Susan absolutely got whatever they wanted. Ah yes, don't forget "Snooks," our beloved boxer!!! Merry Christmas Everyone!!!!!

Asleep At The Altar

As previously stated in Book 1, chapter 1, my parents attended Mount Lebanon Methodist Church in the Thurlow community. In talking with them in later years, it seemed that they were regular church goers.

Revivals in the 1940's were held by most churches at least once annually. The revival at Mount Lebanon in 1941 was held in the summer and the weather was hot to say the least. Even though five years old, I can distinctly remember going to the revival with mom and dad. Depending on the night of the week, attendance was varied. The revival would last for one week with services every evening and culminating on Sunday evening.

The actions of this chapter occurred on a Saturday night which was a big night for attendance as the crowd during the week could be somewhat light since farmers (which comprised most of the church membership) worked late in the fields and many times there was just not enough hours in the day to tend to the farming duties and attend church on the same day.

Saturday evening services before the final day of revival on Sunday would usually find the church "packed" (full). As I said, this was partly due to the day of the week being Saturday and it just seemed to be convenient to go to church on the last weekday of the revival.

As I recall the evening, we entered the church a few minutes prior to the beginning of the service. Mom and dad engaged in conversation with other church goers and we took our seats up front where the choir normally sat. I really did not notice the weather conditions and do not remember a lot about the occurrences prior to the services.

The congregation was unusually large on this night and the service was delayed somewhat as everyone was trying to find a place to sit. The minister approached the pulpit and welcomed everyone which had the effect of quieting the crowd. He quickly acknowledged that the crowd was overflowing and that the people standing in the rear of the church should be afforded a seat as the services were beginning to start a little late. As he made this announcement, the crowd began to shift a little in the pews to make room for the attendees standing in the back.

As the overflow was finding seats, the preacher made the announcement that to provide more seating, any of the children in the congregation could come down and sit on the floor next to the altar. My mother told me, "Go down and sit in front of the altar, so someone can have your seat." I did not like it because I did not want to leave my seat with parents plus I would have to parade in front of everyone to get the seating space in front of the altar. I got up and went down and sat in front of the altar. I was embarrassed because everyone in attendance was looking at me and that no other children came down to sit with me.

There I sat and I guess the service started and proceeded to where the sermon was the high point of the evening. Somewhere in the opening few minutes of service, I laid down and went sound asleep and would you believe slept through the entire service. The next thing I remember was mom waking me up. I remember being very sleepy and people saying something to me, what they were saying I do not remember.

As we were driving home, my mom said something to the effect, "That was nice of you to go down and sit in front of the altar". This did not ring any bells of satisfaction with me. Time passed. We continued to go to church on Sundays, but thank goodness, I never had to sit in front of the altar again and I never saw any other kids sit down there either.

Now, I am firmly aware this is not a very exciting story, but it was an event of my young years that I remember and maybe my children, grandchildren, etc. will get some enjoyment and pleasure of reading about "Granddad" being "Asleep At The Altar."

The Only Time I Ever Heard My Father Curse

As I have relayed in previous stories, my father was the kindest most low-key mature individual that I have ever met. He was extremely well liked by everyone and possessed a quiet demeanor that would make most people envious. Although he did not possess much of a formal education, he was mature and wise way beyond his years.

Many of you may have had the same kind of father and you can appreciate my comments, but mine was special, although it took me several years to fully understand why he was so well liked and why he conducted himself in the manner in which he did.

I never saw him mad but one time in my life and heard his curse only once and believe me I spend a lot of time with him in my youth. As you have read in volume 1, we had a small farm in the Thurlow community in Green County, Kentucky. We raised hay, tobacco, swine and cattle. We lived in town where dad ran the Railway Express Agency, delivering goods shipped by rail to businesses throughout the Greensburg community, but visited the farm every day to take care of the necessary chores and see about the animals.

Dad always maintained a small herd of steers ranging in number from about five to fifteen or twenty or so depending on timing of purchase, price, availability of hay, etc. A steer is a young neutered male calf primarily raised for beef. It was our normal practice to purchase the steers in the spring of the year, provide grain supplements administered through feed throughs and then relying on the fresh grass in the pasture fields to nourish the cattle though the summer where the goal was for them to gain weight when we would then take them to the stock market in the fall for resale.

The price of steers in the mid to late 1940's was from $12 to $15 CWT. (As a comparison, todays price (2021) is about $106 CWT.) Dad would buy the steers somewhere in the 500 - 700 pound weight range. Typical weight gain in a pasture environment is about 1-2 pounds per day.

A lot of years dad would maintain a small herd throughout the summer into the fall and winter months especially if we had an abundance of hay and the price of cattle was somewhat lower than what he desired. The goal here was to turn a profit and sometimes it was just necessary to keep the steers longer than normal.

Tending to the steers, watching them grow during the summer is a quiet pleasant experience. For those of you who have experienced the serenity of cattle grazing in a pasture field in the summertime, you fully understand what I am describing. For my readers who have not had this experience, let me attempt to inject you into such an arena of solitude. So, sit down, rest your head on the back of the chair and visualize a warm summer day, blue skies with scattered floating clouds, and a void of external noise such as cars, trucks, people in conversation, etc. Now, this should place you in a most relaxed frame of mind and complete comfort. Not quite a hypnotic state, but close. Now visualize yourself standing in a green pasture field or leaning on the pasture fence surrounded by several grazing cattle with the only noise being maybe a gentle breeze, the chewing of cud by the cattle and you are now experiencing the phenomena of being submerged in one of the most gentile conditions that exist on this earth.

Now, you can sit in your chair for the rest of the day or like dad and I, although quite content to spend the entire afternoon here, we had other chores to be accomplished.

Now, back to the subject matter at hand. Out of the herd of steers we had raised during the summer, dad selected six head of cattle that seemed to have gained enough weight to realize an acceptable return on his investment, it was time to load the steers in the cattle trailer and take them to the stock market for sale. It is a cool fall rainy day in the early 1950's and we have just loaded the steers in the cattle trailer.

The dirt lane from the highway up to the barn had become quite muddy over the past several days due to the rain and with us going in and out several times in the truck, we had created some ruts. Ruts bigger and deeper than usual I might add. The reader may wonder at this point why didn't you guys have gravel placed on the lane prior to the rainy season thereby avoiding the ruts. Good question. Now, in those days, there were two ways to get your farm lane graveled so as to maintain a good even driving surface. One was to buy gravel from the rock quarry and have the dump truck from the quarry come and spread the gravel, send them a check and the job was done.

The other way was for the farmer to receive gravel for their farm lanes was for the magistrate in your district to provide rock for the lane in return hopefully for your vote in the next election. Be as it was, it was a way of life. There was nothing considered immoral or illegal about such a practice. Well, obviously for one reason or the other we had no gravel for our lane.

As dad was the leaving the barn lot, I had stayed behind to shut the gate. Just as I was shutting the gate, dad had driven just far enough down the lane to reach the deep ruts. As he started through the muddy ruts, the trailer tilted sideway, shifting the load to the driver's side and suddenly the rear tires (especially the driver's side tire) became stuck in the mud.

Dad attempted to rock the truck back and forth to gain enough momentum to pull through the ruts. To no avail. He then opened the driver's side truck door, leaned out, looked at the spinning tire and proclaimed, "*&#%*&@&*!!" Had I heard this correctly? My father cursing!! Yep. Sure had. Wow! A first for me. He finally rocked the truck enough to drive through the ruts, stopped and waited for me to get back in the truck. Silence. Not a word. Dad drove to the stock market, unloaded the steers down the chute, got them weighted, got his cashier's check and left the stock yard.

Instead of going to our home on Henry Street, dad drove to Nally & Gibson rock quarry on Highway 61, ordered and paid for a load of gravel for the farm.

Gravel got delivered, ground dried up and passage up and down the lane was acceptable again. Dad never spoke of the outburst and neither did I. It was a once in a lifetime experience and I have recalled it many times during my life. I suppose it's our little secret.

Doesn't matter. He was still the greatest and I don't care what he said, he was a man among men and although he has now passed away, he is still THE GREATEST MAN AMONG MEN!!

History of The Kozy Korner

Introduction

The Kozy Korner, hereafter referred to as the KK, is a landmark to all Greensburg and Green County residents and to most others who have heard about it. It is not just a restaurant that stands on the corner of Main Street and 1st Alley North. It's not just a place of business housed in an old two-story brick building that was constructed in the late 1800's. It is the molding agent of activities within a small triangle. The building itself has a lot of history as the KK began occupying this building in 1942.

The KK is a standalone landmark as its history and surroundings along with significant county events such as the TGT Pipeline and the Oil Boom of the 1950's makes this such a story that will accurately and adequately relate the events and cover the relationships of other businesses surrounding the KK. This story is developed by presenting it in six segments. The three businesses, KK, Ford Motor Co. and Franklin Theatre form a triangular area that provided in the 40's and 50's a consistent flow (both day and night) of people and auto traffic. The upcoming standalone events are as follows:

Kozy Korner – The Beginning
Background of the Original Owners (Patterson and Mitchell)
Ford Dealership – "Who Gets "The First New Car"?
Franklin Theatre
Construction of Tennessee Gas Transmission Facility At Gabe
Oil Boom

<u>Kozy Korner – The Beginning</u>

I suppose every small town in America and maybe the world has an establishment that serves as a local "shrine" for all those who have lived here and to most who have heard about it. Greensburg was no different from all those other towns, and our landmark is the KK.

The KK had its beginning on Saturday 14, 1937 when it initially opened its doors. It was established by two local businessmen, Floyd Patterson and Walter Mitchell.

<u>Background - Floyd Patterson</u>

Mr. Patterson was born Friday, November 20, 1903 in Green County near Pierce, Kentucky. On Wednesday, June 26, 1929 he was married to Miss Lillian Woodward. The couple had two sons, James Stuart Patterson who died in infancy and William "Billy" Conn Patterson. Floyd was well known, well liked and highly respected by everyone.

He served as Deputy Sheriff of Green County for four years, County Tax Commissioner for eight years and for several years he was the owner and operator of The Chevrolet Sales Agency and Garage. The last elected office he held was Green County Court Clerk which lasted for four years.

I knew Mr. Patterson when he, his wife Lillian and son Billy Conn lived across from us on Henry Street in the 1940's. I have referred to him here as "Mr. Patterson" as that's what my parents told me to call him, however, he was comfortable with Floyd.

This gentleman was one of the most outgoing and friendly man a person could ever meet. Always smiling and greeting everyone, young and old. The thing that I most remember about him most was that he made the best homemade ice cream imaginable. In the spring and summer months, sometimes during the week, after the work day ended, and seemingly always on Saturday, he would get his ice cream freezer from the storage shelf in the garage, take It to the middle of the driveway near the front door of the garage and proceed to manufacture this most tasteful product a human has ever tasted in the form of peach ice cream.

What a name, "ice cream!!" The two words just do not seem to express well each other. Well, maybe a little history will help us here. The origin of ice cream be traced back to at least the 4th century. Early references include the Roman emperor Nero who ordered **ice** brought from the mountains and combined with **fruit** toppings. King Tang of Shang, China also had a method of creating **ice** and **cream** concoctions. So, Ole' King Tang must have given us the name. This dish, appropriately named "ice cream" was likely brought from China back to Europe where over time different recipes were made and finally made its way to the US. The first ice cream parlor was opened in New York city in 1776. Wow, Independence Day and ice cream all in the same year. What a country!! Now back to Floyd Patterson making ice cream.

The manually operated ice cream freezer was invented by Nancy Johnson in 1843 and patented. It was produced by William Young and advertised it as "Johnson Patent Ice-Cream Freezer". This freezer had a four- five quart capacity, takes about forty-five minutes to make and usually requiring two to four adults or a whole bunch of kids to take turns cranking because the longer one cranked the harder the ice cream mix got, making the cylinder harder to turn. No, certainly none of this electricity stuff back then, it just seemed natural to crank, crank, crank.

The recipe for a freezer of ice cream was: 5 eggs, 1 ¾ cup sugar, 1 can Carnation milk, 1 pint whipping cream, 3 teaspoons Vanilla, 1 "pinch" of salt, 1 quart of whole milk and a ten-pound bag of ice cream salt.

The ice cream mixer was a manual device of wooden construction and was operated by cranking a handle. The outer wooden pail contained crushed ice; an inner tin or pewter cylinder contained the ice cream mix to be frozen. A lid was bolted on and the handle inserted through the top of the lid and turned to freeze the milk. The device inside attached to the handle was called a dasher.

After mixing all the ingredients except the last two, any kind of fresh fruit can be added for flavoring, (peach was my favorite) then pour the mixture into container and add a quart of whole milk. Lock the container in the wooden bucket. Pack the space between the container and the wooden bucket with ice cubes and add coarse salt. Tamp the ice firmly between the container and the wooden bucket and add more salt (usually takes about ten pounds) and start cranking. As boys one of us would sit on the top of the freezer while the other cranked and then switch off. The top of the freezer was chillingly cold so Floyd would lay a towel over the top to ward off the freezing effect.

While all this manual labor was delightfully being performed, Mr. Patterson would joke with everyone, and we "young'uns" felt quite comfortable around him. When we could no longer "crank", the ice cream was deemed to be solid. After waiting a few anxious minutes, Mr. Patterson would take the crank off, sweep away some of the ice and salt on top, take the top off the container, remove the dasher and we were ready for the ice cream.

Suddenly bowls would appear, maybe some more neighbors would stroll up and everyone would line up for the treat. Mrs. Patterson would help serve us while Billy Conn, three or four years of age seemed to enjoy all the attention from everyone.

A lot of very pleasant Saturdays were spend eating ice cream at the Patterson's. As I grew older and moved on to other activities on Saturday, it seemed as if the ritual of making ice cream on Saturday just kinda' fazed itself out. But my memories never let me forget the delicious peach ice cream made by our friend and neighbor, Floyd Patterson.

Mr. Patterson died on Monday, October 2, 1950 at age 47. Funeral services were held at the home of his mother, Mrs. S. C. Patterson and burial was in Greensburg cemetery. I do not remember going to the funeral, but I do know that mom and dad went. His pallbearers were Howard Pickett, Dennis Gupton, Colby Cowherd, Paul Calhoun,

Samuel Moore and Boyce Hudson who incidentally is portrayed in my story of "The Most Admired Men Of My Youth" which is presented in Book I, page 286 of Greensburg Memories."

Background – Walter Mitchell

Mr. Mitchell was born on April 14, 1907. Incidentally, the same year as my father. He was a graduate of Greensburg High School. He was united in marriage to Martha Elizabeth Edwards on Saturday, March 7, 1925. To this union was born one son, James Donald Mitchell. Mr. Mitchell was a dynamic and successful businessman as well as a community leader.

Mr. Mitchell served in the US Army during WW II and was a member of Rod Lowe Post 124 of the American Legion. His broad business experience included being a co-owner of the Corner Drug Store, partner in the Green County Livestock Market and Green County Milling Company. He was a successful farmer and raised corn, tobacco, beef cattle and finally operated a Grade A dairy I remember him mostly when he was a partner in the Corner Drug Store as a most friendly and somewhat reserved gentleman. He spoke to everyone and knew everyone by name, young or old.

His involvement in community affairs included serving as Master Commissioner of the Green County Circuit Court, was a Charter member of the Green County Golf Association, a member of the Greensburg Masonic Lodge #54, and the Rotary Club. He was an active member of the Greensburg Methodist Church and served as a member of the Official Board of the church.

Last but certainly not least, he was a member of the Board of Directors for the Peoples Bank and Trust Company for thirty years. Mr. Mitchell died Thursday June 7, 1984 at the age of 77 at the McDowell Skilled Nursing Facility of the Jane Todd Crawford Memorial Hospital where he had been a patient for several months.

Funeral services were held Saturday, June 9, 1984 and were conducted by the Rev. Jack Vibbert and the Rev. Paul Keneipp.

Now that we know all about ice cream and that two smart guys started the KK, let's move on.

Kozy Korner – The Beginning- Continued

The general timeline for the beginning and physical locations of the KK are as follows:

1937	Original opening date
1939	Hattie Hartfield purchased KK
1941	Moved to location inside Picket Hotel Building
1942	Moved to present location from inside Pickett Hotel Building
1954	Lorene Edwards purchased KK from Carl & Hattie Edwards
1989	KK sold to Garth Brobowski

Specifics relative to operations, changing locations and people involved follow.

The KK's original location was in a refurbished trolley car. The original location was located on the property where the W. N. Vaught & Son store once stood. The store burned in 1935. Incidentally, this is the same location where Mr. Abraham Berry operated a Texaco Service Station and where the water fountain is today, 2022. The first KK location was managed by a gracious local lady by the name of Louise Chaudoin. The menu was small and varied but just what our community needed at the time. The main items were hot dogs, ice cream and cokes. What more does one need for good wholesome food, right?

Many of those who remember the KK as it began are now gone and with them are so many fond memories of the way it used to be are now unfortunately part of bygone days.

The Pickett building (Hotel) (KK in 1941 was beside the Pickett building) had housed several businesses over the years. At one point it housed the Greensburg Post Office. The Pickett Building was demolished in 1961.

At this new location the KK began serving hot meals, which is obviously a tradition that continues to this day. Lorene Edwards, Hattie's sister, who had worked there for forty years bought the KK in 1954. Mrs. Christine Jamison was the KK's longest employee as she started working there in 1939.

The building now housing the KK was constructed between 1886 and 1895 to house Buchanan & Phillips Dry Goods Store. The telephone exchange occupied the upstairs space since 1908. The front of the building is decorated with a metal cornice and metal hoodmolds over the windows. A hoodmold (dripstone) is an external molded construction projection of wood, metal or stone from a wall over an opening to throw off rainwater. It is built to fit the contour of the windows whether it be flat or somewhat pointed.

The storefront and wood shingled pentroof (a roof sloping in only one direction replaced the original design some years later. The KK was sold to a local dentist in 1989 Garth Brobowski) whose purpose was to keep the KK as a Greensburg landmark.

Ford Dealership – "Who Gets The First New Car?"

As the KK was located on the northern corner of 1st Street Alley -The building on the southern side of 1st Street Alley was the Ford Automobile dealership. This was a extremely busy site. It contained Goff Motor on the ground floor, a repair garage in the basement and rear and "Oz" Pierce furniture on the second floor.

This was a high traffic area with two solid businesses operating on opposite corners. Both drew a lot of people where they could eat at the KK while getting your car repaired, your vehicle filled with gas or viewing the latest model of a Ford car in the showroom.

The dealership was a very friendly place to visit or just stop in and say hello. I remember going in and looking at the new car displayed on the front showroom floor. Udell Sullivan, Virgil Price and Ray Goff were always very friendly toward me and my friends and we felt comfortable just dropping in as we strolled the streets of Greensburg. Incidentally, Virgil Price (wife Francis) and my mom and dad would occasionally meet and play Rook for an evening of entertainment in the 1940's.

Another connection to the Ford dealership building was that "Oz" Pierce and Phases Pierce owned a furniture business on the east side of the square next to the Deposit Bank. In the early 1950's "Oz" sold his share to Phares and opened his own furniture business upstairs over the Ford dealership. His business slogan was "Walk up to save Money." "Oz" had a very gentle effect on young and old alike, never appearing to lack the time for a story, a bit of homespun philosophy a cheerful word, a broad grin or a shake of the hand. In fact, soon after getting married we (Joyce and I) bought all the furniture for our new house from Oz.

The building was built in 1929 and was occupied by the Chess Motor Company (Chevrolet Dealership) and was occupied by them until 1945. The Greensburg *Record-Herald* occupied the second floor. The Ford dealership history began in September 1945 when Virgil Price and Ray Goff moved their Ford dealership known as Price-Goff Motors into the building. Udell Sullivan bought Virgil Price's interest in 1946 and it became Goff-Sullivan. Then in 1958 Ray Goff bought Udell Sullivan's interest and created Goff Motor Company. Goff Motor Company also provided a new car for driver's education at Greensburg High School.

The building had a sign out front advertising Standard Oil Products and two gas pumps positioned just off the sidewalk directly in front of the building. Self-service gas pumping was unheard of then, so when a customer drove up to buy gas, someone from inside the building would come out and pump gas into the customer's vehicle.

Incidentally, the price for a gallon of regular automobile gas back then was $.21 in 1929, $.26 in 1948 and $.27 in 1951. Economist will relate that gas is cheaper in the 2000's on an adjusted for inflation basis than it was "back then". I don't know 'bout that, as I'm just providing some background information for my story!!

The configuration and size of the Ford dealership showroom was that the dealer could display only one vehicle at a time. This space was reserved for the latest production model fresh off the assembly line of Ford's production facility in Detroit. When the latest new models of Ford's were available from the factory, usually in the spring or summer, one or two were quickly procured by the owners of the Ford dealership and was promptly put on display in the front show room. This allowed one and all to view the latest model of Ford product for sale to the public.

Realizing that small dealerships like this one would/could get only one new car or maybe two for display and sale of the latest production model, new car inventory was limited as the automobile production company in those days did not produce as many new models as they do today. What would now be unheard of in today's world, was that the new car would already be sold prior to delivery to the local Ford dealer. In case of Greensburg's Ford dealership, there was an agreement (informal, I'm sure) that the first new car received would be sold to a Green County resident residing on highway 323 about halfway between Summersville and Gabe. This gentleman's name was Adair Donan. I don't know for how many years this agreement was in effect, but I can assure you that it did exist and I can remember one year probably in the early 1950's that the first car was a red convertible and Mr. Donan drove it with the top down and waving to everybody.

Construction of Tennessee Gas Transmission Company (TGT) Facility At Gabe

During the 1950's the two most talked about events occurred in Greensburg and Green County that had significant impact on the KK. First was the announcement that Tennessee Gas Transmission Company (TGT) headquartered in Houston, Texas would build and operate a natural gas line and pumping station in the Gabe community to supplement and support their existing pipelines in Kentucky and other states.

Why place the plant in the Gabe community? According to sources somewhat familiar with the operation it was described that it represented a strategic location for natural gas to temporarily be diverted from the pipeline into the plant at Gabe where certain properties of the natural gas were changed or reconfigured and returned to the pipeline, albeit rendering a better product for the consumer further up the line in other states. Please realize now, that we are more interested here in the effect of this project on the KK than we are discussing the processing of natural gas.

Tennessee Gas represented a set of natural gas pipelines that run from the Texas and Louisiana coast across Arkansas, Mississippi, Alabama, Tennessee, Kentucky, Ohio and Pennsylvania to deliver natural gas in west Virginia, New Jersey, New York and other New England states. The pipeline totaled some 11,900 miles in length.

Was this a big deal for Greensburg? You bet it was! To put it mildly, lots and lots of people came to Greensburg to design, manage and construct the pumping station for the pipeline during the proposed timeframe. The parent company purchased one hundred and ten acres in the Gabe community and construction began about 1948. Construction was completed and pumping operations began in May 1950. The work force that descended on Greensburg was large and varied to say the least ranging from laborers to engineers, accountants, concrete masons, security fencing personnel, building contractors, paving services personnel, etc.

A significant portion of the local work force was employed in the construction of the pumping station installation as well.

Once the plant started production it was continually manned twenty-four hours a day, seven days a week for three hundred sixty days for thirty-six years. Just as an aside here, the total operating hours for thirty-six years would calculate to 315, 360.

It was a very stable employer for residents in Greensburg and Green County. At closing, TGT employed forty-six employees.

As soon as the external professionals and non-professionals

began to descend on Greensburg, accommodations in the form of housing, food, laundry and dry cleaning, automobile gas, etc. etc. became a priority and a growing concern and of course, a great opportunity to increase the financial status of local businesses.

The Wright family took advantage of this opportunity as well. We, the Wright family rented rooms to two different contractors on two different occasions who were working on the Tennessee Gas construction project. I was required to relinquish my bedroom to the "new temporary resident of our home" and I was relegated to a roll-away bed in the dining room for sleeping. For a more detailed review of gentlemen, I have presented some additional comments in Volume I, page 512, "Greensburg Memories" entitled "Bennie and Mike." I think you would enjoy learning about Bennie and Mike as they were two colorful gentlemen.

At the outbreak of the announcement concerning the construction, the KK became the focal point of feeding the large volume of workers constructing the pipeline facility, at least for the evening meal, while continuing to provide excellent meals and service to residents. There were, of course, other restaurants in town that served great food and service as well, however the crowd just seemed to congregate at the KK for food, lots of table talk and I'm sure some elements of business were discussed along the way.

In addition to the dining clientele, who were waiting in line for an available table or already seated in the restaurant, there was an additional crowd gathering outside (weather permitting) of the KK. Every evening in the spring and summer months, weather permitting, a crowd of young people (mostly boys and young men) in their late teens and early twenties would begin to gather in front of the KK, sitting on the benches (never on the seat but on the top railing of the back of the bench) placed along the front windows of the KK and taking up sidewalk space while engaged in whatever conservation happened to be the topic of the moment.

I can never remember, a Saturday or a Sunday that the KK was not inundated with customers. It was not only a local establishment for relieving the pains of hunger, but a meeting place for all concerned to have open and private conversations culminating with a mixture of business and personnel matters. Due to everyone working at the construction site during the day, normally the largest crowds would occur in the evenings starting about 5 p.m. and continuing until 9 p.m. or after. In addition to the fine cuisine of not only the evening meal, but every meal, the KK has always been a place to meet, eat and greet for breakfast and lunch. Crowds for this event will vary as will the conversation, but the event has always been a stable of the KK operations.

Standing, sitting, walking around and just mingling were very natural to this crowd. The crowd would generally begin to develop around 5:00 p.m to 5:30 p.m. The evening "show" (movie) always attracted some of the group and others would just "hang out" for a bit, then go their separate ways. The construction crews, engineers, managers, etc. began to exit our fair city in late 1949 and early 1950. As the operation of the facility was absorbed by residents, one might seem to think that our famous restaurant would return to the days of yore relative to providing food for the locals and occasional travelers through our fair city. Not so, after we talk a little about the Franklin Theatre, we are going to review the next major event relative to the KK, Greensburg and Green County.

<u>Franklin Theatre</u>

The major entertainment outlet in Greensburg at that time was the Franklin Theatre which was housed directly across the street from the KK and completes the triangle of business success revealed in this story. The theatre opened Saturday, July 27, 1946 replacing the Mossland Theatre which had burned down in 1944.

Depending on the weather and in the spring and summer, Saturday evening would be the evening that the largest crowd of young people would gather outside the KK awaiting the evening performance at the Franklin Theatre. The program at the movie theatre always provided a highly advertised western saga complete with cartoons, news reel and previews of coming attractions. Prices to attend the show were $.15 for those under thirteen years of age and $.25 for those attendees over thirteen. A bag of popcorn was $.10. Even before growing into my teens, I remember mom and dad would give me a twenty-five cents for movie admission and popcorn and off to the show I would go. The group would disperse usually about ten to fifteen minutes prior to the movie, make our way across the street, buy a movie ticket, then some popcorn and make our way down the left side of the theatre where we would occupy a seat. At the conclusion of the movie, a small gathering of youth would sometimes again congregate in front of the KK, talk for a bit, then say "Goodnight" and make our way home.

Just as an item of interest here, the movie theatre consisted of a main floor, a stage up front for presenting live performances and a balcony in the rear. The balcony had maybe ten to fifteen sloping rows with about twenty seats wide. The main body of the theatre consisted of a middle section of about twenty seats across and two side sections of about five seats across. Capacity was estimated at five hundred and seven seats. Just a minute, why are you telling me, the reader about the seating in the theatre when the topic of this story is the KK? Well, the theatre was an integral part of the triangular beehive of activity around the KK.

Open seating was available except the theatre participants of color who would automatically make their way down the right side to a frontal section of approximately twenty seats deep with five additional seats from the aisle to the wall. Although this was the seating arrangements, I never heard anyone comment as to why as this was just the way the seating arrangement and was informally established and I never saw or witnessed any instances of confrontation. When the movie was over the segregated section would make their way to the rear of the theatre and exit the side door into the alley which would lead to the front of the theatre. The theatre closed in 1968. The last movie shown was Walt Disney's "Jungle Book."

On Sunday, the crowd of young people (mostly boys) would

develop about the same time. Many of the group who had not gone to the "show" on Saturday would gather, attend Sunday evening church services and return for the Sunday version of the "show." One distinctive event on Sunday as well as Wednesday evening was the musical rending of the bells emitting religious songs from the steeple of the Methodist Church.

The sounding of those bells would be our signal to leave the KK and go to church. These bells were a most pleasant sound and seem to provide a serene atmosphere all over town. I must admit that I did not appreciate them when I was living in Greensburg, but when I was in college and after living elsewhere, I would often think of the bells and their peaceful evening sounds. The bells were discontinued sometime in the 1960's. Input as to why the ceasing of the bells has been sparce. One input was from Emily Whitlock (now Ware) is that she played the Sunday chimes during the years of 1955-1959

After discussion with a few people familiar and members of the Methodist church about the bells, no apparent reason could be documented as to why they were stopped.

Oil Boom

In 1955, some five years after the completion of the TGT pipeline pumping station, oil was discovered in Green County with the completion of the Moore Oil Company drill site No 1 on the property owned by Carl Perkins. This and other oil wells to come would show oil somewhere around 800 feet or less. Oil wells within this sphere of depth were drilled and completed for costs ranging from $7,500 to $10,000. When 1958 rolls around and as more wells continued to be drilled and more oil discovered, development of the so-called shallow oil field was revealing up to two hundred drilling rigs operating per day.

In 1959, Green County is producing 10 million barrels of oil annually. In March of 1959, Ashland Oil Company completes a pipeline from Louisville to the oil field at the cost of approximately

$2,000,000. The pipeline was transporting 824 barrels per hour. The oil boom provided additional revenue to Greensburg and Green County and the KK got their share by feeding the oil boom crowd, leasing agents, acidizing company personnel, drillers, etc. etc.

The companies who drilled the oil wells were of course the element in the production cycle that provided oil. Prior to the drilling, financial and legal arrangements had to be made for the drilling for oil to begin.

These arrangements were initiated by a group of people who came to our county in the form of leasing agents. Their job was to seek out the land, with landowners and procure a lease/s on a particular piece of property for the purpose of drilling for oil. Initially, the going lease price for a farm was $1.00. That rapidly grew into much larger amounts when the word got around that individuals or companies were willing to paying more, sometimes quite a bit more, for the privilege of being able to drill for oil. During this boom to our economy the landowner would usually get 1/8th of the proceeds from the sale of oil. This or course can vary, but in the 1950's I understand this was the going rate.

So, in addition to the lease price, I'm told that sometime the owner could negotiate with the leasing agent could get a percentage of the gross sale price of the oil extracted from his farm/property. As one might imagine, this resulted in increased income for the landowner. Sometimes this was a significant amount of money which could enrich the landowner as well as the banking institutions in our fair city.

Now I will briefly discuss acidizing of oil wells, for without this process there would for the most part be no oil. I certainly am no expert on acidizing oil wells and not a geologist, but the following was the preferred method of acidizing in the 1950's in Green County. Most wells required this application to allow the oil to flow into drill shaft so it could be pumped to the surface.

This is a most important part of "bringing in" an oil well and suddenly another three or four companies made their way to Greensburg and established their operation. The local managers of the acidizing companies worked with the drillers to procure the job of acidizing the well. One tact the operators used was to position a member of their sales team in the KK about lunch time, then have the acidizing trucks (most likely empty) slowly drive past the KK in low gear as if they were heavily loaded. The operator could then announce to the people having lunch, "Yep, there goes another acidizing job for us." I have another appointment with a driller, so I'll be going. Enjoy your lunch." The trucks would then come back to the company site, park and wait for an actual job.

The actual acid used was muriatic acid and was shipped to Greensburg in a railroad tank car. The acid from the rail car was cut (reduced by water) from 100% to 7% or some other percentage, depending on the desired quality designed by the driller. The designated amount of acid to be used was pumped from the tank car into tanks mounted on heavy duty trucks. The tank trucks then made their way to the well head based on the time requested by the driller, parked and waited.

As the driller determined he was near the oil reserve, he would take a sample of soil (shale) every foot or so and check for color. The blacker the color the closer to the oil the drillers were. The driller determined when the acid was needed to "frack" the surrounding rock formation thus allowing oil to seep into the well. If the driller drilled thru the shale and burst the oil seam so to speak, oil could be lost.

At that point the acidizing people would attach a pipe to the top of the well head and start to let the acid naturally freefall into the well. When the well was full of acid, the acidizing trucks would start the pumps which would build up pressure in the well thereby forcing the acid into the rocks and usually within a very few minutes, the rock would be "gently" fractured thereby allowing oil to flow into the well from the oil reserve. When this event occurred, the acidizer's job was completed. He gathered his pipe and left the drill site back to the company site usually located somewhere in the city of Greensburg.

The acidizing process described here was developed in talking with professionals who worked in Greensburg during the oil boom.

The oil boom of the 1950's had a great economic impact on Greensburg and Green County. In addition to producing oil, the wells provided a soothing to the countryside landscape in the form of "flash burn off" of natural gas that would accompany the oil. To get rid of the gas to avoid explosions, etc. the driller would install a two to three-inch diameter pipe from the bottom of the well to some six feet above the earth surface which would allow the gas to escape from the confine of the well. As the gas would exit the pipe, the flame would be ignited and produce a small flame about six to eight inches tall.

When driving down country roads and highways one could spot the oil well by the gas being "burned off" or "flared" by observing the small flame atop the gas pipe. Whether it was one or more wells burning off gas, the view from the highway was quite peaceful, providing somewhat of an ambience to the countryside.

And in conclusion, according to an article in the National Geographic, **"The KK is not only famous for its food but also for the oilmen that ate and schemed there"**.

SUMMARY

As I scribe about this hustling bustling triangle of activity that was so dynamic in the 1940's and 1950's, I come to the realization that it no longer exists in the form that I remember it was and that makes me yearn for the times gone by. The "Oil Boom" as such, is essentially over. The pipeline installed by Ashland Oil has been removed, the operational buildings and management housing of the Tennessee Gas Transmission facility have been obliterated. The Franklin Theatre is now closed and the residents can no longer view movies of love stories and powerful action packed westerns. The Ford dealership has been replaced and the owners discussed here are deceased. "Oz's" furniture store has long been closed. Sure, other businesses have taken their place, but that's how I remember it.

Even the Kozy Korner as I knew it is gone, replaced by updated interior decorations and a younger crowd of local customers. But it is still here albeit in a different decorative format, but nevertheless operating. After reading about the bygone glory days, I would hope that one could visualize the crowds, the restaurants, the traffic, the hustle and bustle of visitors and residents intermingling day to day for business and pleasure. Those were the days prior to television, cell phones and other high profile current communication devices and therefore the populous depended and relied on personal communications skills. It was, however, the way we grew up and remembering it always draws satisfaction of memory and **"The Way We Were"**.

^ Documentation to support some estimates is varied.
^ Kudos to my friend Lanny Tucker for providing me Mr. Donan's name.

Site of the original Kozy Korner

Gas process piping at the TGT plant at Gabe, Ky.

Main pumping facility at the TGT plant, housing of some 25 engines that move the gas through the plant.

Photo taken on a Saturday in the summer of 1951
"Stage To Tucson" had a running time of 81 minutes, was
released by Columbia Pictures in 1950 and starred Rod Cameron,
Wayne Morris, Kay Bailey, Sandy Ellers, Carl Benton Reid.

Mr. W. B. Owens

Mr. W. B. (William Burnice) Owens came to Greensburg High School as our principal in 1948 from the Leitchfield Kentucky School System after serving there since 1941. He departed Greensburg High school on Tuesday, June 1,1954 to become Superintendent of Taylor Schools. Why, you say, would you write about a High School Principal. Well, there are two very specific reasons which I will present in the next few paragraphs.

He was more than a high school principal. He was very active in community affairs as President of the Green County Fair Board in 1952, a member of the Greensburg Rotary Club and a member of their Board of Directors, President of Highway Association 68, President of the SCKC Conference and had been Vice-President of the Kentucky High School Athletic Association and Editor of the Kentucky Athlete, a monthly publication of the Athletic Association.

In addition to being a superb educator, W. B. had a background in athletics. First, in addition to understanding that W. B. was a great educator, citizen and he was our basketball coach at Greensburg High School for two years (1952 and 1953).

When he coached at Horse Cave High School in 1937, 1938 and 1939, he coached a young man by the name of Dero Downing. W. B. proclaimed Dero to be an excellent guard and a great rebounder. He also proclaimed Dero to be a very good student in mathematics. Under the tutelage of W. B. the Horse Cave High School basketball team went to the Kentucky State Basketball Tournament in 1937, 1938 and 1939, but W. B. was quoted as saying, "We didn't get very far."

In August 1969, after his retirement and living on his farm in Taylor County W. B. said, "Fishing hasn't been so good lately." He issued this statement while being interviewed about Dero Downing who had just been appointed as the new president of Western Kentucky University. He also stated that Dero "had the very best qualities of leadership from the very start and he will be a great administrator of Western Kentucky University".

While serving as a most successful Superintendent of the Taylor County Schools, in conjunction with Miss Loneta Sublett of Greenburg, W. B. organized chartered bus trips for high school students. Beginning in 1958 he organized trips to Washington D. C. and New York City. In 1964 he took two chartered busses to the New York's World's Fair filled primarily with teachers from Taylor County. Because of the favorable outcome of the 1964 trip, he again organized another trip for teachers to Yellowstone National Park, Salt Lake City and Denver, Colorado.

The Greensburg Grade and High School burned on Thursday, March 2, 1950. This event is covered in greater detail under the chapter entitled "Burning Of Greensburg School" and Mr. W. B. Owens played a most important role in restarting school for both grade and high school and managing the financing of the new school building along with W. C. Burress of the Greensburg Deposit Bank.

W. B. was always very cordial and friendly to yours truly and I relate here two specific instances that I cherish with W. B. In 1953 occurring when the district basketball tournament was to be held at Greensburg High School. Now our basketball team was not the greatest. In fact, we had only one outstanding athlete and that was Larry Dale Gumm, who was the leading scorer for our team, made the all-tournament team several times and later played college basketball at (then) Campbellsville Junior College. After graduating from Campbellsville Junior College, Larry went on to attend and graduate from Western Kentucky University. After graduation from Western he pursed a teaching and coaching career for the Green County Schools. He went on to become the winningest coach in Kentucky high school baseball for several years. See Chapter entitled My Celebrity Friend "A Hero Among Us."

Back to our story

The best basketball team in our region was Campbellsville High School and you would know we drew them as our opponent for the first game of the 1953 District Basketball Tournament. In preparation for that game, W. B. took the entire team to his home on Legion Park Road for the afternoon.

During the afternoon we just sat around, catnapped and read in anticipation of the that evening's game. This was his way of preparing us for the game in the best way possible, by letting us relax and feeding us a light meal prior to the game.

The first instance in my memory occurred late in the afternoon on the day of the basketball game, just after Mrs. Owen had fed us a balanced dinner (supper) in hopes of increasing our performance in the basketball game to be held later that evening. He arose from the supper table and told us he was going to the barn to feed his cattle. He maintained a small herd on the back of his property. I asked his if I might go with him. "Surely," he replied and off to the barn we went. I wanted to go with him because my dad always had a small herd of cattle and I was interested in his herd. Believe it or not, we had a most pleasant conversation. Him telling me about his cattle and me listening intently. He took time and patience to talk with me about the breed, the size of the herd, etc.

Later that evening, we went to the gymnasium for the basketball game and of course, got beat badly. I remembered the game loss somewhat, but most of all I remember the conversation with W. B. in his barn that afternoon and have thought of it often during the years.

The second instance is as follows: I was the catcher on the high school baseball team. The school provided the catchers equipment in the form of chest protector, face mask and catcher's mitt. Some of the players had their own glove but I didn't, and I used the mitt provided by the school, which was not a very good piece of equipment, as it was flimsy and without structure. One afternoon, just prior to the spring baseball season in 1952, I was walking down the hall in the high school and met W. B. in the hall. He said, "Come into the office for a minute, Leo". I followed him and he immediately reached behind his desk and picked up a new catcher's mitt and handed it to me.

"This is for you," he remarked. I was obviously quite pleased and replied, "Thank you very much and I shall return the mitt to you at the end of the baseball season." "No need," he replied. "The mitt is yours to keep. No need to return it to the school." I thanked him again and left the room.

I cannot think of a reason for him giving me the mitt as a personal gift and he did not elaborate, but I have recalled that exchange many times over the years. I have to think that he knew I did not have good equipment and wanted to correct the situation. I asked W. B. on a couple of more occasions if I should return the mitt to the school. "Definitely not," "it's yours," he said. After graduation, I attended Bowling Green Business University where I played baseball with a local semi-pro baseball team for two seasons and utilized the mitt several times during that time. It was a good mitt and I enjoyed using it, but it still didn't improve my proficiency as a catcher. After a couple of years, the mitt just disappeared, I have no recollection of when the mitt and I parted company and frankly, my interest in baseball was no longer on my radar screen.

W. B. moved his family to Taylor County in June 1953. He continued to serve Greensburg Schools until June 1954. Upon his move to Campbellsville, W. B. sold his property to a veterinarian named Dr. Edward H. Page. As I recall, the new veterinarian drove a white pick-up truck with no lettering on the side as I understand in those days advertising of veterinarian services in logo form on vehicles was not permitted.

W. B. died on Thursday, October 31, (my wife's birthday incidentally) 1985 at age 86, in Jefferson County, Kentucky and was interned in Cemetery Hill Cemetery in Springfield, Kentucky. Now, this may not be an overly exiting story to my readers, but his actions and attitude toward me as a high school student will be forever remembered and cherished by me.

Death Fall Into The Rock Quarry

On Highway 68, about four miles south from Greensburg stands a rock quarry that has been abandoned ever since I can remember. The rock quarry lies about ½ mile south of the Vaughn Estate, brick residence on top of the off to the right side of Highway 68 and just across the Russell Creek bridge on the left side of the road.

Although this story occurs some three years prior to my birth, I have heard it repeated man times by many people over the years, and of course, dad and I would pass the quarry daily in the 1940's and 1950's on the way to our small farm a little further south on Highway 68. After one hears about the accident so many times, it just automatically jumps into your mind every time the quarry is passed.

Personal discussion coupled with documentation leads me to be able to develop this narrative, **"Death Fall Into The Rock Quarry"** relating events of the tragedy utilizing timing and movement of participants within a reasonable and appropriate time frame.

The background on the quarry was developed with residents of Green County who are somewhat familiar with the quarry and the property on top of the quarry and a review of ownership record during 1933 and ensuing years through Property Valuation records. The total acreage of the quarry and the land above it totaled some four to six acres.

The rock quarry and land above it were owned by Mr. Tobe Perkins in 1933. Extraction of rock from the quarry was last performed in the early 1940's when the highway 68 was constructed. Mr. Perkins sold the property to Mr. Finis Durrett sometime in late 1940's or early 1950's. Finis Durrett dynamited the quarry wall to create an opening in the left rear of the quarry to access to the bottom land below alongside Russell Creek according to local resident of Green County who were familiar with the property.

A rough estimate of the quarry opening on the left side is about twenty feet high to thirty feet wide. For as long as I could remember this opening was utilized by anyone who chose to do so for the dumping of garbage, trash, discarded items, etc. onto the sloping hillside in the back of the quarry allowing the discarded items to make their way via free fall down the hillside into Russell Creek thereby obviously not generating pure fresh creek water. This condition did not exist in the 1933 as the opening on the left side of the quarry had not yet been completed.

This was the conditions surrounding the quarry in the 1940's and 1950's. Control over dumping has not been activated from 1933 up until the 2020's. The quarry was developed a few years prior to 1933.

The unfortunate and deadly accident presented here in the title occurred on Sunday, July 23, 1933. On this fateful day, three couples were going on a picnic on the property above and to the rear of the quarry. Distance from the bottom of the quarry to the picnic site on top of the quarry is estimated to be approximately fifty feet. The couples were identified as (1) Mr. Ralph Burress of Greensburg and his companion Miss Louise Parrott of Campbellsville (2) Mr. Tom Burress and his companion Miss White of Columbia and (3) Mr. Paul Mitchell and his companion Miss Lola Hill of Columbia. Ralph and Tom Burress were first cousins, Ralph's father was Charlie Roscoe Burress, a brother to Thomas's father, Ruffas Burress.

To gain access to the property above the open quarry today, one must drive to the top of Russell Creek Hill and turn left onto the first lane at the top of hill. Follow this lane about one-quarter mile and that will bring you to the approximate site of the picnic some fifty feet from the edge of the quarry which was not marked at the time and the picnic site was somewhat overgrown by grass and weeds. The three couples left Greensburg a little after 6 p.m., and arrived at the rock quarry at approximately 6:30 p.m.

Indications are that they did not drive to the picnic area at the top of the quarry but drove directly into the quarry itself and ascended on foot from there. **(See Analysis #1).** In their quest to reach the top of the quarry and due to the time of day being late in the afternoon with only a couple of hours of daylight left, it seems unlikely the couples walked from the quarry to the picnic site by exiting the quarry onto Highway 68, climbed Russell Creek Hill, then turned left onto the lane leading to the picnic site (if one existed in those days). **(See Analysis #2).**

At this time of day there was apparently enough daylight left for them to ascend to the grassy field on top and rear of the quarry and still have enough daylight left to build a fire for cooking the hot dogs and having their planned picnic. Upon arrival at the picnic site, the three couples built their fire and set up their picnic site about 50 or so feet back from the cliff's edge, in what would seemingly be a safe distance from which they could enjoy their fire and picnic accordingly.

After building their fire, the couples engaged in eating, bountiful story- telling and laughter, just having a good time. About eight o'clock (some two hours later), darkness had overtaken daylight and the couples decided to leave for their respective homes. Records indicate that their car was parked in the rock quarry, not on top of the hill, which indicates that all arrived at the quarry, in the same automobile.

Documentation surfaces somewhat of a mystery in that the couple's access to the picnic site must have been accomplished by climbing around the sides of the quarry to the top as the steepness and height of the rear wall of the quarry would prevent any other manner of ascending to the top. However, there is no documentation as to the actual route of ascent.

With everyone deciding to leave and return to the car, which sources indicate was parked at the bottom of quarry, Ralph Burress remarked that they should not leave the fire burning. **(See Analysis #3).** He and Miss Parrott remained at the picnic site to extinguish the fire while the other two couples returned to their car parked in the quarry. The other two couples exited the picnic site (How they exited the picnic site and climbed down to the bottom of the quarry is not clear) and reached their parked car where they waited several minutes for Ralph and Miss White to catch up.

With no sign of Ralph and Miss White the other couples started blowing the horn and calling for them to attract their attention. No response was heard so they decided to return to the picnic site **(See Analysis #4)** to investigate the reason for them taking so long. They reached the campfire, (where incidentally there is no documentation available to ascertain if the campfire had been extinguished or was still burning) looked around the immediate vicinity but Ralph and Miss Parrott were nowhere to be found. After calling out numerous times the faint voice of Miss Parrott could be heard from some fifty feet below near the floor of the quarry (Had the two couples just been to the car at the bottom of the cliff)? Maybe they had because documentation indicates they returned from the base of the quarry to the site of the campfire on top of the quarry). **(See Analysis #5)**

At this point they discovered that Ralph and Miss Parrott were lying at the bottom of the cliff presumably on the quarry floor near the cliff's edge. The two couples answered the outcry from Miss Parrott but remained a safe distance from edge from the top of the quarry.

Now, not having a light and fearing to make the descent without one, Paul Mitchell returned to the automobile (Did he reach the automobile by climbing down the inside of the quarry or did he make his descent around the edge)? and drove to a neighbor, Mr. Fred Cowherds to obtain a lantern while the other three members of their party remained at the top edge of the cliff talking to Miss Parrott.

While Paul had gone to obtain a lantern, Tom Burress, Miss White and Miss Lola Hill continued to talk from the top of the cliff. With Miss Parrott attempting to ascertain the location of Ralph. However, in her dazed state she was unable to inform the others of his exact whereabouts and she kept calling for Ralph with all involved summarizing that he was nowhere near her.

When Paul Mitchell returned with the lantern and the four of them made what might be described as somewhat of a perilous descent **(See Analysis #6)** to the bottom of the cliff, where they found Miss Parrott lodged between an Ash tree and the edge of the cliff. Having found Miss Parrott, Tom and Paul now began

64

their search for Ralph and surmised that he had hit the bottom some distance to the right of where Miss Parrott lay and shortly located him. (The logistics and layout of the quarry and the distance between the couple that had fallen start to become somewhat hard to identify at this point).

The boys discovered Ralph and surmised immediately that he was dead, but they did not inform the girls. Dr. H. B. Simpson was immediately contacted and upon arrival summarized that Ralph had died immediately from the fall relating to internal injuries sustained when his body fell onto some large rocks. Miss Parrott was severely bruised but was found to be suffering from shock and exposure more than anything else.

Mr. J. C. Cowherd, the local undertaker was summoned to the scene and due to the inaccessibility to the deceased, it was around three am the following morning before the body of Ralph was brought to the undertaking establishment of Mr. Cowherd in Greensburg where it was prepared for funeral services and burial. (The exact location where the body of Ralph was found remains somewhat of a mystery in 1933. Mr. J. C. Cowherd renovated his South Main Street home into a funeral home. Walter Lee Parrott purchased half the business in 1947.

Speculative as it was not discussed in researched documentation).

A fire had destroyed the Dulworth & Cowherd hardware store and funeral business. The three ladies involved returned to their respective homes in Campbellsville and Columbia.

Miss Parrott, age 19 was taken to the home of her parents, Mr. and Mrs. Fred Parrott of Campbellsville, early Monday morning. Louise was the brother of Walter Lee Parrott Sr. and their family was in the funeral home business. She later became a licensed funeral director associated with the Parrott and Ramsey Funeral home in Campbellsville, in addition to being a teacher at Campbellsville Elementary School for more than 61 years. She was united in marriage to Henry Allen Buchannan on Friday, October 19, 1951. Ms. Louise died Tuesday, August 5, 2003 in Campbellsville at the age of 89 and was buried in a local cemetery.

Miss Lola Hill, age 20 returned to Columbia where she soon graduated from Lindsey-Wilson Jr. college. She was a member of the first All-American Girls Basketball Team, an avid fisherman, golfer, loved boating and water skiing. She was a life-master bridge player and during the 1940's and 1950's played in many duplicate tournaments around the country as well as social bridge with and against the best players of the time. Miss Lola did on March 8, 1999 at age 95. Funeral services were privately held, and the family requested expressions of sympathy be made to a charity of one's choice.

This horrendous event caused quite a stir in Greensburg, Campbellsville and Columbia as residents absorbed a great shock within all three communities. Documentation surfaced describing Ralph Burress as a fine young man with a bright future before him. He was a graduate of Greensburg High School, a Sophomore at the University of Kentucky and had made his mark as a qualified athlete at the University.

His funeral was conducted at the Methodist Church where he was a member and a teacher of the Sunday School class. Services were conducted by his pastor, Rev. J. M. Perryman and assisted by the Rev B. J. Skaggs and J. T. Stuart. One of the largest crowds to ever attend a funeral in Greensburg was in attendance to pay their last respects. He was survived by his father and mother, Mr. and Mr. Charles Burress and three sisters, Marie, Opal and Wilma.

Burial was in the Greensburg cemetery. Pallbearers were Dwight Smith, Samuel Moore, Tate Howard, Owen Phillips, Paul Mitchell, Morris Phillips, Colby Cowherd, Austin Simmons and Perry Marshall. For some reason Ralph Burress was not listed as a pallbearer.

Flower girls were Maxine Tucker, Eva Tucker, Decatur Johnson, Jane Rogers, Elizabeth Gorin, Kathleen Gorin, Mary K. Mitchell, Pansy Wilcoxson, Jan Anderson, Rachel Skaggs and Mrs. Minnie Brummal (nee Lewis) who was not the wife of Greensburg School Professor Jack "Prof" Sanders. She had recently married Mr. Jack Allen sanders just a month or so before in June 1933.

The male survivors from Green County were Tom Burress, who

later served as City Attorney for Greensburg and lead Attorney for the Deposit Bank. He closed his practice in 1982 and died in 1990 and Paul Mitchell managed Mitchel's Hardware Store on the square from 1946 until 1963. Paul died on Wednesday, April 2, 1975.

At the time of this very tragic event, Tom Burress was 20 years of age and Paul Mitchell was 21 years of age.

Documentation of an autopsy report and a county accident relating to the accident were not located.

EPILOGUE

The story is told with the help of documentation and conversations. What the reader must remember, is that **all the events in the story did happen.** I suppose one could have presented the events using pseudonym's or told the story as fiction, but it just would not be the same and would deprive those who have not heard the story and possibly some family members of an actual occurrence in 1933. After all, I'm not trying to rewrite history here but just to leave as an account of the accident as correct as possible from the documentation available. No matter how presented, this tragedy is bound to surface some painful memories.

ANALYSIS OF ASCENTS AND DESCENTS (EXCLUDING THE FALL OVER THE CLIFF) ON THIS TRAGIC AfTERNOON

1. Documentation does not clearly identify how, upon arrival at the quarry in their automobile the three couples ascended to property above the quarry for their outing. It merely states that on their arrival at the picnic site a fire was built. Conversations would lead us to ascertain the lane at the top of the Russell Creek hill was probably not yet constructed.

2. A defined easy access trail has not defined from the bottom of the quarry to the top for the couples to follow, however the picnic area could be accessed by utilizing highway 68, which realistically would take much longer than the daylight hours would be available for the duration of the picnic. In either case there is no defined route of ascent.

3. At the conclusion of the picnic (about 8pm) two couples (Tom and Miss White along with Paul and Lola) would make their way back down to the bottom of the quarry where their car was parked and one couple (Ralph and Louise) would remain at the picnic site to extinguish the fire. The path they traveled to the car is undefined. Upon reaching the car the two couples tried to contact the couple left to extinguish the fire but to no avail.

4. The two couples then returned to the picnic site, and still the stay behind couple could not be located. Shortly the faint voice of Miss Parrott could be heard from the base of the quarry some fifty feet below. Had the two couples just been to the car at the bottom of the quarry? Evidently, they had because documentation defines that they returned to the picnic site to extinguish the campfire.

5. Now it was dark and not wanting to descend back into the quarry without some proper lighting, in this case in the form of a lantern. At this point the two couples were still on top of the quarry.

6. When Paul returned with the lantern, both couples negotiated "the perilous descent to the bottom of the cliff ", located Miss Parrott.

OTHER

There is no doubt that other trips were made from the quarry to the picnic site, but by what route is open for interpretation.

The total number of accents was two, one by all three couples (a)

Ralph Burress and Louise Parrott, Tom Burress and Miss White and Paul Mitchell and Lola Hill. (b) The second ascent was made by two couples (c) Tom Burress and Miss White along with Paul Mitchell and Lola Hill.

The total number of descents was three, two by two couples (8c) Tom Burress and Miss White and Paul Mitchell and Lola Hill in search of Ralph Burress and Louise Parrott, who had already fallen on the cliff into the quarry) (d) after returning with the lantern, the two couples made their final descent to floor of the quarry were Tom Burress and Miss White and Paul Mitchell and Lola Hill.

You Killed My Dog

When I was going up, young people learned to drive early on in life and as for me I learned to drive when I was about eleven or twelve. As I spent a lot of time my dad, it just natural to drive. I do not know which came first the tractor or the truck, but since we did not have a car the truck was much more likely.

One of the jobs my dad had was to pick up cream from "cream stations" around the county and delivery it to the poultry house which was located about five hundred feet behind Woodson Lewis department store.

Cream Stations, as we called them was where farmers would bring their milk from their herd of milk cows to have the milk processed thru a milk separator which would separate the milk into cream and skimmed milk.

The finished product (cream) was placed into what we determined to be "cream cans" which are of steel construction, about three feet high with a handle on each side for lifting. The top portion narrowed into an opening about eight inches across with a top that fit snuggled within the top of the can. Cream cans would quite often be a part of the kitchen decoration. Many times, the cans would be decorated as shown in to be used as decoration and or used as a seat in the event of a shortage of kitchen chairs.

Decorated "Cream Can"

Our job was to pick up the cans filled with cream and bring them to the Poultry House which was located on Main Street where the convenient store is now. The purchaser (usually a dairy or a company that made butter and other milk products) would recover the cream cans from the poultry house. Cream stations positioned in various communities, most usually in the back of a country store. Our route took us to Bloyd's Crossing, Pierce and Donansburg. We made this run twice a week.

When I was fourteen years of age dad began to let me occasionally make the run by myself. I would go to the various cream stations, load the cream cans on our truck which would hold about twenty or so cans of cream and return to Greensburg. The route most traveled by me was going to Donansburg and Pierce then back home. It was somewhat of a circle route but was the best to complete the task.

I would travel North on Highway 61, turn west on Highway 88 and make my way to my first stop in Donansburg. It was an easy drive, a little curvy but easy nevertheless. This summer day I was traveling about 40 to 45 miles per hour which was an acceptable speed on Highway 88 and I was in a curvy stretch of the highway. As I was rounding a small curve, I noticed a house on the right side of the road with children playing with their dog in the front yard.

For some unknown reason the dog decided to chase the truck and before I could get slowed down and stopped. The dog ran under the right front tire. I felt the bump and heard the "thump - thump" of running over something. I immediately pulled to the side of the road and got out. I saw the dog lying in the middle of the road and it was obviously dead.

Now I was concerned as the father was coming out from the front porch followed by his son, about five or six years of age. Neither looked happy. I immediately walked toward the gentleman and said, "Sir, I'm very sorry, but there was nothing I could do". He immediately replied, "I understand, it wasn't your fault, the dog just likes to chase cars and trucks". Whew!!! He was on my side.

His son, however, was not as pleased. He had followed his dad and he ran to the dog, then looked back at me, started to cry and said, **"You killed my dog"!!** I did not know what to say or how to respond, so I said to the father, "I will be glad to get your son another dog". "Oh no", he answered, "I know it wasn't your fault".

At this point I had never told him my name and was undecided on what to do. I then relayed to the father," I will be glad to take the dog with me and bury it if you like". "Not necessary, I know you didn't hit the dog on purpose". I then told him my name and who my dad was. "I know your dad", he replied. Suddenly no one was talking and I remarked, "Well sir, if there's nothing else, I'll be on my way and again, I'm sorry". He didn't answer so I immediately got back in the truck and drove on to Donansburg.

I picked up the cream at Donansburg then made my way south

on New Salem road to highway 218, turned left (west) and made my way to Pierce, picked the cream and drove east on 218 to Highway 68, turn north and headed back to Greensburg. I tell you that I had a lot of thoughts on my way back, very much concerned about what dad would say.

When I got to the poultry house dad was waiting. "How did it go"? he asked. "OK", I said and immediately told him about hitting the dog and my conversation with the father and little boy. He listened and then said, "Those things will happen from time to time, especially when driving in the country". "No one was hurt, were they?". "No sir", I said. "That's good", he said, "Let's get the cream unloaded". And we did.

The next week dad went with me on the Donansburg – Pierce trip. As we neared the house where the dog had run in front of the truck, I told dad, "Here is the house where the dog ran out". He never replied and we drove on, picked up our cream and went back to Greensburg.

The incident was never mentioned again, but every time I passed that house, I hoped I would not see the little boy. I don't know whether he got a replacement pet or not. This happened in 1940 and it is as clear to me today as it was then.

Grandparents

One set of my grandparents (Blakeman's) lived on Locust Grove Road and other (Wright's) lived in "The House in the Woods"

Now that I am a Grandparent and a Great Grandparent, I have a deep appreciation for being allowed to become a "Grand". I feel I am loved by my "Grands" and I certainly know I love them, probably not any more than I did my children but in a different way. I may not have explained that very well, but most every "Grands" will understand what I'm saying.

First, let me talk about the Blakeman grandparents on my mother's side then I will get to the Wright grandparents on my father's side and "The House In The Woods".

Grandparents – Leo & Kate Blakeman- Locust Grove Road

My grandfather, Leo Blakeman was born in Green County on Thursday, February 11, 1886 and died of a heart attack at the age of 47 at his home on Locust Grove Road in the Thurlow Community on Friday, December 8, 1933. My mother called him "Papa" and related to me that he very soft-spoken man, of slight build, a devoted family man, a Christian and a very hard worker.

As my grandfather Leo died prior to my birth, I never had the opportunity to meet and spend time with "Papa". As he was discussed in our house numerous times, I have certainly missed not being able to know "Papa" from listening to stories told by my mother and my uncles. I'm sure I could have learned from him as I understand he was a very patient and methodical man and difficult to show anger. I'm sure he would have helped me as my disposition is beyond patient and methodical. I asked my mother why she was named Earl and she said that "Papa" had the name picked already picked as he just knew she was going to be a boy.

My grandmother, Maderia Catherine "Kate" (Ennis) Blakeman was born in Green County on Wednesday, May 22, 1883. She died as a result of a paralytic stroke suffered two years before at her home on Locust Grove Road on Sunday, December 29, 1935 at the age of 52.

Leo and Kate were married Wednesday, December 25, 1907 at Mount Lebanon Church in the Thurlow community. They took up residence at the farm they had bought and moved in 1904 to the Blakeman farm and spent their entire married life as farmers tending the same one hundred acres of the "ole home place." Leo and Katherine are briefly mentioned in Book 1, page 199, "Greensburg Memories."

To this union was born three children, James Lyman on Sunday, October 18, 1908, Morton Earl, my mother, on Wednesday, April 2, 1913 and Henry Edwin on Tuesday, November 28, 1916. According to my mother, life on Locust Grove Road was quite pleasant being surrounded with loving parents and a good standard of living. Mother tells of a lady of colored lady that worked there, as a permanent house maid and helper by the name of Miss Millie Haskins.

Unfortunately, both my grandparents died at a young age which ended a blessed married life as well. My mother and dad were married on Wednesday, December 27, 1933, just nineteen days after Grandpa Leo died.

Grandpa Leo's funeral service was held on Saturday, December 9, 1933 at the Mount Lebanon Methodist Church in the Thurlow community. The service was conducted by Rev. L. A. Pendleton and assisted by Rev. Rayburn, pastor of the Greenburg Methodist Church. Burial was in what is now Neagle cemetery, Row 10. He was survived by three sisters, Lera McMahan, Hattie Ervin, Mattie Paxton and two brothers Lallie Blakeman and Early Blakeman.

Grandma Kate's funeral was held on Tuesday, December 31, 1935 at the Mount Lebanon Church in Thurlow. The service was conducted by Rev. Thurman Curry. She was survived by her five brothers, Tommie, Ernest, Alvie, Sam and Henry Ennis; one half-brother, Urie Houk and one half sister. Mrs. Harvey Pierce. She was interned in the Neagle Cemetery alone side Grandpa Leo in Row 10.

Grandparents – Mose & Elviria Wright - The House in the Woods

My Grandfather Mose Akin Samuel Underwood Wright was born on Sunday, September 15, 1872 in Green County, Kentucky and died Wednesday, March 26, 1952 at the age of 80 at the Howard Clinic in Glasgow, Kentucky.

My Grandmother Lucy Elviria (Wilson) Wright was born on Thursday, September 21,1876 in Metcalfe County, Kentucky and died on Monday, January 7, 1952 at the age of 76 at the home of her son Earl Wright in the Thurlow community.

They were married Thursday, March 12, 1896 at the home of the bride's parents, Mr. & Mrs. G. T. Wilson in Metcalfe County. To this union four sons, Earl, Tom (my dad), Fred, Jim and two daughters, Sarah and Della were born. Jim and Sarah died at very early age of natural causes.

Near or about 1936 my Uncle Earl constructed a house on his farm in the Thurlow community. The house was placed in a wooded area some one quarter- mile off Highway 68. It was only accessible from the highway by a one lane road. My Grandparents moved into that house sometime around 1937 and Grandpa Wright went to work for my Uncle Earl. The location of the house was hereafter dubbed "**The House In The Woods.**"

I spent my first night away from home with Grandpa and Grandma Wright in **"The House In The Woods."** I was four-years of age and my mom and dad were going somewhere that would require an overnight stay. I distinctly remember saying goodbye to Mom and Dad as they drove down the lane to the highway. They dropped me off sometime in the afternoon and I played until dark, ate some supper and went to bed with Grandpa and Grandma.

My Grandparent's bedroom was on the front left side of the house and the bed allowed one to look out the front window, down the lane and see traffic on Highway 68. That night I had a difficult time going to sleep. I was not aware that my parents would not come for me until morning. I would doze and wake up and see the traffic passing by on Highway 68 and thinking that any minute mom and dad would turn in and come pick me up.

My uncle Earl, his wife Blanche, my uncle Fred and his wife Levy would visit from time to time and not recognizing it at the time, it was a peaceful time for brothers and parents to visit.

I finally went to sleep and slept soundly until morning, had some breakfast and about midmorning Mom and Dad showed up and I was a happy boy. I know what the reader might think, he doesn't remember all. YES, I do. Quite vividly. I know sometimes I cannot remember what I had for breakfast, but I can assure you I remember this.

My Grandmother was of small feminine build about 5' 4". She was very loving to me and would always pick me up, hold me and give me hugs and kisses. I first remember going to their **"House In The Woods"** when I was about three years of age and would chase the chickens around the back yard. We would visit my "grands" on a regular basis.

Grandpa Mose was about 5' 9" and was always dressed in work clothes as he was a fulltime farmer. He had a corn crib where he maintained his supply of corn for feeding the animals. It was constructed of chicken wire inside their small barn. Chicken wire was used to allow air into the corn so it would not rot. It had a solid wooden roof and a door of chicken wire with a latch to keep it shut and to keep unwanted animals out.

One thing I did not like was going to the corn crib with Dad or Grandpa Mose to get scoops of corn for the chickens. Rats were evidently a problem in those days, especially around the barn and to preserve their corn from being eaten by the rats, they kept a black snake in the crib with the corn. The snake was supposed to eats the rats and I suppose it did. I understand that in those days, it was common practice to keep a black snake in the corn crib.

Dad would step inside the corn crib, scoop up corn and put it in a bucket. No matter how many times when he pushed the scoop into the shelled corn he would disturb the black snake and it would slither away either on top of the corn or bury itself deeper in the corn and disappear. When I first observed this scenario, I was about three or four years old and I would slither away, so to speak as well.

I was assured that the black snake was harmless and would not bother me. I was not a believer for a few years and as I observed the scooping of corn and the non-aggressive manner of the reptile, I began to feel more comfortable going with Dad or Grandpa to the corn crib.

Years later when we had our small farm, we had a black snake that was small when we first saw it as it must have come into the barn seeking a nice home, and over time it grew to about three feet long. It stayed near our cattle shed where we stored the hay. We would notice the snake lying on top of the baled hay or warming itself just under the eave of the shed. We never bothered it and it was never aggressive toward us. When we approached, it would slither away not to be seen until later.

I guess it caught some mice as that was good for us as it kept the rodents from eating into the bags of grain stored in the feed room.

Our barn was painted red and after a few years it needed a new coat of paint. When the painters were spraying the cattle-shed they painted the black snake as it was lying just under the tin roof taking in the warmth generated from the sun. Obviously when the spray gun noise and paint hit the snake it quickly slithered away, but alas it was too late, it had been painted red. Until the snake shed its skin later in the year, it was easy to spot with the red and black color. It became an item of smiling conversation when we would see it and remark, "There goes ole' red and black."

In 1947, Grandma Wright became ill, could not care of herself and was confined to a hospital bed. As a result of that illness, she was moved to the home of my Uncle Earl just a short distance away. Grandpa continued to work albeit on a reduced scale. Grandma's illness never improved and on Monday, Jan 7, 1952 she passed away. Her funeral was held at Mouth Lebanon Methodist with burial in the Neagle Cemetery.

Shortly after that, Grandpa Wright came and lived with us for a month. As we only had two bedrooms, I was relegated to sleeping on a cot in the dining room. This was not the first time I had to give up my bed and move to the dining room. The other time was shortly after when the Tennessee Gas Pipeline pumping station was being build, we had two boarders and you may read about them in Book 1, page 512, of "Greenburg Memories."

Grandpa Wright was a handsome man with a handlebar mustache. He was a quiet man, soft spoken and very courteous. When he lived with us, he would walk to town and back just to get out of the house. He buttoned his coat is a manner I had not seen before. He wore what we refer today as a barn coat with three buttons. No matter how cold, he would button only the top button, pull the bottom back and put his hands in his pockets.

I thought that was a little odd until years later in the 1970's and 1980's, I purchased a small farm and we moved to the country, bought myself a barn coat and guess what?

Yep, you guessed it. I began to button my coat in the same way. Joyce (wife), Angela and Susan (children) would ask, "Why don't you button your coat up all the way, Dad?" "Because it feels natural to do it that way," I told them. I relayed that Grandpa Wright had buttoned his coat the same way, but I guess my family still wondered that if a coat came with three buttons, why not use all of them?

After a month living with us in Greensburg, I think Grandpa missed being in the country, so he moved back to "The Little House In The Woods". A short time late in March he was involved in a fatal accident on the farm of my Uncle Earl when a team of mules he was driving ran away, threw Grandpa off, ran over him causing severe injuries. Uncle Earl, attempting to stop the runaway mules suffered an injury to his arm. Grandpa Wright was taken to the Howard Clinic in Glasgow where he lived for only a few hours.

Later that evening after Grandpa had died, Dad came home from the Howard Clinic and I shall always remember him coming in the front door, tears in his eyes and saying, "Well, It's all over now."

I couldn't really appreciate his comment then, but years later when my parents passed away, the meaning became very clear to me.

Grandpa Wright was buried in the Neagle Cemetery alongside Grandma Wright in Row 12. My parent A. T. "Tom and Morton Wright are buried close by in Row 7. Ironic isn't it. Mose and Elviria died some forty-five years after Leo and Kate, yet they are buried in the same cemetery only two rows apart.

Some family pictures below may help the reader in recognizing some of my family portrayed above.

Uncle Fred on Left
Grandpa Wright and Uncle Fred taking a break from
cutting hay. Notice the scythe in rear of Uncle Fred
that has a "cradle" for catching the hay after cutting
and depositing it neatly on the ground.

Grandma "Elviria" Wright

Uncle Earl (age 12) and Uncle Fred Wright (age 5), circa 1912.

Grandpa and Grandma Wright.
House in background is not "The House In The Woods".
Notice wood chips in front from cutting firewood.

My dad, A. T. "Tom" Wright
Circa 1911

Grandma Wright (Elviria) &
Clementine, my first cousin
Circa 1930

A. T. "Tom" Wright (My Dad)
Stapleton Farm
Twanda, Illinois -1930's

My Celebrity Friend –
"A Hero Among Us"

A Celebrity Is

"One who is widely known"

A Hero is

"A person who is admired or idolized for courage, outstanding achievements or noble qualities"

The above definitions set forth the short versions of defining a celebrity and hero. Celebrities and a hero can earn the title by excelling in whatever endeavor's they pursue, or in some cases choose not to pursue. Medicine, education, film and stage actors and actresses, military personnel, husbands, wives, sports, etc. One could list several pages of the categories of people who qualify for these distinctive honors.

My celebrity friend has been my friend since we were six years old as we played together, roamed the streets of Greensburg, and finally grew into what we hope were responsible adults. We spent a tremendous amount of time together growing up. No intent to get mussy here, but one must realize this is a story about a young man in a small country town, where numbers of available playmates were few and who grew up and became a celebrity and hero.

Just as an aside here, he, I and seven other youngsters enrolled as first grade students under the tutelage of Miss Mae Simpson (See "Start of Life & School on Henry Street," page 21, Book 1 of "Greensburg Memories") in the Greensburg Grade School system on Monday, September 7th, 1942 and by some hook, crook and possibly default of the educational system we all graduated together in May 1954.

After graduation from high school our small group of nine and the rest of the graduating class, numbering about thirty-two in total as I remember went our separate ways as we pursued additional educational opportunities, the work force, marriage, etc. and hopefully using our talents to improve society.

Before I go too much further, you should know that my friend, the celebrity and hero of whom I speak is none other than today's Greensburg resident **Larry Dale Gumm** as he is now known, but back in the 40's and 50's then he was **"Pee Wee"**. It just seems that as we met and grew through the year's we just seemed to gravitate toward the company of each other. As young boys growing up in a small town, the reader has probably already realized that our main activity together, except for schooling was basketball in the winter and baseball in the summer.

In fact, Larry has surfaced with me through several of my stories, not necessarily in name but by being there during these documented events presented in Book I of "Greensburg Memories "in the chapters of "Cattle Cane," "Baseball & Fall Over Cliff," "Catching a Major League Pitcher," "Going to Owensboro," "Basketball and Green Hair" and as a pseudonym in "High Banks – Swimming & Camping."

The focus of this writing is to highlight his athletic abilities in high school and college along with his contribution to athletics in general as an educator, coach and mentor to youth engaged in athletics.

Starting in grade school and continuing through high school, Larry was the best athlete in the Greensburg school system, and he has the statistics to prove it.

As I played both baseball and basketball with him during our grade and high school years, I can honestly relate that he was a superb first baseman, both offensively and defensively. One of the best defensive qualities a first baseman can have is to be able to catch the baseball thrown by another member of the infield who had just fielded (caught) a ground ball hit by the batter.

Depending on where the ground ball is hit (usually in the infield) and where its caught will depend on how hard the baseball should be thrown to the first baseman to order to get the runner "out." The speed of the base runner coupled with the timeliness and speed of the baseball being thrown to the first baseman are major factors in scoring an "out" for the home team. Quite often, time elements of a second or a millisecond can determine whether the base runner is safe or out.

Now, with that background, one of the qualities of an excellent first baseman is to be able to reach and stretch as far forward as possible toward the ball to facilitate the catch. Larry was a master of this maneuver. By reaching and stretching far enough to catch the ball as early as possible, time elements of one second or milliseconds could result in whether base runner is safe or out. Perfecting this ability along with his other athletic qualities, he allowed old "Greensburg High" to chalk up a lot of "outs" when otherwise, the base runner would be safe and become a potential score for the opposing team.

He also excelled in basketball as a high scoring, fast moving, floor savvy guard with a tenacious aggressive attitude toward winning. Statistics provided below will testify to his ability.

Highlights of his high school basketball, football and baseball career are:

In High School

^ Scored 1,800 points in his high school basketball career.
^ During one two-week span he scored 43, 45 and 47 points respectfully. He maintained that record until his son, Jeff, broke the record years later with 52.
^ Placed on the All-District tournament basketball team three times. See Footnote A.

- ^ As a senior, scored 36 points in a regional tournament loss to Adair County, was named to all-region team and received a trophy.
- ^ As a senior, scored 36 points in the Campbellsville Christmas Tournament. Ironically, in later years both his sons, Jeff and Greg, also scored 36points in the same named Christmas tournament.

In College

- ^ Obtained a basketball scholarship to Campbellsville Junior College where he was acclaimed "All-State Junior College" athlete in his Sophomore year.
- ^ Attended Western Kentucky University and played first base, on the "Hilltoppers" baseball team his last two years in college.

As A High School Coach

- ^ Employed as a baseball Coach, assistant basketball coach & assistant football coach – Greenburg High School.
- ^ Started the Greensburg Babe Ruth baseball program in 1961 and served with the organization from 1961 to 1968 and coached the American Legion baseball team for several years.
- ^ Established the practice of baseball coaches wearing a uniform as opposed to khakis, tee shirt and tennis shoes when coaching on gameday.
- ^ Established the practice of playing baseball as many days as possible instead of two games a week. This initiative established a playing schedule that is still in effect in the 2020's.
- ^ After some 45 years of coaching baseball, his 1000th victory was achieved on the last day of the 2006 season.

<u>Wide-Spread Recognitions</u>

^ In 1972 "Personalities of the South" recognized him for "Past Achievements, Outstanding Abilities and Service to the Community".

^ He was a member of the first class of the Kentucky High School Baseball Hall of Fame.

^ In 1997 he was awarded a "Certificate of Membership" into the Dawahares Hall of Fame Court of Support.

^ In 2003 he was inducted into the Fifth Region Athletic Directors Association Hall of Fame.

^ Received two citations honoring him from the Kentucky House of Representatives.

^ In 2004, in an awards ceremony in Las Vegas, where he represented the Southeast Section of the United States, he qualified as a finalist for "National Coach Of the Year".

^ In 2006, he was awarded a plaque by the Kentucky High School a Athletic Association "In Recognition of Lifelong Contributions to School Students and the Sport of Baseball."

^ In 2007, he was inducted into the National High School Athletic Coaches Association Hall of Fame. See Footnote B.

^ In 2007, he again qualified as a finalist for National Coach of the Year at the annual meeting in Milwaukee, Wisconsin.

^ And last but certainly not least, from 1961 thru 2007 his total baseball coaching victories totaled 1,006 and losses of 499 for a winning percent of 66.8%.

Now in closing, we say "How 'bout That, sports fans? We all see highly recognizable athletes and coaches in the newspaper and on television, but how many of us get to relate our childhood experiences with such a HERO and CELEBRITY!!

Not bad accomplishments, Larry as you remarked to me "I'm just an 'ole country boy"!!!!!!!!

Thanks, Larry for all the memories!!!!!!

Footnote A

In the 1950's when a high school basketball player was awarded a position on an all-tournament team, in addition to a certificate the awardee was given a small basketball (gold plated and probably ½ inch round in diameter). Larry took the basketballs awarded to him, had them evenly spaced and attached to a gold chain (about fifteen inches long) from which he wore daily as a symbol of success. The chain would be attached securely on one end to the inside the left front pants Pocket on the other end attached to a belt loop on the left side of his trousers.

Footnote B

There were only seven other coaches from Kentucky in the National Hall of Fame and he WAS THE FIRST INDUCTEE TO HAVE COACHED BASEBALL!!

Permastone

When writing stories about your youth, one might wonder why the author would recall a teenager experience about building block, facia, or whatever it is called. That just does not seem like something a young man, fourteen years of age would be interested in. Well, in this case it is called Permastone and the reason for writing is that I have only viewed application of this product once in my lifetime and it was in 1950 or 1951, the best that I recall, in Greensburg, Ky. I can assure all, it created a lot of interest among the populous of our fair city. First a little background.

Permastone was invented and patented by Albert Knight in 1937 and was sold by the Lasting Products Company as a stucco product that was applied to brick row-houses as a renovation improvement in East Coast cities in the United States.

It is a simulated stone product sold in sheets or blocks of varying sizes that are fastened as a veneer layer over a building's pre-existing exterior siding or possibly direct over wall sheathing to provide what looks like a real stone or stone veneer wall. It is installed for reasons such as, peeling, rotting or other damaged wood clapboards and to exterior walls to improve the appearance and hopefully the value of the structure.

This product was contracted to be installed on the front of the former Green River Hotel, which later became Elizabeth Hotel. The Permastone effectively disguised a significant Federal style hotel as the initial construction was sometime prior to 1914. The building housed as of the Permastone installation date, Chester's Restaurant, a TV repair shop owned by Mr. Carl Wilcox on the right. The Permastone was not installed on the Green River Hotel or the building on the corner to the left of Chester's, which was a separate property and later housed Turner & Son, a dry goods store, one in a chain of fifteen stores owned by the Turners.

The week that the Permastone was being installed began on a Monday when the workers drove up in two trucks. The first process was to attach fasteners to the existing wall in the form of projected nails or spikes. The actual mixture of the stone was performed from the back of truck parked in front of the building.

The workers applying the formed blocks of Permastone first attached the spikes or nails as a basis to hold the stone which would be attached. This stone is being attached to a vertical wall and must have something to hold it in place. The stones, which were of irregular shapes to portray a limestone rock formation look. Therefore, they are made in several different shapes.

The crowd of young men did not begin to assemble until school was over for the day and it seemed that the sidewalk in front of Chester's was inundated with gawkers such as myself. The crowd of on lookers was bigger than the work force and I'm sure it interfered with their work.

I can vividly recall that the sidewalk in front of and approaching the building was not coordinated off permitting "rubberneckers" such as myself and a multitude of others to gain access to the installation site. In today's construction climate there would be no way on lookers could get anywhere near the installation site.

As I remember the persons applying the stones to the building would call out a number or a size, etc. and the mixer on the street working from the back of the truck containing the ingredients for mixing and forming Permastone would select a mold matching the size called for. He would then mix various material in three layers. First was the cement mortar about 3/8" to ¾" inch thick. This layer was then scored before it dries. The second layer of mortar is between ¼" to 3/8" thick.

The third layer is again ¼" to 3/8" thick and is applied to the second layer while the material is still flexible. The top layer (third layer) is then hand-sculpted to resemble a rough surface look and then sprayed to make the Permastone have a clean finished look. Variations in coloring could be obtained by mixing coloring agents into the top layer of the stone producing colors such as gray, red, tan, brown, greenish-gray, etc.

As the day wore on the placement of the stones on the building grew higher and higher, therefore ladders and short scaffolding were erected. The mold containing the formed stone had a handle on each end so it could be easily moved from one worker to another without dropping or damaging the stone. The worker affixing the stone would grasp the tray with both handles and push the stone onto the spike embedded into the building therefore securing the stone to the building.

The worker would hold the stone in position for thirty seconds or so to ensure the proper fastening to the building. He then called out for another stone by size or number, return the mold to the mixer on the street where the process would be repeated.

I have no idea how many stones are on this wall, but the company was there about a week, the best I recall. The reason I'm explaining the process is that I and many others had never been exposed to this process and it was interesting to see it being applied.

It's strange how small beginnings turn into greatness. I'm not talking about me, but specifically the Turner & Son dry goods store. At this time Turner & Son owned a chain of fifteen stores. In 1953 they moved to another location in Greensburg and in a few more years, Turner & Son developed into what became the national chair called Dollar General.

And that, my friends is the story of how Permastone came to Greensburg!!!

Chester's Restaurant and and Wilcox TV Repair Shop circa 1953
The Permastone has been removed and the frontage now
presents it's original red brick as it's face.

The building as shown after removal of the Permastone.
Notice that the two picture windows denoting CAFE have
Been removed and replaced 15 pane windows. The awning on the
right side has been removed and windows replaced with 15
paned windows.

The Permastone has now been removed and one may view the original brick that was used to build this magnificent structure in 1820. There is quite a history concerning this building which will be presented in my next book, "Bits & Pieced". But for now, just visualize how this historical building was developed with popular and ash wood for the interior, three brick thick interior walls, all built in the Federal style. For additional information access the following:

Greenriverhose.workpress.com

Mechanical Tobacco Handsetter
"Chuck-A-Luck"

This device, The Mechanical Tobacco Handsetter was invented by Horace T. Walker of Adair County Kentucky. He was born in 1880 and died ninety-seven years and nine days later in January 1957.

He was an aggressive gentleman and gained fame as an operator of a tin shop in as well as Mayor of Columbia, where the local newspaper referred to him as an "eloquent and entertaining speaker", creator, owner of an entertainment emporium, purveyor of Walker's Pure Herb Tonic and inventor.

Tobacco was first discovered by the native people of Mesoamerica and South America and later produced in Europe and the rest of the world. Tobacco known today comes from a member of the nicotiana genus - a close relative to the poisonous nightshade.

Archeological finds indicate that humans in the Americas began using tobacco as bar back as 12,300 years ago, thousands of years earlier than previously documented. Tobacco came to America sometime around 1776. Christopher Columbus traded tobacco with the native American Indians as a bargaining tool.

Tobacco is generally defined withing seventy types knows to be produced around the world. The manner of growing each type may vary with the region of production within the country it is grown. Burley tobacco is knows for its light air-cured finish of sweetness and a variety of tobacco blends.

The type of tobacco grown in Green County Kentucky is Burley. The process for growing is generally as follows: (1) start with seed in a bed (either indoors or outdoors), (2) when seed develops into a "plant" about four to six inches tall, it is extracted "pulled "and taken to the tobacco "patch" to be set," i.e., placed in the ground some eighteen to twenty-four inches apart so it may develop into a full-grown marketable commodity. WHEW!! A more detailed description of tobacco may be read in Book 1, page 488 of "Greensburg Memories."

This story is about how tobacco is "set.". Down thru history, tobacco has been "set" by at least three methods, (1) Tobacco Peg, (2) Early Mechanical Tobacco Setter and (3) Tobacco Setter.

The **tobacco peg** is defined as a short piece wood, metal or plastic, constructed at a ninety-degree angle so as to provide a place where the peg can be gripped by hand, typically tapered and sharpened at one end so it can be inserted into the ground, thereby making a hole to "set" the tobacco plant. The peg has been around since there has been a need to "set" the plant into the ground. This process is generally how it is done and there's no attempt here to teach someone how to manage their tobacco production.

The **tobacco setter** is generally defined as a piece of machine without engine that is pulled behind a team of horses or a tractor. It is designed to seat two people near the back with a cylinder between them to drop the tobacco plants so the setter can plant "set" them into the ground. Yes, there is some more to the setter than what is described here, but this is presented just as a descriptive of raising tobacco and not an integral part of this story. The setter was probably invented for use around 1940.

In between the peg and setter was the **"Early Mechanical Tobacco Planter"**, alias the **"Handsetter"** and was known to us as **"The Chuck-A-Luck"** the developer of tired muscle and much sweat.

The term **"Chuck-A-Luck"** is a game of chance, having originated in English pubs. The game is also known as Crown and Anchor. Originally, it was called Sweat Cloth, and it found its way to the U. S. around 1800 as just Swear. Other names were Chuck-Luck and just Chuck. By 1900 it was called Birdcage. The game was played by Lazar in the James Bond movie, "The Man with the Golden Arm". Now, how the name of "Chuck-A-Luck" became associated with this device, research has not brought that fact to the surface.

No, we were not opposed to sweat if it developed from playing basketball or baseball, etc. but I confess, I did not cater to producing sweat from the "Chuck-A-Luck." The origin of the common name of **Chuck-A-Luck** has not been verified by the author.

However, the patent reads "One-Man Mechanical Tobacco

Setter." So, you can just take your individual choice of words to describe this back breaking monster.

Now that we think we know the background of this "setter," tell us about it. This device was used in two ways, (1) fill in missing plants from the setter attached to the back of the tractor or (2) used as a standalone piece of equipment used to "set" tobacco. We used this as a standalone instrument.

Tobacco fields are prepared for "setting" by plowing, disking and sometime dragging to make the planting surface flat. The last step prior to "setting" was to plow rows or "furrows" as straight as possible or to follow the contour of the tobacco "patch". If a farmer did not have a tobacco setter and his allotted amount of tobacco was relatively small, say one-half acre of less, as it was in our case, the "Chuck-A-Luck" was the primary planting tool used in "setting tobacco."

The "Chuck-A-Luck" was a handheld device about two and one-half feet tall, with two reservoirs, the larger one in front for water and smaller one in the rear for the tobacco plant. The process to "set" the tobacco plant was simple. Setting the plant was essentially a two-person job. One person to drop the plants into the rear reservoir and keep the front reservoir filled with water and other one to hold and operate the setter.

The person holding the setter (Chuck-A-Luck) would approach the spot where the tobacco plant was to be set, thrust the setter into ground hard enough to make a hole about three to four inches deep, depending on the size of the tobacco plant. They would then pull the trigger at the top of the setter, just to the right of the holding handle, which would open the bottom, at which time the tobacco plant, which had been placed in the rear reservoir would drop down into the ground along with an amount of water to accelerate the grown.

The person manning the setter would extract the setter from the ground thereby closing the hole and moving dirt up around the tobacco plant, i.e. having "set" the tobacco plant then move on about eighteen to twenty-four inches and repeat the performance.

This was a back breaking and tiring exercise and switching of jobs would be frequent. For me it was quite frequent as I was never very good at manning this monster. Nevertheless, between dad and a helper or two and myself we would manage to get the tobacco "patch" filled with plants that would hopefully grow into a money-making crop around August or September which we could "cut" depending on weather, growing, etc. and "hang" in the barn on "tier poles" for curing prior to stripping, hand tying and taking to the tobacco market for sale.

Now, the reader might be wondering, why have you told us story? The reason, it was a way of life for small farmers (us) in the 1950's and it provided a good sweaty workout for young men. May you never ever have to man a "Chuck-A-Luck"!!

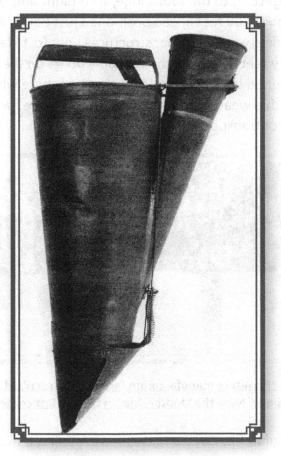

The Mechanical Tobacco Setter
Alias - "Chuck-A-Luck"

Fold-Up Desk

W. T. Boyd, the depot agent in Greensburg and who lived across from the street from us on Henry Street in the 40's and 50's was a maker of fine furniture when not performing duties as depot agent. More on the Boyd family can be found in Book I, page 89 of "Greenburg Memories".

His small "furniture manufacturing facility" (if you can call it that) was located just under the footbridge and was accessible by taking Columbia Avenue to Water Street past the trailer park and just before getting to the footbridge, turn night and the furniture shop was about 200 feet ahead positioned just below a hill.

The building was a one floor structure about forty feet wide and some twenty feet deep with three double doors on the front which could be opened to provide a pleasant atmosphere when working in the favorable weather months and to allow large furniture to be moved out for transportation when finished.

"Furniture manufacturing facility" as described
Above. Note the "footbridge" in the top left corner.

One evening Mr. Boyd and dad were loading a bedroom suite for delivery to some customer. I was tagging along as always and listening to the conversation which had turned for some reason to the subject of office desks, kitchen cabinets or just flat surfaces on which to place paper, read, pay bills, maybe do some filing, sort out things, etc. etc. Mr. Boyd commented that he did his paperwork for the furniture business on A crudely build flat surface attached to the rear wall, somewhat out of the way to provide more space to manufacture furniture.

Dad mentioned he had a desk that he used about every day. "Now Leo here", he commented, "does not have a desk, he is relegated to the dining room table to complete his school assignment when writing is required."

Nothing else was said about a writing surface and the furniture was loaded onto our truck and it was delivered to some home in Adair County. Several months passed and one Saturday in October dad was again getting ready to make a delivery for Mr. Boyd.

As always, I tagged along. When I entered the furniture shop, Mr. Boyd said, "Leo, come here and see how you like this." I went to the back of the shop and Mr. Boyd and dad were standing next to a piece of furniture attached to the wall. It looked to be about five feet high and three feet wide some four inches thick and it had two legs on either side for support that were about two feet tall.

They were just standing there looking at me. "What is it?", I asked. Dad said, "This is for you," Okay, that's good, but what is it? Dad and Mr. Boyd were smiling when dad said, "This is your new desk." Well, I gotta' admit I had no idea what the conversation was and I was embarrassed to say the least.

"Here, let me show you how it works." Said Mr. Boyd. He went to the desk, reached up the top center, released a small latch and the front folded down to where it was at a ninety-degree angle with the back portion of the structure. Yes, it was a desk, complete with an inkwell and a compartment for holding paper clips etc. mounted on the back wall. The desk could be attached to a wall with a bolt to keep it stable and erect. When not using the desk the writing surface could be folded up making the entire structure stick out about four inches from the wall.

The fold out portion of the structure made the writing surface and was attached to the rear of the desk by two small chains, which kept it level and from falling over. There was a swing out "leg" to support the desk surface keep it stable. I get it now. It was something new and I really liked it. We took it home to Henry Street and dad bolted it to the wall. I'm not sure what wood was used for construction, but Mr. Boyd had finished it into a bright mahogany which is a straight grained of a deep -reddish-brown color.

I used this desk all through school, took it with me when I got married, kept it in my study until the late 1980's when we sold our home and moved into a full furnished condo. I sold the desk to one of my neighbors who gave it to their daughter for her room. I happened to see them some years later when their daughter had graduated from high school and had gone to college.

Without me asking, they let me know that it still in their daughter's room and had several people wanted to buy it, but no it's not for sale.

The reason for writing this story is I have never seen a desk like this anywhere else. I have several furniture makers if they ever constructed a desk such as this. I believe it must be one of a kind. Who knows, this may be a valuable antique for someone. Good Luck!!!!

Mumblety Peg

"What did you say?" "Mumblety-Peg" I repeat and yes, I am enunciating it correctly. We (young boys in the 1940's and 1950's) commonly referred to the game as "Mumble Peg". Well, the reader at this point could truthfully say, "I never heard of it." The story that accompanies this game is that it is referred to by this name because, "the player with the lowest score is compelled to *mumble*"-"*extract*" out of the ground with his teeth a small wooden *"peg"* which has been gently driven into the ground with a certain number of soft blows from the handle of a knife. Believe it or not this is how the name of this game was described.

The definition of *"mumble"* is when defined as a noun is *"a quiet and indistinct utterance"* and when described as a verb is *"to say something indistinctly and quietly, making it difficult for others to hear,"* which as the reader can see has absolutely no descriptive qualities of this famously renowned game.

Well, mumble is one thing, mumblety-peg is something else. What a subject!! Where did this tale come from? Well, it's not a tale. The game was developed in the 1650's as a boy's knife-throwing game. It's a game that was still popular in the 1940's when I lived on Henry Street. In fact, it was popular not only among boys but men as well. Cowboys are known to have played the game as well as soldiers in World War II while trying to pass the time. Mark Twain's book *Tom Sawyer* recounts "mumblety peg" as one of the boys' favorite outdoor games.

So, how do you play the game? Well, it's simple. First you need a pocketknife. Preferable one about two to three inches long with two blades. A long blade which is opened and aligns straight with the handle of the knife and a short blade that is opened only halfway and forms a ninety-degree angle from the long blade and attached to the knife handle on the same end as the long blade.

There are numerous versions of playing and scoring the game. Our method was quite simple. First, in keeping with the original game rules, a short wooden peg about two to three inches long is gently driven about one third to one half inch into the ground. The object of this gesture is that the loser would have to "mumble" i.e."extract" the peg out of the ground with his teeth or lips. Right or wrong, this is how we played the game.

The first player places his knife on the ground with the short blade barely sticking in the ground to hold the knife steady while the butt end is resting on the ground behind the short blade. Then with the index finger placed under the back edge of the knife, he "flips" the knife upward hoping that when it comes down one of the blades will stick in the ground. Scoring methods are varied, however our scoring method was as follows: Sticking the long blade in the ground is worth ten points while sticking the short blade is worth five points. If neither blade sticks in the ground, no points are scored. Each player gets four flips. The score is then tallied and the player with the fewest number of points has to "mumble", or extract the peg with his teeth.

And we played the game, probably not consistently but more out of boredom than anything else. I know there is now a question in the readers mind as to just how we, boys, age 10 to 12 get a pocketknife to play with. Well, it was really a common practice back then. My dad bought me my knife at Woodson's Lewis's store. The occasion was that we were delivering some furniture that had been shipped via the Railway Express Agency. Dad had the local contract for REA delivery which was awarded to him in 1948. See "The Railway Express Agency" story in Volume I of Greensburg Memories for a more detailed review of the agency.

As I recall, the display of knives was on the righthand side of the store on top of one of the front counters. The knives were enclosed in a display case with a glass front for easy viewing. I was looking at the knives and dad said something to the effect, "Would you like a knife?" "Sure," I replied. "Which one?" he asked. I had no response for that question. About that time, Coleman Paxton, an employee for the store came up and dad ask if he needed some help. "Leo needs a knife." He said. Coleman opened the case picked up a small two blade black handled knife.

He handed the knife to dad and dad handed it me, "This knife OK?" "Yessir." Sale completed. I do not remember the cost, but it was not bank breaking. I have no idea what the name was and kind of knife my dad bought me, other than it had two blades for playing "mumble-peg". I carried the knife, played mumble-peg, cut small branches, scrapped dirt off my shoes, tried to keep it sharp by using a whet rock my dad had and I suppose a lot of other silly things.

The word "pocketknife" keeps popping up in this story and so to answer the perceived question in the readers mind, "What is the history of the pocketknife?"

The oldest pocketknife ever discovered dates to around 600-500 BC. It was unearthed in Hallstatt, Australia and featured a single blade with a bone handle. A little later the Romans were the next group to really use the pocketknife as a tool. None of the knives at this point had locks or springs but used friction to stay closed and required pressure from the hand or thumb to stay open.

In fact, the Romans invented their own version of the Swiss Army knife that included a spoon, blade, spike, fork, spatula and pick.

Many folding knives have been found from the Viking era and had a catch to hold the blade open. In the 1600's the pistol grip "Gully" knife was the most likely used for fighting. Between 1650 and 1700's the peasant knife or "penny knife" became an affordable knife for that time in history.

Since that time knifes of all different configurations and names have surfaced such as Slipjoint, Barlow, Camper, Canoe, Congress, Elephants Toenail (how 'bout that one?) Laquiole, Okapi, (say what?) Peanut, Penknife, Sodbuster, Stockman, Sunfish, Trapper, Whittler, Butterfly and in 1710 the Switchblade. From 1896 until 1990's, pocketknives were developed like the Japanese Higonokami, Defender, French Douk-Douk, Italian Stilletto, etc. etc.

Now, you fully understand the equipment (a small two blade

knife and a small wooden peg) one must have to compete in a rousing game of Mumble-Peg.

But wait, this long forgotten game could have a comeback as the next most highly talked about and competitive sport in the world-renowned Olympic Games, wherever they are held. With this new-old innovation, it's worldwide acclaim could give us old-timers a chance to be seen "FLIPPING & MUMBLING" on the international stage.

Happy Mumble Pegging!!!

Mr. Charles Bloyd – Volume II

In my first publication entitled "Greenburg Memories" I included a chapter entitled "Mr. Charles Bloyd" where I presented three separate events in the life of Charles. A little while after the book was published, I was in group discussion with friends and someone introduced the subject of time pieces. As the discussion progressed, I remembered an event in the life of Mr. Charles Bloyd that I had neglected to include in Volume I. The stories I wrote about Charles in Greensburg Memories may be found on page 256.

Just to redefine the physical setting relating to this event, Charles lived in the Thurlow community in Green County, some six miles south from Greensburg on Highway 68. He lived with his parents whose home was located on a country lane off the west side Highway 68 near the country store owned by Elmore and Gladys Perkins. This country store, like most others in the 1950's was the local resident hangout where one could purchase gas for their car, truck or tractor, a small line of groceries, numerous staples for the home and farm, etc.

In addition to being a great place for small purchases, it was also a place for conversations, serious in nature or otherwise, covering any subject one can imagine. Residents of the local community (mostly men) would gather, sit around the middle the store on chairs and nail kegs and converse.

On this day Charles was walking from his home on the country lane to Elmore and Gladys Perkins country store on Highway 68 to get himself a Double-Cola, more commonly referred to as a "Big Dub". As he entered the country store, greetings were exchanged all around. Charles then purchased his "Big Dub", found a chair and joined the group.

The present conversation (whatever it was) concluded, the discussion (s) continued to evolve on most every conceivable subject that could be thought of and the group continued to raise more subjects and participate in discussions over the next few minutes.

And then, somewhere along the way one of the group asked about watches and soon the group was deep into the subject of pocket watches, wrist watches, alarm clocks, wall clocks, grandfather clocks, etc. During this conversation, as Charles was enjoying his "Big Dub" and listening intensely to the subject matter at hand.

Soon, one of the men in the group looked at Charles and said, "Join in Charles, we could always use another opinion." Charles remained quiet as he was and was never a long winder conversationist anyway.

One of the gentlemen then asked Charles, "Do you own a watch or timepiece, Charles?" Now remember from the chapter in Greensburg Memories, Charles has a real stuttering problem, but he answered, "Noooo, I doo nooot." In a light bantering way, the men continued to ask Charles why not?

Charles slowly set his "Big Dub" down and replied, "Weeelll, I geettt uuup at daaaylight, Mammmmy riiiinnggs thee bellll at ddiinnneeer tiiiime, and annny dammnn fooolll caaan tteell wwwhheen daarrrkk cccoommes." When Charles finished his reply, he gently picked up his "Big Dub" and took a big swig.

The rest of the group almost fell out of their seats laughing and they kept on laughing for a few minutes until one of the gentlemen stopped laughing long enough to catch his breath and said, "Charles, truer words were never spoken!!"

Charles promptly finished his "Big Dub", said his short words of farewell and exited the store for parts unknows. Charles Bloyd was a fine person and it was my pleasure to have known him!!

Jack Allen Sanders

When I was growing, Greensburg was the home to one of the most colorful characters one could meet. No disrespect is intended by identifying him as a character, but all who were acquainted with this gentleman in Greensburg would somewhat agree that he was most interesting to say the least. This gentleman was none other than Mr. Jack Allen Sanders, hereafter referred to as JA. When I knew JA he was about forty to forty five years of age and a widower.

His home of rock construction occupied the corner of Hodgenville Avenue and 1st Street. At that time in his life, he was pretty much a stay-at-home retiree relaxing in his pajamas at least three out of every five days. He also wore a lightweight robe which was ever open and would gently flap in the wind as he walked. Odd, you say, well maybe for some people, but not for JA.

He was quite friendly to all as he sat on his side and back yard in the summertime with his ever-present walking cane and greeting all who passed by via automobile or walking.

JA was originally from Burgin, Kentucky and was a very prominent businessman in our state. His connection to Greensburg was that he met, had a glorious courtship and married Miss Minnie Brummal Lewis on Friday June 2, 1933 at high noon. High Noon Yet! Sound like a gunfight at the OK Corral. Just kidding, guys!!

Minnie Brummal had been a popular member of the Greensburg High School faculty for several years and had greatly endeared herself to the people of Green County.

She was beautiful, he a handsome young man and they were married in a beautiful wedding ceremony at the statuesque colonial home of the bride located on the north corner of Hodgenville Avenue and Highway 70. The home was beautifully decorated with potted flowers, ferns and roses. It was a magnificent day and all attending were having a grand time.

Miss Lewis was dressed in a pink crepe traveling ensemble with accessories to match. She wore a shoulder corsage of gardenias.

Research did not reveal what JA was wearing but even though I was not present at the wedding, I can assure you he was impeccably dressed. JA was thirty-four years of age and Miss Minnie was thirty -two. Each in the prime of life. Immediately following the taking of the wedding vows, the newlyweds left for a motor trip to Chicago. Unfortunately, their marriage was short lived.

Miss Minnie's attendant was Mrs. Ruth Lewis and JA was attended by his best man Robert L. Edwards. Mrs. Isobel Taylor played Mendelssohn's wedding march as the bridal party entered the room, preceded by Rev. W. Gordon Wise who officiated. Mrs. Taylor also played "I Love You Truly" during the ceremony. Incidentally, Isobel Taylor was the wife of G. B. "Gabe" Taylor, owner of Greenburg Bottling Company and our neighbor living just two houses down from us on Henry Street. You can read more about Gabe Taylor in Book 1, page 305 of "Greensburg Memories".

Just five short years later, at age 37 on May 20,1938 Miss Minnie passed away at their home after an illness of several weeks. Funeral services were held on Sunday, May 22,1938 at the Greensburg Presbyterian Church with the Rev. R. T. Stewart officiating and assisted by the Rev's V. A. Jones and J. W. Reynolds. Miss Minnie was buried in the Greensburg Cemetery. She was survived by her husband JA Sanders, her sister Mrs. W. F. Shadoan of Wickliffe, Ky and her brother, Mr. Woodson Lewis of Greensburg. Miss Minnie and JA had no children.

The funeral must have been a beautiful affair as Miss Minnie was attended by eight active pallbearers, six honorary pallbearers, twenty-two flower girls and six members of her Sunday School class.

After the death of his beautiful spouse, JA maintained his residence in their family home. I began to know of JA about 1948 as I and my friends would be riding my bike around Greensburg. In fair weather, JA would be sitting in the back yard and would wave and shout such comments as, "Good day, boys, out for a little ride?" "Nice day, isn't it?" "Where are you young men off to?"

JA was not a recluse by any means. He just liked his privacy. On occasion, he would make his was into downtown Greensburg for a haircut, maybe some lunch and some conversation with just about everyone he met. On his sojourns from his home to downtown he would dress in a starched white shirt, tie, pressed trousers, matching sport coat, highly polished shoes and of course, his ever-present walking cane.

He would summon a taxi and make the trip downtown. His first stop was usually one of the two barber shops located on the square. The reader may review a story about these barbershops in Book 1, page 275 of "Greensburg Memories". I have had the pleasure of being in the barbershop owned by Ada Kidd and Alton Stearman when JA would enter. His entrance would be unintentionally dramatic, but dramatic it was. He would open the door and enter with a natural swagger and begin greeting everyone. He would then have a seat and ask Ada if he could get a haircut.

The reply was "Certainly, JA, you are second/third in line." That was fine with JA as it provided him with a platform for conversation with everyone in the barbershop. His conversation was engaging to say the least. He could discuss any and everything in a very pleasant and somewhat natural authoritative voice.

JA carried his money folded in his left front pocket for easy access. He would quite often pull out a five or a ten -dollar bill, look at a particular person and remark, "Here young man, go buy yourself a new shirt" or "Here is a fin, I'll pay for your haircut today" and other remarks as they would surface when he was in a conversation mode. These comments were not intended to be abusive or negative in any way and they were not received as such.

After some time in the barbershop where he purchased a haircut and possible a shave while continuing his conversation, he would exit onto the sidewalk and greet who ever passed by. He would make his way around the square and stop in various business establishments based on his own whimsical fancy. I do know he liked to visit the Corner Drug Store where he could always get a bite to eat and drink and continue his conversation.

After making his rounds, about two to three hours, talking and occasionally handing out money for whatever reason he fancied, he would walk across the street where a taxi was usually parked and procure a one-way ride back to his home where he would resume his relaxing style of lounging in his pajamas, not to be seen in downtown Greensburg for another month or so.

He was a colorful man, a great conversationist, a snappy dresser and always a welcome sight to merchants and street strollers as well.

I left for college in June 1954 and didn't see much of JA after that, but I'm sure he continued to be his affable self. JA died suddenly at his home Sunday, October 17, 1965 at the age of sixty-six. He had been without his beautiful bride for twenty-seven years. He was a retired businessman, a veteran of World War I and a member of the Cumberland Presbyterian Church. He was a native of Taylor County.

Funeral services were held at the Foster-Jones Funeral Home on Wednesday, October 20, 1965 with Rev. Walter Swetnam officiating. Pallbearers were Woodson Lewis III, William Lewis, Victor Griffith, Brooks Edwards, H. H. Durham and Bill Lile. Burial was in the Calvary National Cemetery in Lebanon.

I never had the pleasure of meeting Miss Minnie or observing her and JA together, but I believe it was truly a benefit for the people of Greensburg to have Miss Minnie and JA in their midst.

Cross And Easter Sunday - Buckner's Hill

There are four ways to enter the city of Greensburg, (1) Highway 61, 68 and 70 running north and south, (2) Hodgenville Avenue off Highway 61 running east and west, (3) Columbia Avenue of Legion Park Road, Highway 417 from the east and (4) from the "Burma Road" to Buckner's Hill from the west.

All these highways form routes from which you can reach various points of interest within our fair city. In writing about various sites in Greensburg, I have briefly brought these avenues of approach into these stories in the descriptive sense to include Buckner's Hill which is referenced in Book 1, page 252, "Greensburg Memories."

Buckner's Hill is the focal point of this story because of the activity at the crest. Buckner's Hill begins at the intersection of 2nd Street and Columbia Avenue just a short distance from downtown Greensburg and rises steeply for about one-half mile where it crests at the entrance to the main house of the Garnett Milby farm and the field in front of it. Entrance to the Milby home was reached by turning left onto a small lane at the crest of Buckner's Hill. The home was built between 1810 and 1925 originally owned by Richard Aylett Buckner, alas the name "Buckner's Hill." Now, who would ever guess that?

At the top of Buckner's Hill, the road curves slightly to the left (west) and that road in the 1940's and 1950's was called "Burma Road". It seems, that the road was named by W. L. "Dick" Kessler after he had personally paid for reconstructing about one mile of the road. He said it was in honor of a famous road built in the far East in the early part of World War II. Thus the "Burma Road" became known far and wide.

By 1941, the family of William Cantrell had owned the property for decades. The Garnett Milby family later purchased the home and it remained in the Milby family during the 1950's where I attended the Easter sunrise service.

The significance of this crest is that a cross, of a religious nature, measuring about twenty feet tall with the top span being about six feet across was erected each year about fifty feet in the field just off the lane to the Milby home. The field in front of the cross contained a multitude of March lilies. The formulation of the Easter Sunrise Service and the cross is not readily ascertained nor neither is who constructed the cross. There was no lighting on the cross. Nevertheless, it was there and well attended.

The origin of the lilies has not been determined but it could have been from the flowers people attending the sunrise service who were asked to bring flowers to place around the bottom of the cross. Perhaps the flowers were already growing on the hill and do you think that could have been the reasoning behind the cross and Easter sunrise service? I don't know but it seems logical to me. The first sunrise service was held in 1941 and was attended by about one hundred and twenty-five people.

All distances and number of attendees are estimates on the part of the writer and have not actually been measured.

The cross was quite visible to various points in Greensburg. I believe the cross was erected about two weeks prior to Easter and remained until two weeks after Easter.

The cross was of wooden construction, painted white and quite possibly of four by four inch square posts. It was an impressive sight to say the least and even quite stark when looking up and view the cross silhouetted against a beautiful blue sky of the day or the bright orange setting sun in the evening.

The biggest attraction I believe was that it provided the perfect setting for the sun rise service on Easter Sunday morning. The service was conducted probably on a rotating basis, one of several ministers of selected Greensburg churches. There was on open invitation to anyone that wanted to attend. Just show up about 6 a.m. on Easter Sunday at the top of Buckner's Hill and be sure to wear a warm coat, gloves and a hat as the weather atop the hill was cold to say the least, if there was any wind blowing, and there usually was and it could be quite miserable.

I remember driving my dad's truck up Bucker's Hill about 6 a.m., parking and gathering with the crowd awaiting to hear the sunrise service. The crowd that gathered was multi denomination and usually numbered nearly one hundred people in attendance.

Once the crowd gathered, the minister would begin the service and due to several factors, such as time of day, weather, a need for coffee, etc. the message was usual short but very powerfully given.

Crosses as a religious symbol are displayed all over the world in various forms and sizes. The one cross I viewed that immediately brought back memories of our cross on Buckner's Hill was the cross in Rio de Janiro, Brazil. This magnificent cross is displayed in the form of Jesus Christ with outstretched arms. It stands ninety-eight feet tall, and the outstretched arms span ninety-two feet.

The statue is immense to say the least. The corner stone was ceremonially laid on April 4, 1922 to commemorate the centennial on that day of Brazil's independence from Portugal. Construction began in 1926 and was completed in 1931.

So, it's a little bigger than our cross but ours was enjoyed by me and a lot of others in our hometown. The Easter sunrise service was moved from Buckner's Hill to the town square in 1969. I wonder what beauty a public square would possess that would overshadow the beautiful hilltop at Buckner's Hill with a cross and blooming March lilies covering the hillside? Well, it does not matter Leo as it happened anyway.

The March lilies can still be viewed on the hillside atop Buckner's Hill each spring. It is still a wonderful site. Just another memory of youth in a small comfortable setting in Kentucky.

March Lillies pictures on Buckner's Hill with the Milby Residence in the background. Downtown Greensburg would be on the left side of the picture.

Construction Of A "GATE" across a "GAP"

A "GAP GATE" you say! "What on earth are you talking about?" "And why would you write about such a thing?" Some professionals would say, "I don't know anything about a **GATE**, but a **GAP** is a "General Accounting Procedure." That's true, but that's **not** what I'm talking about.

Common definition of a **GATE** is:

(a) A hinged barrier used to close an opening in a wall, fence or hedge.

Common definitions of a **GAP** are:

(a) A break or hole in an object or between two objects.
(b) A pass or a way through a range of hills or an unfilled space or interval.

You would agree that normally gates are constructed out of wood or metal with either closed or spacing between the boards or metal, being hinged at one end to a post or structure with a closing bracket on the closing end.

Now we're getting closer. I also realize that a lot of people are not familiar with my definition of a **GAP** and the accompanying **GATE**. The definition of **"my GAP"** is this:

"An opening between two fence posts usually when the location is on a farm used in an opening of a pasture field but could be used for any field and a **"GAP GATE"** is the object that closes the distance between two fence posts."

A **"GAP GATE"** is usually made of 4 wooden sticks (of varying size) approximately 3 feet high. The sticks are attached to usually three strand of barb wire (not your best barb wire but some that has no apparent use and can be rusted). The 4 sticks will be placed as follows: One on the left side of the opening, one on the right side of the opening and the other spaced evenly in the middle.

Construction of the **GAP GATE** usually begins with the barbed wire being wrapped around the stick on the left progressing to the right and wrapping of the one stick in the middle and ending up being wrapped around the stick on the right. Obviously, you need to measure the opening to get the spacing and length fixed so as to fit the opening where the **GAP GATE** will be installed.

The purpose of the **GAP GATE** is normally to keep cattle from getting out of the pasture. For this, you do not need a fancy or heavily constructed gate.

The barbed wire is somewhat evenly spaced from top to bottom so that the **GAP GATE** is high enough to prevent livestock, cows etc. from climbing over the top and exiting the enclosure (usually the pasture field).

Now that the **GAP GATE** is finished, it must be attached to the fence post on the left and the right sides of the opening. A round piece of barbed the stick on the left side through the "hooped" barbed wire and pushing down so the stick is firmly placed inside the hoop. Then pulling wire (hooping) is placed around the fence post on the left. This is required for both the bottom and top of the fence post.

To operate the **GAP GATE,** you would (working from the left side) place the bottom of the stick to the left, insert the top of the stick into the hoop on top of the fence post. This stabilizes the left side. Dragging the **GAP GATE** across from the left to the right side of the opening, repeat the same procedure for securing the **GAP GATE** and apply to the right side. Properly place sticks in the barded hoops will leave the **GAP GATE** firmly attached to both posts and thereby prevent the cattle from exiting the pasture.

That's really all there is to it. One might say, why did you write this? And I say why not, I understand how a **GAP GATE** is constructed and used as they were in use on our farm and I guess I wanted everyone else to understand as well.

Telephone Calls In The 50's

As I began thinking about the way one made telephone calls prior to today's massive electronic systems, it suddenly occurred to me that that the 1950's was somewhat of mid-point in the evolution of the telephone.

Briefly, in the 1870's Elisha Gray and Alexander Graham Bell independently designed devices that could transmit speech electrically. Both men rushed their respective designs for these prototype telephones to the patent office within hours of each other. Bell got his telephone patented first and later emerged the victor in a legal dispute with Gray.

Alexander Graham Bell was born on March 3, 1847 in Edinburgh, Scotland. He was family educated in sound from his youth as his father and grandfather were authorities for speech therapy for the deaf. After the deaths of Bell's two brothers, the family immigrated to Canada in 1870.

After a brief period of living in Ontario, the Bells' moved to Boston, Mass. Where they established a speech therapy practice. One of Bell's pupils was a young Helen Keller who when they met was not only blind and deaf but was also unable to speak.

By October 1874, Bell's research had progressed to the extent that he could inform his future father-in-law, Boston attorney Gardiner Greene Hubbard, about the possibility of a multiple telegraph. Bell proceeded with his work and by June 1875, the goal of creating a device that would transmit speech electrically was about to be realized.

On June 2,1875, while experimenting with the harmonic telegraph, it was discovered completely by accident that sound could be transmitted over a wire. Over the next year the work was accelerated and one day, Mr. Bell shouted into the mouthpiece, "Mr. Watson, come here – I want to see you". The first telephone had just been made.

The device was patented, and success began to spread. By

1877, the first regular telephone line was established. By the end of 1880, over 49,000 (a) telephones were in the United States. The Bell Telephone Company was founded in 1877. Bell quickly bought out competitors and after a series of mergers, etc. American Telephone and Telegraph (AT&T) was incorporated in 1880. Because Bell controlled the intellectual property and patents behind the telephone system AT&T had a de facto monopoly over the young industry (b).

The first regular telephone exchange was established in 1878. The early telephones were leased in pairs. The subscriber was required to ensure his own line was connected with another. Progress continued to be made and in 1899, the coin operated telephone (payphone) was patented by William Gray of Hartford, Connecticut and was installed and used In the Hartford Bank. Unlike today, the users paid after they had finished their call.

The first telephone book was published in New Haven, Connecticut by the New Haven District Telephone Company in February 1878. It was one page long and held fifty names; no numbers were listed, as an operator would connect you. The page was divided into four sections: residential, professional, essential services and miscellaneous.

In 1886, Reuben H. Donnelly produced the first Yellow Pages-brand directory featuring business names and phone numbers categorize by the types of products and services. Caller ID and 911 did not come along until the 1960's.

By 1905 there were about 2.2 million phones, but did we know how to use them? Well, take telephone number "**Mu**rray Hill 685-9975. Using the telephone keypad, here's the way it worked: **MU** represents 6 and 8 on the telephone keypad, 5 was added and that number represented the "East Side of Manhattan's" telephone exchange. This system also allowed the call to say to the operator, "Murray Hill 685-9975, please". This is also why four letters with the number nine. Check it out!!!

As an aside here, on July 2, 1961 the Record Herald ran a short article stating, "Greensburg phone customers will be able to use seven digit phone numbers instead of the two letter and five number in December of this year".

In the 1950's full words for making phone calls were abolished and area codes were established, but they were used mostly by operators and not customers.

The design of phones in the 1940's and 1950's varied from desk phone to wall phones, etc. and not much of a style change. One thing all phones had in common was color. I'm reminded of the story of Henry Ford's reply when some employees asked, "Mr. Ford can we paint Ford cars and trucks different colors"? "Certainly, replied Mr. Ford, "as long as they are all black".

Now that we are all aware of the dramatic changes in telephones and the operations thereof through the years, I'm gonna' go back to my story of telephones in the 1950's. First, we did not have a phone in our home, and I don't know that a lot of people did. Businesses had them for obvious reasons.

The telephone exchange in Greensburg was first housed upstairs over the Kozy Korner in the early 1900's, however in the 1950's it was located upstairs over the Shuffett Dry Goods store. Access to the telephone office was via stairway between the dry goods store and the Corner Drug Store. After ascending to the top of the stairs, one would enter the office of Mr. Tom Burress, Attorney on the left which was located over the Corner Drug Store and entrance to the telephone office was on the right.

There was a narrow passageway with a banister on the stairwell side to prevent one was falling back down the stairs. Upon entering the telephone office, the operators were on the left sitting in front of a massive keyboard (see photos).

The telephone operators were Lynxton Pickett, Louise Chaudion and Iona Patterson. These beautiful and well-respected ladies are not the operators pictured in the attached photos. As an aside, every day at precisely twelve noon, the "twelve o'clock whistle", denoting the noon hour, would be activated utilizing a preset time element. The noon whistle was not sounded on Sundays as churches services would probably still be in process. While the whistle was blowing all telephone service would be suspended due to the noise and as a courtesy to whomever might be on the phone at the time.

In addition to the "twelve o'clock whistle" the telephone office played a crucial role in engaging the all-volunteer fire department. The process was that, whomever discovered a fire, the first order of business was to call the telephone office, who would sound the fire alarm, and then call the fire chief who would then proceed quickly to the fire house where other members of the fire department would meet and off to fight the fire they would go, all because of very informative and some very efficient telephone operators.

If one did not have either a home phone or access to a phone, a telephone call could be made from the telephone exchange. In the right front corner of the exchange there was a telephone booth constructed of wood with a wall mounted phone in the rear. The booth has windows for viewing and a door for privacy. The costs of a phone call equaled $.10. That's right ten cents!!!

The procedure was that the caller would relate the appropriate number to the operator who would begin connecting the call, then tell the caller when to enter the booth. When the caller entered the booth and picked up the receiver the phone would start ringing. The caller would answer, engage the called party in conversation and when finished hang up and exit the booth, at which time payment could be made for the phone call.

I know it seems like a cumbersome process and thinking back on the subject it was, but back then it was just the way things were. We had not yet heard of Dick Tracy's talking wristwatch and were not totally consumed by the phone as some of us are today.

And so, my friends, just another "Memory" is documented just so later generations will know "how it was back then"!!

(a) The number of telephones in the 1950's was approximately forty-four million households with about two thirds (twenty-nine million) having a telephone. Telephones were rented during that era as opposed to ownership today.

The number of phones in the 2000's is 4.88 billion and 62% of people worldwide are cell phone owners. More people have cell phone around the world than those who have access to a flush toilet.

(b) AT&T would maintain its control over the U. S. telephone market until 1984 when a settlement with the U. S. Department of Justice forced AT&T to end its control over state markets.

The attached photos are not of the Greensburg Telephone Office but do present the type of equipment used in the 1950's.

An aside to the above was surfaced to me recently and I think it's perfectly acceptable to include here. Our community had a population of around seventeen hundred in the 1950's and to put it mildly, "everyone knew everyone else" and certainly I was acquainted with the telephone operators. However, I was more acquainted with Lynxton than the other two ladies. She, her husband Howard and daughter Martha Howard lived directly across from the high school on Hodgenville Avenue just to the right of "Stuffy's", the local hangout during recess for every student in Greensburg High School

One Saturday in the spring of 1954, I happened to be at Martha Howard's home with a group of our friends. I must have asked Howard (Mr. Pickett) if I might borrow his car so we (me, Martha Howard and friends) could take a joy ride. The car was returned "undented" which was in our favor and we obviously thanked Howard (Mr. Pickett) for permitting us to take a joy ride. The Pickett's rented the home from Mr. Frank Cantrell. Shortly after the joy ride Martha Howard and parents moved into their newly constructed home on Columbia Avenue. I wonder if he thought that if he moved, I wouldn't know where he lived and would ask him for his car anymore? You recken'? Probably not, he was a very nice man!!

**A bank of telephone operators processing phone calls in the 1950's
(Not in Greensburg)**

**Telephone operator manning a single operator telephone system
(Not in Greensburg)**

A New Car & Death On The Double "S" Curves

In 1947, the grand finale at the American Legion picnic in Greensburg, Kentucky was the drawing to win a new car. How the tickets were obtained I'm not sure as the reference material is not real clear here, but the method of being qualified to win the new car is not germane to the story.

The picnic, as usual was a success. This was a big day for the picnic as it was a beautiful warm sunny rain free day and was crowded with children and grown up alike. About 5 p.m. or so, word began to circulate that the drawing would be soon and to gather around the speakers stand which was manned by two local officials, the Mayor of Greensburg and the County Judge of Green County. Directly in front of the speaker's stand sat the grand prize, a new Ford automobile, black in color and boy was it shiny. It had obviously been washed just prior to being brought to the speaker's stand and gleamed in the sunlight.

The crowd gathered with much mummering with talk centering around comments such as, "What would I do with a new car?", "Boy, wouldn't it be nice to win that", "If I could win that car, it would simply be wonderful" and "I just feel as they are going to draw my name," etc. etc.

The crowd around the speakers stand continued to expand in size and the word was passed that "It's almost time for the drawing!" The big wire cylinder holding the tickets was full and was being slowly turned by two young men to keep the tickets shuffled, so to speak, and to allow everyone a fair chance to win.

The Mayor kept talking with the crowd, "Is everyone ready for the drawing?" "Yeeaah", the crowd answered. "Get everyone down here near the podium as we don't want anyone to miss this event." "Come on in closer folks so those in the back can hear the winner."

"Whose gonna' draw the winning ticket"? shouted the crowd. "The Mayor and County Judge, of course". "Well, let's do it",

125

the crowd responded. Finally, after much talk and enthusiastic prompting, it was time for the drawing. As the boys continued to turn the big wire cylinder, the Mayor and County Judge made their way down to the basket.

The turning of the wire cylinder stopped, the door to the cylinder was opened and both officials reached in and together selected a ticket which contained the winner. The two officials looked at each other and then looked at the crowd, who shouted, "Well, who is it?"

The mayor held the winning ticket in the air and said, "The winner of this year's grand prize is." Halted his voice and looked at the County Judge who loudly proclaimed, "Howard Jones!!!!!"

Some of the crowd looked at each other and said, "Who is Howard Jones?" "He's Leo and Grace Jones's boy," someone answered. "Is he even old enough to drive"? "I thought a grown up should win" and on and on and on. Off to the side of the crowd, a group of high school age boys and girls stood watching the drawing. Howard Jones was in that crowd. As the announcement was made, all the students cheered and started hittin' Howard on the head and shoulders. Howard was as stunned as anyone.

"Is Howard Jones here?" asked the mayor. "Here he is," answered one the young people. "Come on down here, Howard and get the keys to your new car," the mayor announced. Howard made his way through the cheering crowd to the podium. The Mayor and Country Judge welcomed Howard to the podium by shaking his hand and relating, "Congratulations, young man, on winning this new car." Like most teenagers, Howard did not have a lot to say, but was constantly eyeing his new car.

He was presented the keys by the Mayor and was escorted from the podium to his new car. Everyone crowded around congratulating Howard and looking inside the new car. Not far from the car stood his family, mother, father, sisters, brothers. All were talking, amazed and surprised when Grace, his mother said, "That car will be the death of Howard*."

After winning the car, Howard and his friends had a grand time that spring and summer riding around and experiencing a once in a lifetime experience. Howard was 17 years old when he won the car.

School started in September and students were still talking about Howard winning the car. School progressed into fall and on Friday, November 28, 1947, three young men, Howard, Billy Lingle and Henry Hall, all GHS students rode in Howard's car to a basketball game in Campbellsville, Kentucky. They watched the game, had some popcorn and cokes, and conversed with their friends and spectators sitting near them. After the game they made their way to Howard's car and started home to Greensburg.

Campbellsville is about twelve miles from Greensburg on highway 68 & 70. The road is generally composed of a few hills, some curves and short straight stretches and is a relatively easy drive. About one mile from Greensburg the highway suddenly turns into two steep curves known as the double "S" curves. It is highly advisable that speed should be reduced when approaching and executing these curves.

On this Friday night when Howard and companions approached the double "S" curves something happened. The auto did not negotiate the curves, instead it crashed over one embankment into another. The car was demolished except for the right front section where Billy Lingle and Henry Hall were sitting.

Howard Jones was killed instantly. Billy Lingle was critically injured, suffered a fractured skull and concussion. He was transferred immediately to the Lebanon hospital. Henry Hall was also transferred to the Lebanon hospital with a broken shoulder and bruises. Both Billy Lingle and Henry Hall survived their injuries.

Apparently, the boys were all good friends and athletes as Howard was a first team basketball player at GHS. Billy Lingle was a starting guard on the first team and Henry Hall plays on the second team.

The Greensburg community was obviously shocked to hear of such a tragedy and it mourned its youth for some time. Howard's funeral was held on Sunday morning, November 30, 1947 at the Greenburg Methodist Church with the Reverends E. G. Sidle and V. A. Jones in charge of the rites. Howard had united with the Greensburg Methodist Church three years before in 1944. Pallbearers were Marshall Lowe, Hardin H. Durham, Jeff Vaughn, Ben E. Burress, Brooks Edwards and Sonny Pickett.

Honorary pallbearers were Tommy Jones, Joe Jones, Doug Pickett, Austin Pickett, Bobby Cooke, Leon Upton, Rollin Beard, William R. Blakeman, Gordon Pierce and Charles Shuffett. Flowers girls were from the senior class of GHS.

Howard was interned in the Curry Cemetery near Pierce, Kentucky.

Memo

(1)

Just a little info here, future occupations of the pallbearers were: Marshall Lowe became principal of Greensburg Grade School, Hardin H. Durham worked in the family owned Durham Grocery & Department Store and was later an executive at the Peoples Bank, Jeff Vaughn (unknown), Ben E. Burress, owned a lumber company and was a State Representative, Brooks Edwards became a farmer and Sonny Pickett worked at Tennessee Gas Transmission Company in Gabe, Kentucky and lived on Penick Avenue, two doors up from my mother.

(2)

At the time of the accident, the Jones family resided at 202 Shreve Avenue which is short hilly street left off Depot Street. A few years later their home was purchased by Joe and Marue Bundy, the father and mother of my wife Joyce (nee) Bundy Wright.

*Comments by Howard's mother result from numerous conversation and expressions by various people dating down through the years.

Another Use For Shaving Lotion

What does a male apply to his face after removing his whiskers with a razor? Well, for a lot of us, we apply shaving lotion, or it might be called cologne today. The lotions of old (won't name brands here) would sting the face upon application (and that was expected) but did allow the man to have a nice masculine smell emitting from his face, at least for a short time.

Well, I guess every book needs to have a screwy story and this one will probably qualify. In the 1950's there were a numbers of house painters in Greensburg and it being a small community everyone knew everyone else.

The painters of that day, for the most part wore white shirts and trousers when they were working. Some even wore white painter's caps. Also, like all young lads of that day we roamed free around town and through the streets of Greensburg.

I began to know this gentleman (name whose name will not be revealed here) who was a house painter. I don't know how the acquaintance occurred other than just be riding my bike by the house where he might be painting we would wave and I might stop and exchange a few words occasionally.

One day as I was riding by, he hailed me down and ask me to come over to where he was working. He said, "Leo, I need you to do me a favor." "Yessir," I replied. "Here's two dollars, go to the drug store and buy me a small bottle of shaving lotion, (again, brand names excluded) and go by the grocery store and get me a loaf of white bread." "Sure," I replied and off I went. I went to the Corner Drug Store and bought a small bottle of saving lotion, then to Freeman Faulkner's grocery across the street for the loaf of white bread and returned it to the gentleman, he thanked me and off I went. As time went by he would occasionally ask me to buy shaving lotion and or a loaf of white bread for him. I never gave it a thought.

On day I was talking with my dad and the subject of me buying the shaving lotion and the bread came up. "Do you know why he

129

wants those two items?" "No Sir, I have no idea." Dad then went onto explain the process as it apparently was common knowledge (mind here not common usage) among the adults of the community. I can assure you it was not the practice of <u>MY</u> father!!!

He related that sometime people tend to use these and other products as an alternative to legal whiskey. This made no sense to me as I had never had a drink of an alcoholic beverage and was totally unfamiliar with the subject. Being somewhat inquisitive I asked him how this worked. He explained that first of all he had never undertaken of these products (shaving lotion and bread) and I could certainly believe that knowing my father as I did, but he had heard that the following is the process.

He said that he thought that the process was to take about five or six slices of bread, hold it over a jar and pour the shaving lotion through it. This is supposed to make the liquid gathering in the bottom of the jar consumable and provide somewhat of the same effect of drinking legal whiskey. So, I guess the bottom line is that instead of buying legal whiskey, one can make their own alcohol by utilizing the process described above.

Well, bottom line is this. (1) My father told me in no uncertain terms that my days of buying shaving lotion and bread were over. (2) He further informed me that should I be riding my bike near a house where this man was working, do not speak, keep riding and don't look back. Yes sir, as the message was loud and clear. So my career of being the procurer of shaving lotion and milk was over.

And so ends another story in my youth and presentation of "Greensburg Memories."

And, as I said at the beginning, every book needs a screwy story and I would submit to you, this is it!!!!!!!!!!!!!!

Money Made And Lost

The summer of 1948 was like any other in Greensburg. Hot, humid with lots of nothing to do for the youth of our town. Some of the youth had part time jobs, running errands, mowing lawns, etc. and some were not what you might call gainfully employed. Well, that didn't matter, we were young, twelve to thirteen years of age and just glad to be out of school for the summer.

We could play a little baseball among ourselves but that too became boring. So, we rode our bikes, (at least the boys did), drank "Big Dubs" (Double Cola) and just enjoyed the summer. But, alas, some of our parents were wondering when we were going to do something constructive. So, mowing yards became the most sought-after occupation because almost everyone had a lawn mower, and the adults would rather pay a small fee than to get all hot and sweaty. (That's what we though anyway).

During the summer I had accumulated several yards to mow at a reasonable price. I could use our lawnmower as it was the old reel type push mower whereas power mowers were a far thinking piece of equipment of the future. What a deal, all the sweat one could produce at no costs. Wow!!!

So, on this occasion, for the past week or two I had mowed a few yards and collected somewhere around $3.00 plus change. Not bad for 1948. I had developed a habit of carrying my money in the watch pocket of my jeans. Just as an aside, I kept this habit for the next several years as it just seemed to be a convenient place to carry what little money a young lad could make.

Now, not to make a distinction here, as all boys of our age knew each other, but each group sought their own level of association. Let me explain a little here. Some of our parents had let it be known to us that we were not to be keeping too much company with certain other lads in the community. The ones we did not "run with" so to speak were not evil by any means but by association or other means some of our parents just let it be known loud and clear, keep your distance.

Well, enough of that as it is only mentioned to set the stage here. So, on this particular hot summer day, two or three of us decided to go swimming. We had two places on Green River where we would swim. Both places have been previously referred to in Volume 1 of "Greensburg Memories", pages 335 thru 346.

The two places were "High Banks" which is located slightly upriver from highway 68 and the Green River bridge, giving access, egress to and from Greensburg. The other local swimming hole was located on Green River but some five or so miles as the crow files to the east, just off Legion Park Road and below the American Legion Hall, and that was where we decided to go swimming on this day.

The river was easily accessible with a large sand bar for easy access into the water (when the river wasn't on the rise) and was surrounded by shade trees all up and down the river thus provided a cool and pleasant atmosphere for relaxing and swimming. This sand bar was often used for washing cars as one could pull out say fifteen or so feet from the bank.

This day we left from my house on Henry Street, riding our bikes down Hodges Street to Columbia Ave, turned left and the road soon turned into Sardin's Ford Road (Now Legion Park Road) and made our way to Green River for a swim.

As we arrived, there were already several people swimming and we talked with a few of them and decided to change into our bathing suits. You could do this behind some big trees on the high riverbank without anyone noticing and this was a common practice. As we were conversing with the crowd, we noticed a couple of our neighbors whom we were not supposed to associate with conversing as well with other swimmers.

As we change into bathing suits, we rolled up our clothes and pushed them under a big tree root for safe keeping. We all wondered if our clothes would be safe. My two friends had a small amount of money as well and were concerned about the safety of it as well as me. Not feeling comfortable at all but not having a pocket in our bathing suits we decided that our clothes, etc. would probably be ok. So off to the river we went, swam for awhile and then decided that we had enough so we traced our way back to where we had tried to hide our clothes and lo and behold when we reached the tree where our clothes were supposedly hidden, the ugly truth hit us.

We saw our clothes scattered around on the ground and of course, when looking for our money, it was gone. Sick, was hardly the word for this occasion. Without seeing who did this deed, we knew immediately that our "friends" who we were not supposed to run around with were missing. Alas, along with our money, etc. Although we didn't see the theft, but we knew exactly who had taken it. What do we do now?

As we went home, we decided to ask our parents what to do. As I relayed the story to Dad, he simply stated that yes it was bad that you lost your money. However, if you didn't see who stole it, it would be a difficult task to ever prove. He further remarked, "You can always replace the money, so just let it go."

So I did and my friends parents had told them the same thing. After that for a few years we would see our apparent thieves, we would look at them and they at us, both knowing what had happened, but no words were exchanged. Time heals a little and as we grew a little older, we realized it just wasn't worth the hassle over a few bucks. So, we all graduated from high school and went our separate ways.

After graduation and a few years passed, we had a couple of class reunions and invariably as we chatted with each other, the subject of our theft would find it's way to the surface. As years passed, as I would return to Greensburg for a visit, I would always run into my swimming friends and joke about have you lost any money lately. Our "friends" who stole the money stayed in Greensburg and lived a peaceful and successful life I suppose, and I wish them well.

Moral of this writing is, never leave your money in the watch pocket of your jeans and hide them under a tree root as your money will surely be gone when your return.

My Last Year On Henry Street

Well, I guess everything must come to an end. I had lived on Henry Street since 1942 when I started to grade school and here it was now 1954 and I would soon graduate from high school. I did not finish high school as the valedictorian but was not the last in my class either. I was somewhere in the masses and that's OK. The following thought came to me years later that I somehow gotta' give it some credence: "As the education system continued to default, I was somehow allowed to move from grade 1 through grade 12 along with my contemporaries in the allotted time."

During this time span I suffered no grave illnesses, did not commit any crimes, and now have brought with me lots and lots of good memories. My parents were good to me, I was permitted to play sports, roam the streets of Greensburg without supervision, was encouraged to seek parttime work for spending money and even got to go to Louisville one summer day in 1953 to see the Louisville Colonels, a minor league in The American Association in Cardinal Stadium located in Kentucky Fair and Exposition Center.

The minor league clubs were independently owned and developed affiliations with Major League teams. Professional baseball in Louisville goes all the way back to 1876 and the Louisville Grays, charter members of the National League.

There is a rich history of the Louisville Colonels in terms of names, affiliations and leagues. In 1999, Louisville adopted the name River Bats, in 2000 they moved to Slugger Field, then shortened the name to simply Bats in 2002. However, back in 1953 I knew was that this was my first trip to a professional baseball stadium, and I was excited.

Mr. Joe Guthrie, owner of the Greensburg Firestone Store invited Larry Gumm, Freddy Estes and me to go with him and some other Greensburg gentlemen to a night game with the Louisville Colonels. It was quite an exciting experience for the three of us. Not only did he take us to the game, he purchased our food (hot dogs and cokes) while we were there. This was the first trip to Louisville for me and possibly Larry and Freddie as well. In any case, seeing the city, the massive ballpark, the enormous amount of traffic, etc. it was a once in a lifetime experience and I have recalled it many times during the ensuing years.

Sometime in the early spring of 1954, mom and dad decided to move. We moved to a home on North Main Street. Our house was located about nine hundred feet north of The Peoples Bank and our neighbors were Mr. & Mrs. Ray Shuffett. The home was larger than the one we had on Henry Street, in that it had an upstairs (my bedroom), two bedrooms downstairs, an enclosed back porch and a carport to park our truck. The home has since been town down as well as the Shuffett residence.

My senior year in 1954 was filled with the usual activities of the senior class. Junior – Senior Banquet (no prom then), ordering class rings, hoping to pass all subjects so we could graduate, etc. One of the classes I took during my senior year was Bookkeeping and I immediately was drawn to the numbers, the system and the results from recording each transaction in the proper format. Mrs. Fanola DeSpain was the teacher and was very helpful and encouraging to me.

In fact, she talked with Mom and Dad to see if I was interested in attending college at the Bowling Green Business University which offered Bachelor of Science Degrees in Accounting and Business Administration. Absolutely I was interested. Shortly after graduation, Mrs. DeSpain took Mom and I to Bowling Green where we met with the Administration Officials of the college which was referred to as "BU". We had a tour, got me enrolled beginning in the summer semester and found me a place to stay. BU did not have dormitories and students stayed in individual homes that offered rooms to college students.

In early June 1954, I left home for college and basically never returned (except to marry a beautiful lady, my dear wife of fifty-seven years and leave again) as I attended summer school and graduated in 1957, a mere three years after first leaving Henry

Street. Life on Henry Street had come to an end and another phase of my life was beginning.

I must say in all candor, that the memory of Henry Street has never faded and has remained strong with me throughout me entire life!!

Whoa now, there is life **AFTER** Henry Street. Actually, there is more life after Henry Street than there was on ole' Henry. You know, here are some stories that might be of interest such as: Yellow Dog & Gus The Cat, John Christopher, Angie and The Grenade, Jack & Fernie, Hogan, Shotgun & Trick and others. Now the titles might not sound exciting, but I can assure you they are entertaining, and I will be presenting them in my next book entitled "Bits & Pieces."

Until then, "Thank You" so much reading about my "Memories" and I hope yours were as pleasant as mine.

PROCUREMENT & AWARDING OF PRISONER OF WAR MEDAL

United States military service members have been detained as Prisoners of War beginning with the Revolutionary War where some 20,000 Americans were held in captivity by enemy forces, following by The War of 1812 with 5,000. The Civil War added another 408,000 and World War's I & II accumulated another 98,120 more. Korea, Vietnam and The Middle East rounded out the total with 8,966 for a grand total of 540, 086.

The Prisoner of War Medal is a military award of the United States Armed Forces which was authorized by Congress and signed into law by President Ronald Reagan on November 8, 1985.

The idea of creating a military award to recognize prisoners of war was first put forth in 1944. However, the military services opposed the idea, claiming that other medals could be awarded in such cases. Congressman F. Edward Hebert (D-LA) submitted a bill to create a POW lapel button in 1971, but the bill was defeated. The Defense Department told Herbert that the pin could have an adverse impact on the morals and pride of those families whose members are or were still missing in action, it also claims that it was inappropriate to seemingly reward soldiers for having suffered with such an undesirable status "as prisoners of war." Photo of Prisoner of War Medal shown below.

This medal was authorized by Congress which was passed via Public Law 99-145 on November 8, 1985, as amended by Public Law 101-89 on November 29, 1989 and codified at Section 112B, Title 10, United States Code. The POW Medal is authorized for any person who, while serving in any capacity within the U. S. Armed Forces was taken prisoner and held captive after April 5, 1917.

The POW Medal is of Bronze construction measuring 1 & 3/8 inches in diameter, the front being designed presenting an eagle with wings opened and surrounded by a circle of barbed wire and bayonet points. The reverse side has the inscription AWARDED TO --"FOR HONORABLE SERVICE WHILE A PRISONER OF WAR- UNITED STATES OF AMERICA".

In addition to other medals awarded for exemplary service, Corporal Willie Orville Paxton & Staff Sergeant Omar Lyle Shuffett are entitled to a Prisoner of War Medal. This medal was not authorized during the time of their imprisonment and subsequent military service.

The author has procured Prisoner of War Medals and presented them to the children of both Corporal Paxton and Staff Sergeant Shuffett. Presentation have been made to Willie Sharon (Paxton) Head and to Fran (Shuffett) Stroud and Marilyn (Shuffett) McDaniels in honor of their respective father's service. It is with great pleasure, honor and pride that the author has the privilege of presenting these medals Prisoner of War Medal to both families.

In the process of compiling this saga for Willie Orville Paxton and Omar LyleShuffett, various documents and articles of war were provided to the author through the courtesy Corporal Paxton's and Staff Sergeant Shuffett's children.

SECTION 6

DISCLAIMER

As the principal subjects of this writing, the subjects are deceased and the information provided comes from discussions with family members, together with related documents, such as newspapers, U. S. military historical records, Internet presentations, etc. The author has used these various writings and quotes to develop related stories and timelines, all intended to present a most believable concept of this presentation.

There is no intention to portray anything but the story of two true American's who served his country in a more than acceptable manner, without fanfare and who went on to become solid citizens and family men.

S E C T I O N   7

—⟡—

THE STORY OF WILLIE ORVILLE PAXTON PRISONER OF WAR SERIAL NUMBER 35 708 735

Contents

Background: In Memory of Willie Orville Paxton - Prisoner Of War
Homage: Corporal Willie Orville Paxton
Youth In Rollinsburg
Beginning Of Military Career
Military Deployment To Europe
Capture By German Army
Life In Stalag 7A - A German Prison
Repatriation From Stalag 7A
Arriving Home
Life After World War ll-Returning Home & Ensuing Years
Tragedy
Aftermath
Procurement & Awarding Prisoner Of War Medal
Appendix's 1-8A

Background: In Memory of Willie Orville Paxton - Prisoner of War

In developing the background information to supplement the factual conversations between Willie O and his daughter Willie Sharon (Paxton) Head on which this story is based, it becomes necessary to review the landscapes, organizations, time periods, geography of country and corresponding time periods to dove tail the entire story into a realistic scenario.

After consideration of all the above elements plus additional considerations that may arise, one may then apply all these elements to the very basis short conversation to develop a realistic scenario and to present this story in actual occurrences. The history of the 357th Infantry also provided information as to the locations and timelines for this writing.

"On July 12, 1973, The National Public Records Center at 9700 Page Boulevard in St. Louis, Missouri was the victim of a disastrous fire destroying some sixteen to eighteen million military personnel records. What records of Willie O were destroyed cannot be ascertained."

Homage:
Corporal Willie Orville Paxton

While standing on the public square awaiting the return of Staff Sergeant Omar Lyle Shuffett, unknown to me and seemingly unrecognized by others as well, there was another Green Country resident and former prisoner of war who was working that day on his family farm and birthplace in the Rollinsburg community. The farm was located just down the road from Bethlehem Baptist Church, which is located just off Highway 61 (East) about halfway between Greensburg and the Green-Adair County line.

On the premises of the Bethlehem Baptist Church property is the church cemetery where he was interned with his spouse of some 57 years on August 18, 2002 only one day after his spouse of some 45 plus years was buried in the same cemetery. Both had suffered terminal injuries resulting from a fatal automobile car accident approximately one week prior.

On Tuesday in November 1945, the day that Staff sergeant Omar Lyle Shuffett returned to Greensburg, Corporal Willie Orville "Willie O"- "Bill" Paxton had been repatriated from a German prisoner of war camp some seven months prior after having survived 325 days as a prisoner of war July 7, 1944 through May 1, 1945. Upon repatriation, he was returned to the United States to complete his enlistment with the US Army and the Reserve Components until his discharge from the Organized Reserve Corps Armory Building, Bowling Green, Kentucky on June 30, 1952.

Now that you know that Corporal Willie Orville "Willie O" - "Bill" Paxton was the other ex-prisoner of war from Green County during World War ll and whom this story is about. Now as I was standing on the square in 1945, it would be another 77 years before I would be more acquainted with the story of "Willie O and would be able to relate to you this man's horrific story and how he became a solid citizen of Greensburg and Green County. It is my pleasure to relate this story through research and conversation. 'ERE WE GO!!!!!!!"

Youth In Rollinsburg

Willie Orville Paxton, known as "Willie O" or "Bill" was born at home on the family farm in the Rollinsburg community of Green County, Kentucky on May 6, 1925. The family farm had been in the Paxton family for some years when his grandfather died in 1911, Millard, his father took charge of the farm. In addition, his father owned and operated a country store at Rollinsburg from about 1920 until 1934. He also served as the Postmaster at the store. He ran for Sheriff but was defeated in the Democratic Primary.

The above has just surfaced a bit of history relative to the Paxton family that will be used as a backdrop for the life of Willie O presented as follows in the ensuing stories.

The Rollinsburg community is located just off Highway 68 (Columbia Road) some ten or so miles from the city of Greensburg. Access is gained by turning right at George Sharp's store and proceeding past the Bethlehem Baptist Church Cemetery, where after expiring on August 18, 2002, he was buried by the side of his wife, Lera Ruth (Douglas) Paxton of some forty-three years who had succumbed to death a few short days earlier on August 13, 2002.

His funeral was made complete with a military honor guard rendering last rites in the form of a twenty-one gun salute. The day of burial was hot, with temperatures in the high 90's degrees which caused one of the members of the honor guard to succumb to the heat and pass out just after the ceremony. The honor guard member was revived quickly and ascertained that no after- effects of the mild collapse due to the excessive heat were evident.

The stories in this publication are about events occurring in the 1940's and 1950's as opposed to 2022, so what is the connection here? Answer!!!! I did not realize that "Willie O" or "Bill" was a prisoner of war until later in life when a family connection revealed the experience which had been kept under wraps so to speak, prior to the 1970's. Wille O was a quiet man and was never known to have talked of his experience in captivity except for his daughter and maybe to his wife.

To bring one up to speed, let's revert to the childhood of Willie Orville Paxton, born on May 6, 1925. The day was a Wednesday, four days prior to Mother's Day and fourteen days prior to May 30th Memorial Day. His parents were Millard Garnett Paxton and Ethel Aurora Paxton (born Powell) Paxton. His siblings were Bernard Walker Paxton, Woodrow Willard Paxton, Nettie Adeline Tackett (born Paxton) and Stanley Garnett Paxton.

While growing up in the Rollinsburg farming community he attended school at The Temperance School. The location of the Temperance School is unclear, but the curriculum of the school was dedicated to moderation, and more often, complete abstinence in the use of intoxicating liquor.

Research is sketchy as records of that era were somewhat lacking and two versions of educations surfaced; one depicting he completed school through the sixth grade (age of twelve) and the other depicts him dropped out of high school in the early years. The level of education he attained is immaterial to his contribution to the cause of sustaining freedom in this great country of the United States.

Beginning of Military Career

Whatever the length of his formal education was, he was a very smart man as I was able to hear him in family conversations during the 1970's. He registered for the draft on his eighteenth birthday and was drafted into the US Army on September 3, 1943, some 117 days past the age of eighteen and entered onto active duty on September 24, 1943 and was sent to Camp Blanding Military Base located near Starke, Florida.

As an aside here, Willie O's service was preceded by that of his two brothers. The oldest Bernard Walker "Sleepy" Paxton, born November 26, 1917 was a World War II veteran. The next to oldest was Willard Woodrow "Hump" Paxton, born May 17, 1919 and served in World War II and earned a Bronze Star for his bravery. His father, Walker Paxton registered for the draft during WW I, but was exempt from service due to being the sole provider for his wife ad mother and because of injuries to his hand which were incurred at age 19 in the year 2007 resulting from an explosion.

Thus, when Private Willie O Paxton arrived at Camp Blanding it was bursting at the seams with freshly minted Army draftees and enlistees by the thousands being trained in the arts of infantry warfare such as marksmanship, patrolling, basic unit tactics, etc. for use in providing a formidable army for the United States which was rapidly preparing for expanding forces within the European Theatre of War. The course of military study is (was) called Basic Training, which lasted for a period of approximately eight to ten weeks during which the application of the afore mentioned skills taught that were designed to keep the individual soldier alive in the concept and application of war.

The establishment of Camp Blanding originally established in 1939 and called for accommodations of a regiment of infantry comprised of approximately 1,000 military personnel, but by 1940, with a world war looming, as Hitler invaded Poland and France and Britain declaring was on Germany, it was decided to increase the capacity to an infantry brigade, approximately 3,000 to 5,000 soldiers. By the end of 1940 the design was enlarged again to support two infantry divisions of some 12,000 to 25,000 military personnel and various support elements. Florida's Governor and the Florida State Armory Board approved naming the complex after Major General Albert Hazen Blanding, a former commander of the 31st Infantry "Dixie" Division and Chief of the National Guard Bureau.

After basic training in the schooling of the individual soldier, Pvt. Paxton received a seven- day furlough at home prior to being transferred to Fort Meade, Maryland for advanced individual infantry training a ten week (AIT) Advanced Individual Training and after completion of that segment of his training, March10, 1944 he was deemed to qualified as a combat ready soldier, he was transferred along with several hundreds of other highly trained infantry soldiers to Camp Shanks in New York state to await deployment to Europe which was the boiling point of warfare in Europe and was being manned to the fullest as quicky as possible with qualified soldiers in order to halt the advance of the Third Reich in the European community. During AIT was probably where he was assigned the BAR (Browning Automatic Rifle) as his individual weapon.

Camp Shanks comprised one of the three staging areas on the eastern seaboard. The other two, Fort Hamilton in Brooklyn and Camp Kilmer in New Brunswick, New Jersey when combined with Camp Shanks, make the area the largest pre-war staging area in the world. One of the primary functions as a staging area was to ensure that each soldier and WAC (Women's Army Corp) left the US fully equipped before crossing the Atlantic. The final field inspection at Damp Shanks identified any problems, made any necessary repairs, and replaced anything that which could not be repaired in a foreign environment. At the beginning of the war, no large depots existed in England from which soldiers could get their equipment. Therefore, the individual soldiers carried their essentials with them in their backpacks or barracks bags.

When the soldiers were notified that they were on "Alert" statue, they knew they would be shipping out within twelve hours. The soldiers removed their division sleeve patches, and their helmets were chalked with a letter and a number indication the proper marching order from the damp to the train and the railroad car to ride in. It was a short train ride to the New Jersey docks and a harbor boat ferried the troops to a waiting troopship.

Military Deployment To Europe

On the movement from Camp Shanks, there was sometimes a short stopover in New York City and so it was for Willie O. He related to his daughter some years later that some of the troops were able to tour certain parts of New York city and while there he conveyed to her that he had a shot of whiskey at Jack Dempsey's bar in Times Square prior to boarding his ship for passage to England.

After the short stopover in New York City for one day, April 2, 1944 several thousand soldiers boarded ships for transport to various parts of Europe. Willie O boarded a ship bound for England. The original time at sea for a troop ship in the early 1940's was some 230 to 250 days, an incredibility long period of time. However, over a short period of time the US Navy was able to make numerous logistical adjustment which lowered the average time for sailing from the United States to England was about 60 days.

Research did not reveal the specific ship, duration of sailing time or port of entry in England that Willie O was transported on. This lack of information is most likely due in part to the security elements in place at the beginning of war related to tensions within the European community. History will note that shipping routes, duration of travel time, cargo identification and port of entry to England, etc. was not made public and whatever records were made their contents remain classified or unavailable to the external researcher.

In researching the various time elements which are derived from the conversation with his daughter, Will Sharon (Paxton) Head and the History of the 357th Infantry Regiment as complied by S-Sgt George van Roeder, the deployment movement were from the United Stated to England via Atlantic Ocean where the voyage began on April 2, 1944 and ended on May 15, 1944, then to France where the sea journey concluded on June 1, 1944 where he was housed at Camp Lucky Strike located in Valery, France 45 miles from the port of Le Havre. Camp Lucky Strike was a massive tent city housing US troops heading home from the war. Troops headed home were in the category of (1) wounds having been inflicted via action in combat and therefore were being reassigned to stateside duty in the United States or being processed for discharge (2) having accumulated enough "points" (eighty-five) to warrant an assignment away from a combat zone (3) rescued prisoners of war and others.

The trip from England to the port of Le Havre, France, June 4, 1944 through July 10, 1944, a duration of thirty-three days was obviously by transport ship. The timelines for the development of this story are displayed below and after as much of a through review as was practical based on fact and conversation.

Upon arriving at the port of Le Havre, France, elements of the 90th Infantry Division and more specifically selected elements of the 357th Infantry were formed into formable fighting units and proceeded to move the combat element to the city of St Lo, France, considered to be a hot bed of German aggression and began a movement to contact. St. Lo was about 103 miles from Le Havre and the troop travel time was approximately three days. Upon arrived at the outskirts of St Lo, a heavy presence of German forces was evident.

The makeup of the surrounding area was of a somewhat hilly nature, prone to making the advance of troops who would use the tree covered terrain a most advantageous avenue of approach to engaging an enemy. As the German Army had entered St Lo from the West, it had obtained a distinct battlefield advantage by securing the high ground.

In reviewing the elements of attack by the 357th Infantry, as sparse as it may be, there is more than ample reason to ascertain that the German advance contained a more staple and superior fighting force as compared to the newly induced 357th into the field of battle. Mind you now that the 357th was a so called "green" element of the US fighting force in that they were new to the continent and never been tested in combat. Their total time of working and training together as a unit prior to this point was somewhat limited.

At this juncture in the European conflict, it should be recognized that the German Army was well trained in aggressive combat scenarios and well equipped in terms of both uniforms and weapons as they had been well organized and professional trained long prior to the invasion of France.

Considering that the inferior forces of the 357th that were soon to be engaged with the more stable and experienced German fighting force, it is entirely conceivable the 357th contained smaller fighting elements and was more highly disbursed over the battlefield, so the capture of certain elements of the 357th would appear to be easy to accomplish. In addition to the inexperienced fighting skills of the components of the 357th, it is highly probably and more likely that this inexperience element could be a significant factor in the capture of elements of the 357th Infantry.

The 357th Infantry reported to the 90th Infantry division for operational and logistical support along with the 358th and 359th Infantry Regiments. A short history of the 90th Infantry is provided in Appendix 8.

Capture by German Army

The description by Willie O on how the capture by the German Forces occurred is wholly understandable as he stated, quote: **"we were headed for St. Lo when all of a sudden we were surrounded by German soldiers,"** in that the sparse number of US troops was highly likely to have been a factor in the capture of our inexperienced soldiers.

Now in dealing with the actual capture by the German Armed Forces it is highly likely that the capture of the 357th Infantry and Willie O went very smoothly. Why, would you say, the takeover of our fighting men went without incident? The basic philosophy in removing a creditable captured force from the battlefield, is that the first element of capture is to surround the opposing forces with stealth. Having attained a formidable field position, capture usually can be accomplished with a minimum of force.

Up to this point in the narrative, there is somewhat of a thorough description of Willie O's activities from birth to the date of capture by the German Army on July 7, 1944. Although details may be somewhat sparse, it can be reasonable ascertain that the following scenario occurred on that fateful day of July 7, 1944.

This day began as any other, daylight breaking slowly through the black sky waiting for a bright sunshiny day with high temperature. Being awakened around 4 a.m. for another day of hopefully advancement against the German Army who had occupied the lower easter part of France was getting to be the normal routine for the men of the 357th Infantry. First activity was breakfast, served from a personal "Mess Kit". Next came the forming up of selected personal who were assigned a specific territory [re]ady to deploy to their assigned positions along the "Front Lines". Appendixes 1 & 2 will further describe and explain function of "Mess Kit and "Front Lines."

Being assigned specific territory to advance through the hilly countryside, it can be reasonably assumed that the 357th Infantry was briefed by section leaders on the planned aggressiveness of attack against the German Army, who was undoubtably occupying high ground directly in front of the US advancing forces.

The movement from the rear assembly area to the secured static line of defense where the aggressive attack scenario on behalf of the US Army would begin would generally be performed via walking as the history of the 357th Infantry indicates no vehicles allocated for transport. Neither is there any rear echelon supporting fire.

Upon reaching the stabilized defense line. Willie O and his fellow soldiers began to move forward to the low-lying hills where they were expected to engage the superior German Army for control of the designated territory some five to six miles south of St Lo. The actual scenario would most like play out as follows: As the initial advance began, the American forces became spread out over a wider range of real estate. This re-distribution of fire power over a larger area could possibility account for the German Army being able to surround the small inexperienced US Forces and thus an undetermined number of 357th Infantry soldiers became prisoners of the German Reich.

Neither Willie O nor the history of the 357th Infantry indicate a fierce or even a small conflict. I would be thoroughly convinced that the capture of Willie O and his fellow Americans was accomplished with precision, calmness and without major incident as the captives were quickly removed from the battlefield to a rear area for processing, etc. The advance of the American Army would have gone smoothly during the morning hours and the early afternoon hours as the day of capture as described by Willie O to Willie Sharon **"it was a gorgeous day on July 7, 1944"** a hot humid afternoon with the temperature in the high 95 percentile. I suppose a soldier would not easily forget the conditions under which he goes from being a free fighting man to captured status and being totally controlled by one's enemy.

The first order of control by the capturing forces that weapons and ammunition are confiscated, excess clothing taken away, therefore leaving only the barest of necessities to be retained in the form of a battle uniform, and such sustainable gear such as a Mess Kit and a small supply of medical supplies. Segregation of leaders from the captive American soldiers was a common practice to expedite control over the captives. As leaders were segregated into their separate groups sorted by ranks which would relate to managing the movement of the captives as they were away from the line of battle to a more secure location under control of the German army.

The captured soldiers would be ordered to line up in columns for control and marching behind enemy line. Conversation between the captives was not permitted and a lot of loud commands would be given in German thus adding additional confusion to the situation. It is a normal practice to remove the captives from the active battlefield as soon as possible.

Life in Stalag 7A - A German Prison

Immediately after capture the US troops were quickly removed from the arena of war where the capture of US troops was made and were moved to a location some three miles to five miles in the rear of the combat arena. A review of the 357th Unit History does not readily surface how many total members of the 357th personnel were captured.

Willie O remarked to his daughter Willie Sharon (Paxton) Head the following: **"We marched for three days and nights without food and water across the Normandy peninsula."**

The 357th Infantry unit history does not provide a breakdown of the enlisted personnel vs. the officer personnel that were captured. That information would have been most beneficial in developing this scenario, however as we know where he went, we just need to determine how long it took to get there. Willie O was sent to Stalag 7A in Moosburg Bavaria 48-12 (Work Camp 3324-46, Krumbachstrasse 48011, Work Camp 3368 Munich 48-11)

A bit of clarification here, (1) St Lo France is some 73 miles from Normandy, France (2) Normandy, France is some 639 miles to Bavaria Germany, the location of Stalag 7A in Moosburg, Bavaria. Now, per Willie O's statement that "**We walked for three day and nights, etc."** This walking would probably have covered the 73 miles from St Lo to Normandy, France

How the remaining trip was made to Bavaria, Germany (Stalag 7A) is quite unclear. He further stated that, **"We were moved from camp to camp. We slept under cow barns and in air raid shelters. We were made to dig potatoes in below zero weather which were buried under three feet of dirt and straw. We were given only potatoes, black bread and occasionally some cabbage soup to eat."**

In developing a timeline for transfer from St Lo to Normandy to Stalag 7A could be as follows:

St Lo to Normandy - 73 miles - 3 day - average 24 miles per day. From July 7,1944 to July 10, 1944.

Normandy to Stalag 7A in Moosburg Bavaria, Germany = 640 miles {at 15 miles (reduced from 24 to allow for breakdowns, weariness, etc. {per day} equaling number of days in the final march to be about 43. (640/15= 43 days) July 10,1944 to August 19, 1944.

The above of course is an estimate but not unreasonable when considering the total time of imprisonment, as the following possible conditions: Germans needed to get the prisoners to Stalag 7A as quick as possible so (1) the prisoners would be permanently confined and (2) the German fighting force guarding the prisoners could return to fighting for their cause. The longer the march the slower the pace and more breakdowns in personnel, transporting equipment, weather, prisoner control, etc.

Stalag 7A was opened in September 1939 and was designed to house up to 10,000 Polish prisoners from the German offensive in September of 1939. The first prisoners arrived while the wooden barracks were under construction and for several weeks lived in tents.

Stalag 7A was the largest prisoner-of-war camp in Nazi Germany during World War II. It was located just north of the town of Moosburg in southern, Bavaria. The camp covered an area of 86 acres. In addition to housing a POW work force, it also as a transit camp through which prisoner, including officers, were processed on their way to other camps. At some time during the war, prisoners from every nation fighting against Germany passed through it. At the time of its liberation on April 30, 1945, there were 76, 248 prisoners in the main camp and 40,000 or more in Arbeitskommando's working in factories repairing railroads or on farms.

Arbeitskommando's are sub-camps supporting the main facility at Stalag 7A to hold prisoners in the vicinity of specific work locations, factories, coal mines, quarries, forms of railroad maintenance, etc. Sometimes the capacity of these camps held more than 1000 prisoners, separated by nationality.

For identification purposes at Stalag 7A, all prisoners wore an ID tag (See Photo Appendix 7A) with their name and service number engraved on the round disc while the bottom portion of the tag identified the name of the prison. Evidently Willie O did not retain his as it was not in his effects collected after the war. A complete listing of his "Keepsakes" from the war are attached in Appendix 3.

A review of the prisoner listing of Stalag 7A and all Aarbeitskommando's do not reveal Willie O's name as having been a prisoner. This is not unusual as the prisoner listing in the internet data base lists only a few hundred prisoners. There is not a reference from either him or the history of the 357th Infantry that he was located anywhere other than at Stalag 7A proper. Some of his comments as to the conditions in Stalag 7A were:

"While in prison, I incurred frostbite".
"During prison tenure, all my hair fell out".
"My weight was 79 pounds upon my release from prison".
"I was interrogated by the Germans. I was hit, kicked
and threatened to be thrown out a window".
"They held a gun to my nose asking for
information, but I only gave
them my name, rank and serial number which
was the only information I was required to give
per The Geneva Convention. As they held the gun
to my nose, I could smell the gun powder".

While this is the extent of his comments to his daughter concerning his captivity which has been supplemented by the previous commentary on his military service and capture, it doesn't seem to be of further value at this point to delve into additional speculation and commentary upon Willie O's duration of captivity. So, at this point, we can relate some generic and general comments as provided by research as to the overall conditions of Stalag 7A.

Willie O's stay in Stalag 7A was 250 days when he was released on May 1, 1945. As noted on Appendix 4 and as of May 1,1945, 46.6% of his time in the military he had been confined in a German prison camp.

Living conditions at Stalag 7A were not surfaced by Willie O in any of his comments. For example, he did not discuss sleeping arrangements, housing arrangements, work schedules, medical care provided, replacement of threadbare clothing, transportation to work sites, how many days per week were prisoners required to work, etc. This list is not intended to be complete, just to relate to the reader that life in a prison facility is controlled in every aspect of day to day living.

Health care for prisoners was deemed to be above adequate in that a healthy work force is highly instrumental in maintaining a satisfactory output of work relative to the requirement of the German Army.

A further description of Stalag7A denotes that the camp was surrounded by hills and divided into three compounds, which in turn were subdivided into smaller stockades. The stockades held newly arrived POW's for two days while they were searched, medical examined and deloused. Although nationalities were segregated by compounds, intercommunication existed. Barracks were rectangular wooden building divided into two sections, A and B, by a central room used for washing and eating. In it was a water faucet, a water pump and some tables.

The barracks chief and assistant had a small corner room to themselves. POW's slept on triple-deck wooden bunks and gunny sack mattresses filled with excelsior (softwood shavings used for packing fragile goods of stuffing furniture). Gradually as the number of men per barracks increased from 180 to 400, prisoners slept on floors, tables and the ground.

Prison guards were drawn from the German army designed to manage the day -to- day operations of Stalag 7A. Four officers and two hundred enlisted men were employed on general duties. Ten men with the officer rank were designated to act as interpreters. Twenty civilian men and women were employed as clerks in the camp.

Repatriation From Stalag 7A

Finally, on April 30, 1945, the New York Times reported, "Huge Prison Camp Liberated some 110,000 Allied prisoners of war at Stalag 7A (Germany's largest prisoner of war camp) at Moosburg, Bavaria Germany by the US Fourteenth Armored Division."

The German proposal for surrender was "an armistice" instead of a uncontested surrender. This proposal was rejected by the US Command and an attack on Moosburg was ordered. German resistance was established 1 mile west of Moosburg. This resistance was quickly disposed of and the US forces made their way into Stalag 7A. Immediately upon entering the prison enterprising American soldiers raised an American flag and amid thunderous cheers from the prisoners, ran it to the top of the camp flagpole.

The prisoners rushed to greet their liberators. So many prisoners flowed around and over the tanks, peeps, and half-tracks, that even the huge Sherman tanks completely disappeared beneath a mass of jubilating humanity. Some of the comments recorded during the liberation were:

"You damned bloody Yanks, I Love You!!," shouted a six-foot four Australian and threw his arms around a peep driver. (Peep is defined as a World War II jeep attached to an armored regiment).

A weary bearded American paratrooper climbed onto a tank and kissed the tank commander. Tears streamed from his cheeks.

An American Air Corps Lieutenant kissed a tank, "God Damn, do I love the ground forces."

"This is the happiest day of my life."

"You were a long time coming, but now you are here!!"

At this point, Willie O would have been begun to be "processed out" along with all other prisoners. The primary function of the of the repatriation force was based primarily on the objective of accounting for and returning the POW's of Stalag 7A back to the United States in a safe and expedient manner as possible. Again, there is no indication of the time lapse here but one can assume that the transition was made as quickly as possible. The route of travel from Stalag 7A to the US was via Camp Lucky to the US would have been conducted by US Military processing companies and total travel time would fit nicely into a time frame of ten days which would have placed the former prisoners in Pennsylvania USA on about May 10, 1945.

Upon arriving stateside at Camp Reynolds, Pennsylvania, which was a huge Personnel Replacement Depot in northwest Pennsylvania during World War II, Willie O related to Willie Sharon **"I was able to send a telegram to my family in Greensburg to let them know I had been released."** (May 11, 1945). He and other former POW's were then transferred to Camp Atterbury, Indiana for a brief stopover, then flown to Miami, Florida (about May 15, 1945) for final processing where he was granted a sixty day leave which was designated to end on July 17, 1945.

The processing agency in Miami would have made sure that the former prisoners would have as much of the sixty-day furlough to spend at home as possible worked through the administrative requirements quickly and probably would have had them on their way with a day or so.

<u>**Corporal Willie O Paxton - Miami, Florida**</u>
<u>**Shortly after being given a 30 day**</u>
<u>**Furlough - May 1945**</u>

He was flown via military aircraft from Miami, Florida to Louisville, Ky on May 17, 1945. He along with other military personnel were experiencing very long wait times for bus availability. While waiting at the bus station in Louisville he began to converse with another soldier who was on military from Fort Knox and traveling to his hometown of Tompkinsville, Ky. He and his new acquaintance took turns waiting in line to purchase their bus ticket.

Fate would have it that Willie O would be the first one to get to the ticket counter only to be told he could purchase only one ticket, so Willie O bought the ticket, took it back and gave it to his newly made military friend and said**, "Here, you use this one and I will**

wait for the next available ticket". He was overheard by an MP (Military Policeman).

Let's pause here and go from reading this story to thinking and processing the situation that has just been described. We have here, Willie O, a combat tested veteran who has just spend 46.6% of his military career in a German Prison Camp, now getting to come home for the first time since being drafted on September 3, 1943 is giving away his bus ticket home to another military person who he does not know. "Where do we get these men?" See Appendix 5.

The MP proceeded to take Willie O by the elbow, escort him to the ticket window and demanded that the ticket agent permit Willie O to purchase a ticket. After purchasing the ticket, he boarded the bus for Elizabethtown, Ky. Upon arrival in Elizabthtown, at approximately 1 a.m. on May 18, 1945 he discovered the lack of bus service to Greensburg. Anxious to get home Willie O then hired a taxi to drive him to Greensburg, then to Rollinsburg.

According to Willie O, this was a most harrowing ride, as the cab driver appeared to be most interested in the wartime experience, including his prison camp experience as he kept asking questions and turning his head around to see into the back seat waiting for the answer, thereby narrowly avoiding a wreck several times during the journey.

With good speed and lack of traffic on the highway at this time of the morning, he arrived at his boyhood home in Rollinsburg about 4 a.m. Willie O expressed his thoughts of this trip when he said, **"What an ordeal I had just been through and this cab driver is going to kill me before I get home."**

Arriving Home

The reader must now transform from present day environment to that of 1945 when in the early morning May 18, 1945 was one of serenity. The balmy temperature of 72 degrees in the early morning under a cloudless sky with the earth's surface being illuminated of 37% by The Waxing Crescent of the moon, which is defined as percentage of the moon being illuminated by the Sun was about to be interrupted by the soft purring sounds of a taxi making its way to the home of Willie O in Rollinsburg. In those days, families in the country and elsewhere as well would quite often leave the solid front door open to take advantage of the pleasant soothing night air moving through the screen door which undoubtedly would permit one to fall asleep faster than normal.

It was in this atmosphere that Willie O returned to his boyhood home, paid the taxi driver, made his way through the front yard to the front porch where he quietly opened the screen door, entered the house and made his way stealthily up the steps to a bedroom where his older brother Stanley was enjoying a peaceful sleep.

Willie O undressed quietly and eased himself in bed beside his startled brother who set up erect in bed and loudly proclaimed, **"What the hell are you doing here?"**

Obviously, everyone in the house heard Stanley and the welcoming whoops, screams and rejoicing began now that the prodigal son was home. I don't know who all was in the house but there was no more sleep as everyone wanted to welcome Willie O home and hear everything about the past year or so.

Willie O quoted, **"By noon of the next day every woman in the community had baked me more pies and cakes that one human could ever consume."** Throughout the 60day furlough he got reacquainted with his family, did a lot of visiting and meeting with new and old neighbors and of course, ate a lot of pie and cake while entertaining the female population of Rollinsburg and probably Green County as well. This time at home would be expanded and discussed at great lengths many times, but each time it would get the same events on different days with different audiences.

Nearing the end of the 60 day furlough, the time to report to Fort Knox came all too quickly. Alas, a good soldier must return to his duty station and bittersweet as it may have been, Willie O donned his freshly ironed khaki uniform as that was the requirement in those days in anticipation of the trip to Fort Knox. Willie O's brothers drove him to Fort Knox on July 17th, 1945, where they entered the Post from Dixie Highway to Chaffee Avenue and proceed to the in-processing station where he presented himself as **"Private First Class Willie O Paxton, Serial Number 35 708 735 reporting for duty as ordered, sir!"**

And with that action, Willie O was assigned to an out-processing company where he would wait for his discharge from active duty. Shortly after arriving at Fort Knox, he was notified that per orders originating in The Fourth Services Command in Atlanta, Georgia he had been given a "temporary appointment to the rank of Corporal", effective date August 17, 1945. Being promoted to Corporal would authorize his net pay to be increased from $39 per month to $51 per month, an increase of 31%.

How he spent his extra money is not clear, but it certainly was earned. There is no documentation relating how he was compensated for his time while confined to Stalag 7A prison. Extra payments for front line troops did not begin until 1952 as it was first granted to service members deployed to Korea. This payment was known then as "the first modern form of direct combat compensation".

It is now the practice for the US Government to compensate US service members confined to foreign prisons during war time. Today (2022) soldiers who are in a POW status are authorized payment of 50% of the worldwide average per diem rate for each day held in captive status. The Secretary of Defense may authorize more that 50% of the worldwide average per diem rate if requested by the Secretary of the Army.

However, even though extra compensation was not a normal practice in WW II, privates serving in a German prison were paid $50 per month. It seems like toppling three fascist dictators would pay better than that doesn't it? However, that being the case, Willie O would have been paid (255 days in captivity /30=8.5 months at $50 = $425). There is no accessible record of when or even if he was compensated for his time in Stalag 7A.

His duties at Fort Knox were mostly "just stay busy work" as the post had hundreds of personnel to out process. After spending some 173 days at Fort Knox, Kentucky, Willie O was awarded a formal document officially awarding an Honorable Discharge from active-duty status effective November 19, 1945.

A report from the New York Times on Dec 17,1944 reads, "By a vote of 387 to 0 the House of Representatives adopted today, the mustering-out pay bill for veterans of this war, as amended by the Committee on Military Affairs. The mustering-out compensation amount was presented being from $100 to $300 or $200 to $500, depending on which source one may use. No mention of mustering out pay is revealed either in discussions or a review of records. Payment records for soldiers being discharged at the end of WW II are not available or no longer exist.

As Willie O was granted his discharge from active duty, he was assigned to continued service of National Defense through enlistment in Enlisted Reserve Corps. This is documented in an undated letter signed by Major General Edward F. Witsell, Acting The Adjutant General. (See Item B - Appendix 6). For a complete listing of Military Records see Appendix 6.

As of now, November 19, 1945 we have reviewed Willie O's complete military career and he is being discharged. I have listed all the documents provided to me re-his rank and active-duty time served. He is now being assigned to Enlisted Reserve Status for the next six and one-half years until he is discharged from Enlisted

Reserve on June 30,1 952 which will have ended Willie O's total military time served i.e., active and reserve nearly nine years. An admirable feat for any American. His daughter, Willie Sharon (Paxton) Heads quotes, **"To say my dad was a tough old bird is definitely an understatement. He was part of the greatest generation that returned from war and went right back to his life as if nothing had happened. I am so proud of Daddy!! He will always be MY HERO!"**

Life After World War II - Returning Home & Ensuing Years

After being released from active duty, Willie O returned to his boyhood home in Rollinsburg. Even though he had a US Army Reserve obligation there is no indication that he attended meetings. If he did, meetings were once a month for a duration of two hours and were held in Bowling Green, Kentucky according to relevant military documents presented in Appendix 6. The United States Army Reserve meeting requirement was changed to one full weekend per month sometime around the mid 1960's.

After being away from home under trying situations i.e. German prison camp, Willie O returned to working on the family farm for several years and then found permanent employment with the Nally & Gibson rock quarry as a heavy equipment operator. The quarry was located on Highway 68 about three miles from Greensburg traveling east toward Columbia, Kentucky. This employment began in 1955 and lasted some 40 years until he retired in 1995 at the age of seventy.

The transition from military to civilian environment can only be factually related by those who experienced it. In Willie O's case, he held everything "close hold" and did not discuss his military or prison experience easily. The effect of a confined environment appears to be extremely difficult for those who experienced it which is evidenced only by the few who speak openly about it. Oh, maybe a quick off the cuff remark or a brief period of silence in the middle of a conversation which will probably hardly noticed by others may signal a brief re-election of past horrors over the years. However, on a pleasant sunny Sunday afternoon on his front porch on Russell Avenue in Greensburg, Kentucky with somewhat of a quiet sigh Willie O said**, "This day is as beautiful as the day I was captured by the Germans on July 10, 1944."**

Willie Sharon relates that without being prompted he relayed the stories that are presented here in a quiet voice seemingly to relive the instances of that fateful day and the ensuing 325 days after that before being repatriated. Willie Sharon has managed to obtain and keep select documents and pieces of personal equipment Willie O had salvaged from his captivity and other military documents.

Somewhere along the way Willie O met, wooed, chased and courted a beautiful young lady from Greensburg by the name of Lera Ruth Douglas from which a marriage occurred on July 18, 1959 and lasted for 43 years. If the details to their meeting and courtship were available, they would surely be presented here, but they are not. And so, another chapter of this amazing man's life begins with a steady job, a new bride and internal peace, at least from the standpoint of not having to incur hate, hunger, torture, nights with no sleep and uncertainty about what might happen when the sun again rose.

Willie O's and Ruth's first and only child, Willie Sharon was born on December 24, and life thereafter for the Paxton family settled pretty much to nurturing and raising a child, going to work every day and living what one might call a normal life, if there is such a thing in today's robust America.

In 1959, in Green County Kentucky an event occurred that changed the landscape of the community and that was termed "the oil boom" which has presented in the chapter entitled, "The History of the Kozy Korner." This was time of serious money flowing into Green County which along with the influx of new residents, etc. etc. taking up most available housing and a shortage of housing developed quickly. Seeking a place to live, Willie O & Ruth discussed with Mr. Joe Bundy, the author's father-in-law and Willie Sharon's uncle about the construction of a new home.

An agreement was made, construction began and in October 1960 Willie O and Ruth moved into their new residence on Shreve Ave. A short two months later, on December 24th the blessed event occurred with the birth of Willie Sharon, their first and only child. The residence and the surrounding neighborhood was a pleasant one, with the family of Joe and Marue Bundy, Willie Sharon's aunt and uncle, living next door. The best times recalled were when both families, many times joined by neighbors would sit in the back yard under the big shade tree having pleasant conversations covering the entire spectrum of local and worldwide events. This home was constructed at the rear of 202 Shreve Avenue in Greensburg and was inhabited by the Paxton family from 1960 until 1981 when they purchased a home on Russell Avenue.

Over the years, time passed peacefully, their daughter Willie Sharon was married to Charles Head on April 17, 1980 and soon made their way to Florida for employment. Their son and only child, Charles "Chas" Paxton was born on September 23, 1985 while they were in Florida and then in 1988, a new employment opportunity provided them an opportunity to return to Kentucky.

When Charles "Chas" Paxton made his new home along with his parents in Kentucky in 1988, he and his "PaPa" developed a relationship that both had wanted for a very long time. Chas visited very often and the visits were equally enjoyed by both.

When Chas was nine years old, he interviewed his "PaPa" for a story to be read in school to read in front of the class. He wrote and presented the following story, which I though was quite through and understanding for a lad of his young age.

<u>Chas Head Relates The Story of Grandfathers
Prisoner of War Experience</u>

Today I want to you a story about my grandfather.
My grandfather served in World Was ll. He entered
the army in 1943. He was 18 years old.
During the war he operated a Browning Automatic Rifle. He
was on the front lines for a month. The average life expectancy
for a frontline combat soldier was only 3 months.
On July 7, 1944 he was captured by the
Germans and sent to a prison camp.

The Germans were mean and made him work on a potato farm and didn't give him very much food. While he was a prisoner of war he had to sleep under a cow barn in an air raid shelter. On May 1, 1945 my grandfather was released and returned to Camp Lucky Strike, France. He only weighted 79 pounds. On May 7, 1945 the war was over.

I am very proud of my grandfather!!

Chas continued to visit his "PaPa" frequently on Russell Avenue until 2000 when Willie O and Ruth purchased the home of the author, the late Mrs. A. T. Wright located 207 Penick Avenue. At this point, a final residence was established in the same neighborhood and just down the street. Life was good, and as Willie O had now been retired five years, life was getting more and more settled.

Tragedy

The years from 2000 to 2002 were filled with contentment in a relaxing atmosphere and a thorough enjoyment of life. The morning of Tuesday, August 13, 2002 dawned a sunny balmy pleasant 70 degrees. As the Paxton household began to rise and begin a new day around 8 a.m., things were quiet as usual for a Tuesday, however a major tragedy storm was brewing and would be much in vogue in early afternoon of the same day.

Willie O and Ruth may have read the morning paper, relaxing on the outdoor deck taking advantage of the pleasant early morning as the temperature by late morning would reach some 80 + degrees with high humidity. For whatever reason, just after lunch Willie O and Ruth left in their auto, a Ford Tempo and proceeded to their perceived destination. The undefined task, or errand, maybe a short joyride or whatever reason for the trip apparently was completed and they were driving north on Highway 68/70 about 1:15 p.m. or so and presumably making their return to Greensburg and their home on Penick Avenue.

As they crossed the bridge over Green River coming back into Greensburg, they just started to make their way up the slight rise in the highway when tragedy struck. The right side of the highway was populated by a restaurant, Famous Recipe, a home and a little further up the highway on the right was Cowherd - Parrott Funeral Home. At 1:30 p.m. as they traveled at an acceptable rate of speed and passing in front of Famous Recipe restaurant, a Chevrolet pickup truck suddenly exited the parking lot of the restaurant at a high rate of speed and smashed into Ford Tempo "head on." The results were devasting.

Obviously, time stood still at this point. Cars stopped, restaurant patrons and onlookers rushed to the scene and funeral home personnel came immediately to the scene. The Greensburg Fire Department, City Police, Green County Sheriff and Green County EMT's (Emergency Medica Personnel) quickly arrived, prepared to administer medical assistance, only to find that Willie O and Ruth were unresponsive. EMT personnel determined quickly that Ruth should be taken to the Jane Todd Crawford Hospital, a mere three miles to the south. They quickly and professionally extracted Ruth from the vehicle, loaded her into the EMP ambulance and hurriedly sped away to the hospital.

While Ruth was being admitted to Jane Todd Crawford Hospital, EMT's were examining Willie O and determined that the seriousness of his condition warranted treatment in a larger medical facility. An urgent request was initiated for a medically equipped helicopter from Fort Knox to transport Willie 0 to The University of Louisville Hospital, the nearest primary trauma center.

And so, at approximately 2 p.m. on the Sunday afternoon of August 13, 2002 the medical helicopter lifted off from Greensburg amid scattered showers and 35 mile per hour moderate winds to begin the 35-40 minute flight to Louisville University Hospital. Upon arrival Willie O was rushed immediately to the Emergency Room where examination, testing and treatment began immediately.

Back in Greensburg, relatives and friends notified Chuck, Willie Sharon's husband, who came to the school in Elizabethtown where Willie Sharon was working. In one of her well-organized efforts to "round up" and notify family members, she recalls that "Chas" who attended John Hardin High School in Elizabethtown was scheduled to play in a soccer match in Campbellsville that night.

She asked her sister Pam to drive to Campbellsville and retrieve Chas off the team bus. Pam then transported Chas to Hodgenville when she met Gregg Cobb, her cousin by marriage who brought Chas to Jane Todd Crawford where Ruth had been taken. Things were happening so fast and time being the precious factor, Willie Sharon rushed to the Jane Todd Crawford Hospital to see her mother but unfortunately, Ruth died at approximately 2:15 p.m. Tuesday afternoon, about 45 minutes after the accident. Beset with grief and the swiftness of tragedy, it was to say the least, a rough afternoon.

Willie Sharon accompanied by friends and family decided she

now needed to get to Louisville University Hospital where Willie O was being treated. When she went by the house on Penick Avenue to retrieve Willie O's medications, she noticed that two glasses of iced tea still sitting on the picnic table on the deck. As she made her way to Louisville, she began to process the events of the day. The thought process did not reach any conclusions of where and why the trip was made. The glasses of iced tea seemed to indicate that the departure might have been a hasty one, but again no apparent conclusion could be reached.

Upon arriving at the hospital in Louisville, Willie Sharon was met by family members that had made their way to the hospital to show their support. There, she was able to discuss the status of Willie O's injuries with the medical staff. The discussions ware not refreshing. Multiple injuries throughout the body had placed Willie O on the critical list. After a short visitation, she reviewed the tragic events of the day with the hospital doctors and staff and understanding that Willie O was in quite capable hands and as funeral arrangements were to be made for Ruth she returned to Elizabethtown for the evening, as it was now nearing about 10 p.m. and many chores were awaiting to be completed tomorrow.

After a restless night, the following morning she and husband Chuck returned to Greensburg and Cowherd-Parrott Funeral home to plan the funeral arrangements for Ruth. Working with the funeral home staff she planned the funeral, pallbearers, casket selection, etc. and decided that the funeral would be conducted at the funeral home Wednesday, August 14, 2002 with burial in the Bethlehem Baptist Church Cemetery. With the obituary being written, including visitation, it was posted in the Green County Record-Herald and the wait was on. The funeral was conducted with brothers Les Bullock and Jimmy Knifley officiating.

On Friday evening, August 16th, (the author's birthday) there was a large crowd of visitors including the author in the funeral home and all wanted to talk with Willie Sharon. At about 7 p.m., the author along with a lot of others heard a funeral home employee announced to Willie Sharon, "You have a call from

University Louisville Hospital." This was an obvious surprise and she proclaimed, "Oh, I can't lose them both." She answered the phone and appeared very distraught. She immediately left the premises to return to Louisville as evidently there was concern enough with the health status of Willie O for the hospital to get in touch with Willie Sharon.

Thursday and Friday passed and with the funeral of Ruth just completed and Willie O still in critical condition, both days were filled with anxiety and on Saturday, August 17th, the funeral for Ruth was conducted with burial as planned. The visitation and funeral were attended by a huge crowd of family and mourners and the reality was beginning to set in and on Sunday, August 18th, Willie O died and was returned to Cowherd-Parrott Funeral Home for funeral arrangements. Wanting to give him the best burial with related honors possible, Willie Sharon was wanting an honor guard to fire a final twenty-one gun salute to the fallen hero. Unfortunately, there was not such an organization available in this part of the country.

A friend of Mary Ellen Berry, Willie Sharon's cousin relayed that he could procure a color guard from Middletown, Kentucky and with Willie Sharon's approval and thanks, he proceeded to procure the appropriate honor guard. On Wednesday August 21st, the final rites were held for Willie O at the funeral with burial in the Bethlehem Baptist Church Cemetery alongside Ruth.

The funeral was conducted by Brother Les Bullock and the Reverend William Karnes officiating. The grave side ceremony was augmented with the nine-man honor guard dressed in appropriate military uniform to perform the final salute. Honorary military pallbearers from Campbellsville's Bravo Battery, 1/623rd MLRS Field Artillery also participated in the military funeral.

Aftermath

Families and the funeral crowd dispersed, tearful goodbyes were said, promises made to stay in touch. The grave site was closed and the burial grounds soon resumed their eerie silence prior to the ceremonies of August 21, 2002. Memories will only build from here and will take on a deeper meaning as time progresses. Appropriate monuments will soon be installed to permanently identify the final resting place of a true hero, a faithful father accompanied by a loving and supportive spouse and grieving family members.

As time goes by, the events of war and local tragedy will always be in the forefront of painful memories sustained by family members and close friends.

My readers are encouraged to visit the Bethlehem Baptist Church Cemetery and find their way to the permanently engraved epitaph of a truly dedicated American. Criminal charges were never filed against the young man who ran into Willie O and Ruth in a head on crash!!!!!

This photo speaks volumes in that the smile on Willie Sharon's (daughter) face openly relates the love for her father, former Corporal and Prisoner of War, Willie Orville "Willie O" Paxton with his signature hat. Lookin' sharp, trim and alert for a seventy-seven year old American Hero!!!

Time passes and people tend to let the bygone days become subdued and quiet as to the verbal overtones and praise we once used for the service of these men!!!!!

Appendix Listing

1.   History & Definition Of A "Mess Kit"

2.   Front Lines & Browning Automatic Rifle

3.   Personal War Memorabilia Collection Listing

3A.   Photo   -Top Left Down:
                        Mess kit
                        Canteen
                        Identification (ID) Dog Tags
                        Good Conduct Medal
                Top Right Down:
                        Brown Cloth Bag w/Draw
                        Cigarette Lighter
                        Top of a Fountain Pen
                        Spoon
                        Fountain Pen (Ink)
                        POW License Place
                        Twenty-one shell casings fired by
                        Honor Guard from Grave Side @
                        Burial - Bethlehem Baptist Cemetery

4.   Timeline of Life for Willie Orville Paxton

5.   "Where Do We Find Such Men?"

6.   Listing of Military Records & Pictures

7.   Establishment of Prisoner of War Medal

7A.   Photo of Prisoner of War Medal/Stalag 7A ID Tags

8.   History of 90th Division

8A.   Photo of cover of 90th Division History Booklet

Apppendix 1

HISTORY & DEFINITION
OF A "MESS KIT"

To properly understand how and why the "Mess Kit" is an integral part of military life particular in WW II, the following descriptive analysis is presented.

This steel "Mess Kit" was the personal property of Willie O and he carried it through captivity, release from captivity, discharge from active duty and is now in the possession of his daughter Willie Sharon (Paxton) Head. This "kit" was used as an instrument to receive food that was distributed through a feeding "chow" (food) line. The "kit" is shown in the photo as the two-part instrument in the upper left corner. This "kit" still contains the dirt and grime of captivity however structurally is in pristine condition. This GI (Government Issue) was made available to all soldiers during the war years, continuing through the 1980's including the Vietnam War.

In addition to the "Mess Kit", the other two terms seemed to be discussed most often were "Food Lines" and "What type of Individual Weapon was assigned to each soldier?" Both items are discussed in Appendix 2.

The US Military Individual Mess Gear is constructed and depicted in the attached in Appendix 1 with photo representing the basic eating instrument for a soldier to feed himself in the field in WW II. The contents of the "Kit" consists of the two-part "meat can" plus knife, fork, and spoon. The knife is missing from the attached photo. The "Mess Kit" is based on design that was in use before WW I. The depicted "Kit" consists of a pan with a hinged handle plus a lid that fits over the pan and is held together as one unit when the plan handle is folder over.

This design is made of "corrosion resistant" galvanized steel. Now that one had the "Kit" in hand, the two halves of the "Kit" must be linked together with the ring of the plate slipped over the handle of the pan and as you pass along the serving line, the cooks served hot items first, often meat with vegetables, potatoes, and other side dishes on top. A piece of pie and or a spoonful of mixed fruit went on top of everything else. Now you were on your own to balance the two parts of the "Kit" plus a canteen cup of coffee or tea and consume your meal.

Now one had to find a place to sit and then eat your food from the top down from the "Mess Kit". In essence, the desert would be eaten first, followed by the side dishes and then lastly the main course. After eating, the cleanup began. The "Kit" is dipped into a heated trash can for ten seconds, one can with soapy water and the other can with a rinse and then finally one dip in clear hot boiling water. This may seem to the reader to be a most cumbersome eating utensil and clean-up method and it was, but this "Kit" and process managed to feed some sixteen million service members over a period of forty years.

Appendix 2

DESCRIPTION OF "FRONT LINES" AND INDIVIDUAL WEAPON "BAR "BROWNING AUTOMATIC RIFLE

At the time of capture, Willie O had been on the "Front Lines" (Appendix 2) for a period of some three months and his weapon of assignment was a "BAR" "Browning Automatic Rifle."

A "Front Line" or "Front Lines" in military terminology is the position closed to the area of conflict of armed forces personnel and equipment. This is the area where each side's forces are currently in controlling a particular piece of ground or village, i.e. which sometime results in armed conflict. Leaders have often fought at the "Front Lines" either purposefully or due to a collapse in battle formation.

Life at the "Front" can usually be described as soldiers being rotated in and out of the "Front Lines" in defensive or attack positions to provide a break from the stress of combat. Depending on the static and/or fluid conditions of the battlefield, some soldiers may spend four to six days in the "Front" trenches before moving back and spending a few days recuperating in the secondary. However, it is not uncommon for soldiers to be fighting on the "Front Lines" for thirty to sixty days or more, depending on the current circumstances of war.

Job descriptions of Combat soldiers stationed at the "Front Lines" are defined by a combat MOS (Military Occupation Specialty). In addition, cooks, clerks, medics, truck drivers, etc. (support personnel) are also assigned an MOS but in many cases are not issued nor do they carry a personal firearm.

Now, in the case of Willie O, he was a designated BAR team leader. His duty was to operate the BAR, shoot the BAR and care for its maintenance. He would normally be assisted by an Assistant

BAR man and Ammo Bearer. The BAR team was a part of a squad consisting of some six other combat arms soldiers armed with various individual weapons.

The BAR was developed by John Browning in 1917. It is designed to fire a sustained rate of fire of 550 rounds per minute with a slow cyclic rate of 350 rounds per minute or it can shoot single shoots to improve accuracy. Ammo is 30.06 armor piercing. The weapon is forty-seven inches long with a weight of approximately 19.4 pounds. The rifle has a bipod under the front end of the weapon to provide a more stable positioning for firing the weapon from the Prone position.

Apppendix 3

WILLIE ORVILLE PAXTON

Listing of Personal War Collectible Items
Retained from Military Service

Photo Of All Items Is Attached As Appendix 3A

Number	Item
1	Mess Kit - US Military Issue (a)
2	Canteen - US Military Issue (b)
3	Identification Tags - US Military Issue I
4	Good Conduct Medal (Red Background w/six white stripes)
5	Three other medals awarded and issued to Willie O
6	Light brown draw string bag stamped "RED CROSS @ ST. JOHN WAR ORGANIZATION, LONDON", containing (a) 1 small eating spoon (b) 1 "round" cigarette lighter (c) 1 ink writing pen (d) top of a fountain pen I 1 damaged bullet- caliber unknown.
7	Twenty-one shell casings from the 21 gun salute fired at Willie O's funeral 21 August 2002.
8	1 Kentucky POW license plate - expiration 2003-number POW P56

(a) Complete description provided in Appendix 1
(b) Issued to Willie O during his first few months in the military
I The first item issued to Willie O during his initial reporting date in the Army.

   The ID tag issue of WW ll consisted of (1) two tags with name and service (serial) number of the individual soldier (2) the chain was of a more delicate issue than those of today and was brown in color so as to not portray a shiny object at the soldier's neck. Both tags were constructed with a notch in each end so that in case of a battlefield death, the tag was inserted between the upper and lower teeth to provide immediate identification.

(d) (1) European African Middle Eastern Ribbon w/Bronze Service Star

(1) American Theatre Ribbon

(1) World War II Victory Medal

By very definition alone it takes a strong man to operate the BAR and such a man was Willie O. He was about 5'8" tall weighing about 160 pounds as depicted on military records such as Report of Separation Discharge dated 19 November 1945. He was exceedingly strong for his statue, which is probably one reason he was given the BAR as a personal weapon. How he became assigned to the BAR is not defined anywhere in conversation or documentation, but I would ascertain it was due to his determination, strength, etc

Appendix 3A

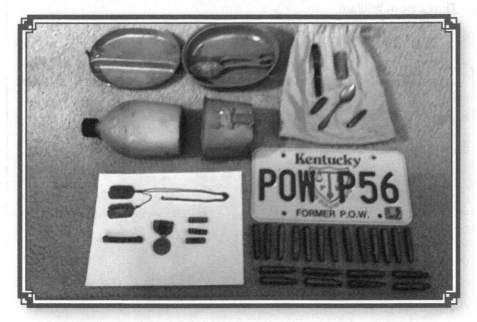

Mess Kit, Canteen, (ID) Identification Tags, Good Conduct Medal, Three Other Medals, Light brown draw string bag, fountain pen, small eating spoon, "round" cigarette lighter, top of a fountain pen, 1 damaged bullet-caliber unknown, twenty-one shell casings from the 21 gun salute fired at Willie O's funeral 21 August 2002, 1 Ky license plate, expiration 2003 and Identification number POW P56.

Appendix 4

Time Line of William Orville "Willie O" - "Bill" Paxton	Appendix 4	Through Age 27		Cumulataive	Cumulative
		Elapsed	Time	Years	Years
Event	Date	Days	Years	Of Life	In Military
Birth	May 6, 1925	N/A	N/A		
Registered - Draft	May 6, 1943		18.00	18.00	
Drafted - US Army	September 3, 1943	117	0.32		0.32
Entered Active Duty (Camp Blanding Starke, Florida)	September 24, 1943	21	0.05		0.37
Concluded Basic Training	January 10, 1944	106	0.29		0.66
One Week Furlough - Greensburg	January 17, 1944	7	0.02		0.68
Advanced Invidual Training - Fort Meade, Maryland	March 10, 1944	52	0.14		0.82
Camp Shanks, New York	April 1, 1944	20	0.05		0.87
Drank Whiskey - Jack Dempsy Bar New York City	April 2,1944	1	N/A		0.87
Boarded Ship To England -	May 15,1944	43	0.12		0.99
Transfer to France - Port of Le Harve - Camp Lucky Strike	June 1, 1944	15	0.04		1.03
Transfer from Le Harve to St Lo France	June 4, 1944	3	N/A		1.03
"Front Lines" France - Captured by Germans	July 7, 1944	33	0.09		1.12
Immediately after capture - marched from St Lo to Normandy	July 10, 1944	3	N/A		1.12
Movement from Normandy to Stalag 7A in Bavaris, Germany	August 19, 1944	39	0.11		1.23
US 14th Armored Division liberated Stalag 7A	April 30, 1945	250	0.68		1.91*
Realesed from Stalag 7 A prison camp	May 1, 1945	1	N/A		1.91

Trf'd to Camp Lucky Strike-Flown to Pennsylvania - USA	May 10, 1945	9	0.02	1.93
Sent telegram to family about freedom from Stalag 7A	May 11. 1945	1	N/A	1.93
Trf'd to Camp Atterbury then to Miami, Florida	May 15,1945	4	0.01	1.94
Issued a 60day entucky by the Miami Processing Station	May 17,1945	2	N/A	1.94
Flown to Lousville Ky via military transportation	May 17,1945	N/A	0.16	1.94
Military transportation to Elizabethtown, Ky	May 18, 1945	N/A	0.16	1.94
Taxi from E-town to G-burg, the on to Rollinsburg	May 18, 1945	N/A	0.16	1.94
Spent all authorized leave time at home -	Rpt'd to Fort Knox	July 17, 1945 **	59	0.16	2.1
Promoted to temporary rank of Corporal		August 17, 1945	30	0.08	2.18
Discharged from US Army and released from Active Duty		November 19, 1945 ***	84	0.23	2.41
Discharged from US Army Reserve Corps (Final Exit)		June 30, 1952	2,241	6.59	9.00****

* At this point, having spent a total of 1.91 years in the military and .890 years (33+3+39+250=325/365=.890) (.890/1.91=46.6% years of total time

spent in Nazi Prison
Camp - Stalag 7A)

** Reporting date for return to active duty
status at Fort Knox, entucky.

*** Recorded in Veterans Discharge Book #3, Page 100, Green County Clerk's Office, this November 23, 1945 (Floyd Patterson, Clerk)

**** In reconciliation of age vs. military time (18.0 + 9.0 + 27 years)
Discharged 1952, born 1925 (1952-1925= 27 years)

Appendix 5

"WHERE DO WE FIND SUCH MEN"?

I present to you, in support of the action by Corporal William Orville Paxton, the answer to "Where Do We Find Such Men"?

The following are excerpts from President Ronald Reagan's speech to military personnel at Hickam Air Force Base in Honolulu, Hawaii on April 24, 1984. And I quote.

"-----I have to take a moment to say to you here, in this particular place, what it means to me to be here with you men and women in uniform and with all of those who are not in uniform but who also serve; those who know some of the privations and hardships, inconveniences - your families, your wives, your children - they, too, serve."

There are some among us who say that the military is one of the causes of war. I'm sure they're sincere in their belief, but they're dead wrong to believe that the uniform, that the military could be among the causes of war is like believing that the police department is responsible for crime. You are the peace makers. The better you perform, the less likely it is that we will ever see combat or hostilities directed against our nation.

You know, many years ago in one of the four wars in my lifetime an admiral stood on the bridge of a carrier watching the planes take off and out into the darkness, bent on a night combat mission, and then found himself asking with no one there to answer, just himself, to hear his own voice, he said, "Where do we find such men?"

A decade or so ago, after spending an evening with the first returning POW's from Vietnam, Nancy and I found ourselves as the evening ended, having heard the stories of horror and brutality by men who had been confined as prisoners of war longer than any other fighting men in American's history--found ourselves asking that same question, "Where do we find such men?"

We find them where we've always found them when we need them. We find them where we found you--on the main streets and the farms of American. You are the product of the freest, the fairest, the most generous and humane society that has ever been created by man."

And so dear readers, after reading and absorbing the above, it is my pleasure to present to you William Orville Paxton, hero and veteran!!!!!

Appendix 6

A CHRONOLOGICAL LISTING OF MILITARY RECORDS & PICTURES FOR CORPORAL WILLIE ORVILLE PAXTON - SERVICE NUMBER 35 708 735

A.   Promotion as a temporary appointment to Corporal - Letter dated 17 August1945

B.   Undated Letter delegating Willie O Paxton (no rank indicated) to continued Service in the Enlisted Reserve Corps -headquartered in Bowling Green, Kentucky

C.   Cover letter indicating PFC Willie O. Paxton is discharged at the expiration of current enlistment, as extended. Letter dated 2 July 1945

D.   Letter of Discharge to PFC Willie O. Paxton from the Enlisted Reserve Corps, dated 31 August 1948

E.   Separation Qualification record issued to Corporal Willie O Paxton - 19 November 1945

F.   Certificate of Honorable Discharge to Corporal Willie O. Paxton - dated 19 November 1945.

G.   Letter from Organized Reserve Corps, Bowling Green, Ky that PFC Willie O Paxton's enlisted in the Enlisted Reserve Corps expired on 30 June 1952. **Note here that Willie O's rank has reverted to PFC indicating that the promotion to Corporal was a temporary one.**

H.   Photo of Honor Guard @ burial site - Bethlehem Baptist Church Cemetery, August 18, 2002.

SAVE

FOR VICTORY
BUY
UNITED STATES
WAR
BONDS
AND
STAMPS

ARMY SERVICE FORCES
HEADQUARTERS FOURTH SERVICE COMMAND
ATLANTA 3, GEORGIA

SPIPE 201 - Paxton, Willie O.   17 August 1945

SUBJECT: Promotion of Personnel of Projects P and R.

THRU   : CG, AG&SF Redistribution Station, Miami Beach, Fla.

TO   : Corporal Willie O. Paxton, 35 708 735.

    1. Under the provisions of paragraph 1, TAGO letter, AG 383.6
(31 May 45) OB-S-A-SPGAM-M, 22 June 1945, subject; "Change No. 2 to
POW," announcement is made of your (promotion) (temporary appointment)
to the following grade, effective this date:

                 CORPORAL
    2. The original of this letter will be furnished the above-named
EM as special orders will not be issued.

      BY COMMAND OF MAJOR GENERAL BROOKS:

                          H. L. Watts
                          H. L. WATTS
                          Colonel, FA
                          Acting Adjutant General

A

1-15-19

WAR DEPARTMENT
THE ADJUTANT GENERAL'S OFFICE
WASHINGTON 25, D. C.

SUBJECT: **Appreciation.**

To: Willie O. Paxton

1. It is desired to express to you the appreciation of the War Department for your continued service to National Defense through enlistment in the Enlisted Reserve Corps. Your aid and that of other veterans who, like you, are displaying an active interest by enlisting in the Reserve will be invaluable in building and maintaining a sound and effective postwar Army.

2. AR 150-5 and the other Army Regulations governing the Enlisted Reserve Corps will be revised to conform with such statutes as may be enacted to govern the post-war Army. Revised regulations and other information concerning the Enlisted Reserve Corps will be made available in the future.

BY ORDER OF THE SECRETARY OF WAR:

EDWARD F. WITSELL
Major General
Acting The Adjutant General

B

195

HEADQUARTERS
KENTUCKY MILITARY DISTRICT
425 South Fifth Street
Louisville 2, Kentucky

AICZR-R 201   2 July 1952

SUBJECT: Discharge from Enlisted Reserve Corps

TO: Pfc Willie O. Paxton INF, USAR
          Rt 1
          Greensburg, Ky.

          Inclosed is your discharge from the Enlisted Reserve Corps,
which has been granted for the reason checked below:

     ( ) a. Reenlistment in ERC. Discharge covers last period of
service, inasmuch as Army regulations require that a discharge certificate be awarded for each separate period of service.

     ( ) b. Enlistment, induction or commission in Regular Army,
National Guard, Navy, US Marine Corps, Coast Guard, or US Air Force.
This discharge should be presented to your personnel officer for entry
of time in service for pay purposes on your records.

     ( ) c. Physical examination for active duty, indicating that you
are disqualified therefor.

     ( ) d. Affidavit submitted by you, listing four (4) or more de-
pendents.

     (x) e. Expiration of current enlistment, as extended.

          (1) You are eligible to reenlist in the ERC in the grade
held at time of discharge, providing you reenlist within ninety (90)
days from date of discharge.

          (2) Individuals who do not reenlist until after the ninety
(90) day period following date of last discharge may be reenlisted in
grades commensurate with their training and experience, as authorized by
SR 615-120-8. In most cases such grade is limited to Private First Class.

     ( ) f. Under provisions of SR 140-133-1, you were determined to
be not available for active military service. You may apply for a new
enlistment in the Enlisted Reserve Corps, should the cause of your non-
availability be removed at some future date.

          BY ORDER OF COLONEL LYON:

                                          Thomas C. Brasfield

1 Incl: T. C. BRASFIELD
  WD AGO Form 55 or   1st Lt,   AGC
  WD Form 256A   C   Asst   Adj

  KMD-ERC Form # 15

SECOND ARMY
HEADQUARTERS KENTUCKY MILITARY DISTRICT
Third Floor - Kenyon Building
112 South Fifth Street
Louisville, Kentucky

AICZA 201 Paxton, Willie O. (ERC)   31 August 1948

SUBJECT: Discharge from the Enlisted Reserve Corps

TO: Pfc Willie O. Paxton, Inf-Res
        Route # 1
        Greensburg, Kentucky

1. Inclosed herewith is your discharge from your previous enlistment in the Enlisted Reserve Corps.

2. This document has no effect on your recent reenlistment.

3. Your records will be maintained at this headquarters as long as you reside in the state of Kentucky.

4. Always advise this office of any change of address you may have.

FOR THE DISTRICT EXECUTIVE:

1 Incl.:   V. WYNN
WD AGO Form 55   CWO USA
                           Ass't Adjutant

D

197

19 15 19 CL

Army of the United States

SEPARATION QUALIFICATION RECORD

SAVE THIS FORM. IT WILL NOT BE REPLACED IF LOST

This record of job assignments and special training received in the Army is furnished to the soldier when he leaves the service. In its preparation, information is taken from available Army records and supplemented by personal interview. The information about civilian education and work experience is based on the individual's own statements. The veteran may present this document to former employers, prospective employers, representatives of schools or colleges, or use it in any other way that may prove beneficial to him.

1. LAST NAME—FIRST NAME—MIDDLE INITIAL				MILITARY OCCUPATIONAL ASSIGNMENTS		
Paxton Willie O				10. MONTHS	11. GRADE	12. MILITARY OCCUPATIONAL SPECIALTY
2. ARMY SERIAL No.	3. GRADE		4. SOCIAL SECURITY No.	4	Pvt.	Basic Tng. Inf 521
35 708 735	CPL.		None.	5	Pfc.	Rifleman. 745
5. PERMANENT MAILING ADDRESS *(Street, City, County, State)*				1 yr.		
Rt 1 Greensburg, Green County, KY.				3 Mo.	Cpl.	Automatic,
6. DATE OF ENTRY INTO ACTIVE SERVICE	7. DATE OF SEPARATION	8. DATE OF BIRTH				rifleman. 746
24 Sep 1943	19 Nov 1945	6 May 1925				
9. PLACE OF SEPARATION						
Fort Knox., KY.						

SUMMARY OF MILITARY OCCUPATIONS

13. TITLE—DESCRIPTION—RELATED CIVILIAN OCCUPATION

Automatic Rifleman:

Servid in the ETO., France as an automatic rifleman with the 357th Infantry Regiment. Attacked enemy isstallations with rifle and granades, supported the infantrymen with high speed rifle, and rode tanks as an outside protection man.

E

WD AGO FORM 100
JUL 1945

This form supersedes WD AGO Form 100, 15 July 1944, which will not be used.

16—45815-1

Recorded in Veterans Discharge Book
#3, page 100. Green County Clerk's
Office, this Nov. 23, 1945
Floyd Patterson, Clerk

Army of the United States

Honorable Discharge

This is to certify that

WILLIE O PAXTON 35 708 735 CORPORAL

COMPANY L 357TH INFANTRY

Army of the United States

is hereby Honorably Discharged from the military service of the United States of America.

This certificate is awarded as a testimonial of Honest and Faithful Service to this country.

Given at   FORT KNOX KENTUCKY

Date   19 NOVEMBER 1945

W J ULLENBRUCH
MAJOR CAVALRY

F

OFFICE OF THE UNIT INSTRUCTOR
ORGANIZED RESERVE CORPS
ARMORY BUILDING
BOWLING GREEN, KENTUCKY
Telephone No. 9828

7 July 1952

Pfc Willie O Paxton, INF, USAR
Rt # 1
Greensburg, Kentucky

r Reservist:

The records of this office indicate that ~~you were notified by the Kentucky~~
~~~~ your enlistment in the Enlisted Reserve Corps (expired)
~~~~) on ___30 June 1952_____.

ce you reside in a locality which is under the jurisdiction of this
ice, and since you are eligible for reenlistment in your present grade, I am
m ing this effort to let you know the members of this office are here to help you
with any of your problems at any time. In the event you were directed to any other
office and you were not assisted to your satisfaction, please feel free to write,
phone or visit this office and you will be properly assisted.

There are many advantages and tangible benefits to be derived from the con-
tinuance of your reserve enlistment, in addition to the knowledge and personal
satisfaction that you are doing your part in the peacetime defense program for the
protection of your country, your community and their people. The time you have
already spent and any future time served in the reserve will be counted for lon--
gevity pay purposes in the event you should ever return to active duty in any of
the services.

If you decide to reenlist before your present enlistment expires on the
date shown above, the Army has authorized the payment of five cents (5¢) per mile
for travel to and from your home to the place previously notified or to this office,
as well as $1.50 per meal for the time required for travel. If for any reason you
are held over at the place designated for reenlistment, you will be paid an additional $2.00 for quarters.

In the event you do not accomplish your reenlistment by the expiration of
your present enlistment, you can still reenlist in the Enlisted Reserve Corps in
your present grade provided you do so within 90 days after the expiration of your
present enlistment. In this case the provisions of the above paragraph would not
apply to you.

I am also taking this opportunity to determine whether or not you already
have reenlisted or whether you intend to reenlist at a later date. You will find
a self-addressed Post Card enclosed for this purpose. Please complete this card
and return it to this office immediately.

Sincerely,

Joseph H Miller

JOSEPH H MILLER
Maj   INF
Unit Instructor, ORC

OFFICE HOURS
Weekdays - 8 AM to 4:30 PM
Saturdays - 8 AM to 12 Noon

G

Military Honors

Veterans from VFW Post 1170 in Middletown, Ky., fired a 21-gun salute in honor of Willie O. Paxton, who was a POW, last Wednesday at Mr. Paxton's funeral. Members of the honor guard are Commander Marvin Meyerhoffer, Vice Commander Bob Ernst, Frank Taylor, Andy Singer, Leon Smith, Joe Hinton, Don Kohler, Charles Kleinhans and Joe Burden. Military pallbearers from Campbellsville's Bravo Battery, 1/623rd MLRS Field Artillery also participated in the military rites funeral.

H

Appendix 7A

Prisoner of War Medal

Stalag 7A Identification Tag

Appendix 8

HISTORY OF THE 90ᵀᴴ INFANTRY DIVISION "BLOOD RED FOR TOUGH 'OMBBRES"

The 90th Infantry Division was reactivated at Camp Barkeley, Texas, March 23, 1942. The letters T-O of the insignia stood for Texas and Oklahoma, being a carryover from World War 1. Today, the T-O stands for "Tough 'Ombres".

The combat elements of the division are the 357th, 358th and 359th Infantry Brigades, with the 357th obviously being the unit that Willie O served during the invasion of Europe. The division deployed to England on March 23, 1944. Willie O embarked for England on May 15, 1944, just two-month after completing his combat training in April 1944.

As the 90th had been re-activated two years and two months prior to being deployed to England for ultimate participation in combat related operations against the Nazi regime, combat efficiency would most unlikely not have attained the high level desired by the command structure.

When activating or re-activating a division combat size unit with three maneuver Brigades, the overall strength fluctuating between 10,000 and 20,000 soldiers, the organizational buildup, personnel turnover, implementation of effective combat, etc. etc. is time consuming and requires training and re-training.

The capture of Willie O on July 7, 1944 would reasonably fit with the scenario above. However, after Willie O's capture, the division gained additional combat experience and was able to contribute significantly to the winning of World War ll in the European Theatre.

Later in 1944, it is documented that the 90th Division took 12, 335 prisoners and killed an estimated 8,000 Nazi soldiers from August 16 through 22. In addition, 308 German tanks, 248 self-propelled guns, 164 artillery pieces, 3,270 motor vehicles, 649 horse drawn vehicles and 13 motorcycles were destroyed.

This documented combat efficiency speaks extremely well for the command structure for US forces in manning, training, deploying and obtaining conclusive combat results.

Although, there may have been other Kentuckians serving with the 90th during this period, however the pocket size history booklet, pictured in attached Photo 8A, only one other than Willie O is identified as Pfc William L. Smiley of Centertown, Ky. Pfc Smiley and his fellow soldiers were pinned down by a Nazi machine gun nest behind a twenty-five foot hill.

Pfc Smiley proceeded to scale the hill, fired point blank into the enemy causing them to retreat and or surrender.

Appendix 8A

PHOTO OF COVER OF 90TH DIVISION HISTORY BOOKLET

Front Cover & Back Cover

❧

BACKGROUND - OMAR LYLE SHUFFETT

Serial Number - 15 046 357

Omar Shuffett was born on Tuesday, February 20, 1922, to James Robert Michael Shuffett and Daisy Bird Lile in Liletown, Kenucky. The attending physician was Dr. H. Shively. Over the years Omar inherited a middle name-Lile or Lyle-although it does not appear on his birth certificate. The fact that his mother was Daisy Bird Lile may be the reason it came to be used as his middle name.

It is thought that Omar's fourth great grandfather, Melchior Shuffett, immigrated to the United States from Bavaria sometime before 1765. His great, great, grandfather, Mikiel Shuffett, was the first to migrate from Virginia to Kentucky, settling first in Harrison County before 1820 and then to Green County between 1830 and 1840 where he died in 1857. He and his family first settled in Donansburg.

Omar's grandfather, Michael Larkin Shuffett was a private in the 13th Kentucky Infantry during the Civil War. He was wounded in the battle of Resasa, Georgia, which was fought on Saturday and Sunday, May 14, 1864. He is buried in the Judd Cemetery I Grab, Kentucky.

Photos of the Shuffett residence where Omar spent his formative years on the Liletown-Pierce Road which runs in a westerly direction from Highway 68/70 to Highway 218 near Pierce, are shown here. The top photo shows how the home looked in the 1920's or 30's, and the bottom photo how it looked in 2010.

His high school diploma refers to him as Omar L. Shuffett, but his death certificate refers to him as, simply Omar Shuffett. The first mention of Lyle surfaces when Omar entered the military. He continued to use Lyle as part of his signature throughout his life. For the purposes of this narrative, I will use his name as Omar Lyle Shuffett.

He was the eighth of 10 children born to James Robert Michael Shuffett, (born Wednesday, March 27, 1872) and Daisy Bird Lile (born Friday, August 17, 1877). James died of pneumonia Saturday, January 15, 1927, when Omar was only 15. Omar and his mother became exceptionally close and she succumbed to a stroke Wednesday, January 10, 1940.

Two family pictures of interest shown here, are Omar's father and his grandfather (born 1843 and expired on Friday, August 16, 1872). Omar's grandfather was a Union soldier and, not only was he injured at Resaca. He contacted a bad case of measles in the war which may have led to his death from "Brights disease". (Bright's disease is an archaic term for what is now referred to as "nephritis," an inflammation of kidneys, cased by toxins infection or autoimmune conditions. It is not strictly a single disease, rather a condition with different types and causes).

Omar's Grandfather
Michael Shuffett

Omar's Father
James Robert Michael Shuffett

The picture below is of the Shuffett family before Omar was born. Considering that Omar was the eighth of 10 children and judging by the size of the participants, the family members are as follows: (1) Omar's father with mustache, (2) Omar's mother, holding baby Avery, who would become the business partner with Omar in the automobile parts and repair business upon Omar's return from captivity. (Note the dress on the baby. This was not an uncommon practice up through the 1930's.), (2) Merle, standing in black suit with necklace next to Omar's mother, (3) Flossie, standing on right with white dress, (4) Vernon, standing in rear between Omar's father and mother, (5) Raymond, (6) Lillian, standing to the left of her father with her hand on his left leg.

This photo was most likely taken in 1910 as Elsie, child number seven, was born August 18, 1911 and obviously not included in the picture.

The pictures below represent an assortment of photo's at different times in the life of the Shuffett family.

(1)   (2)   (3)

**(1) Daisy Bird Lyle, (Omar's Mother, (2) Avery (Omar's Brother, Omar and Velma (Omar's younger sister)
(3) Velma Strong (Omar's sister) and daughter Brenda.**

(1)   (2)

**(1) Daisy Bird Lile, Omar's Mother in black dress,
(2) Omar and wife Maxine, circa 1946 or 1947.**

(1)
(1) Shuffett Motor Parts, early days,

(1)   (2)
(1) Omar and Maxine's Wedding picture
(2) Avery (left) and Omar at the station.

Omar most likely attended grade school at Liletown, although other grade schools in the vicinity were Manilla, Lone Oak and Chinquapin (pronounced "Chink-ah-pin)." The word Chinquapin is a derivative from the eastern-dwelling Algonquians.

Chinquapin trees are known as far west as Texas. They produce edible nuts, much like the chestnuts, which are eaten whole as a snack. The nut is the only part of the tree that is consumable as the leaves contain toxic tannins.

At the class reunion of 1986 celebrating 55 years since graduation, the Record Herald produced a photo of the eighth-grade class taken in 1927.

The Greensburg High School Class of 1931 as eighth graders in 1927. Front row, left to right, Virgil Price, Boyce Marcum, Russell Phillips, Austin Simmons, Paul Mitchell, Omer Shuffett; second row, l-r, Lucille Pickett Guthrie, Eva Tucker Cheatham, Elizabeth McMahan, Opal Burress Hoover, Esther Thomps Davis, Jane Rogers Allen, Lottie Smith; Third row, Howard Smith, Louise Simpson Larimore, Lill Gumm Skaggs, Mary Price Beams, Anis Gupton Shi William Cox Teacher, and Raymond Peterson.

Thru this and other stories that are related in this chapter in a hero's life, I am reminded that members of his family said, "Omar was a reserved and sensitive person. It was very difficult for him to speak of his prison experiences. It was painful. He had to be tough to have survived and he was mentally tough, but he did not return the same person. There were nights after he returned home that he would have nightmares."

His family members further commented, "He was kind and loving husband and father, and we don't ever remember his raising his voice." His daughters also quick to declare, "Dad was a hero to me." Having spent over 50 percent of his military service in Japanese prison camp, his resilience and hindsight in recalling diversity, trauma, tragedy and threats is phenomenal

Omar Lyle Shuffett joined the Army Air Corps on September 28, 1940. He was released from active duty on November 18, 1946, a total of six years and two months totaling 2,250 days.

He spent a total of three years and four months in captivity for a total of 1,215 days. This period of confinement calculated to be 54% of his military service where he was interned by The Imperial Japanese Army.

I first saw Omar Shuffett on Tuesday, November 6, 1945, when he returned to Greensburg for the first time since entering the military. I was there, along with approximately 3,000 other Green County residents who filled the public square to await the return of a distinguished war veteran. To honor this returning hero, all businesses and schools were closed.

We walked from the school down Hodgenville Avenue to Depot Street, then crossed the footbridge to the square where we lined the street awaiting the motorcade. Being nine years old, I and my other "little" school mates were placed in the front row of the reviewing crowd. Not completely understanding all this, but there we stood.

I really had no idea what I was doing there, but we "wee ones" were certainly placed strategically for good viewing. It was in the early afternoon right after lunch. The crowd assembled and waited patiently for Omar to arrive. I remember seeing my mother on the other side of the square and her waving to me.

The escort vehicle in which Omar was riding was met by Green County officials at the Green-Larue County line and escorted to the public square in Greensburg. As the vehicle made the right turn down to the public square, huge applause from the crowd began. The closer the vehicle came to the center of the square the louder the applause.

Upon getting to the middle of the square, the vehicle stopped, and Omar made his appearance. He was so weak that he had to hold on to the passenger side door to stand. He was presented a huge bouquet of chrysanthemums and red roses bound by red, white and blue ribbon by Miss Ann Lewis, a majorette with the Greensburg High School. After receiving the bouquet, he sat back down in the car and was driven away. No speeches, just the recognizing of a true Green County hero. The high school band was present and played "On to Victory". The color guard was present, standing at attention at the car paused. The color guard was formed of men from both wars, some wearing overseas ribbons, some the Purple Heart. There were soldiers, sailors, and marines honoring the returned veteran.

A longtime resident of Greensburg, Suzanne (Turner) Taylor recalls that when Omar raised up from his seat on the passenger side of the automobile in which he was riding to receive the roses from Anne Lewis and tipped his Hat--a true gentleman.

Sure, he was a veteran, but so were a lot of other guys, so why him? Well, it seems he underwent the most catastrophic experience of any veteran of Green County. Hearing parts of this story was hard for me to grasp the full meaning and understanding of the suffering that was involved. It was only as I grew out of my youth and became associated with the military that I had much better understanding of this horrendous action.

As the years went by, Omar settled into a somewhat normal life in Greensburg, opening an auto repair shop with his brother, Avery. It was several years after his safe return home I began to learn of his captivity. When I was a youngster, I would see Omar around town, working in his business or in church. My father would occasionally mention something about Omar's war experience, As time went on, I began to hear "war stories" to which Omar had been exposed.

Upon Omar's return, his brother Vernon Shuffett, a local attorney, offered to pay the tuition for Omar to become a veterinarian. Although this was Vernon's plan for this brother, upon his return Omar was too ill at the time to accept the offer.

Since publishing the first book, I learned a bit more about Staff Sergeant Omar Lyle Shuffett, and in fairness to the Green County hero, I am presenting here additional respectful information. I knew this man in my teen years and was respectful of his ordeal although I was missing many details. In attempts to learn more about Omar, I have since talked with member of his family and other close neighbors and friends and all agree he was very reticent in relating his captivity experience.

Omar met the love of his life Rachael Maxine Kemp shortly after returning home and they were married on Sunday, October 20, 1946 in Glasgow, Ky. He shortly thereafter began to partner with Avery in a parts and auto repair business just south of the Greensburg square. Maxine was a beautician on the square. Over the years they became the parents of two daughters--Carolyn (born Sunday, July 27, 1947) and Fran (born on Saturday, May 24,1952). Omar taught Sunday School at the Greensburg Methodist Church where he also served as Chairman of the Official Board, was a lay leader and a delegate to the annual conference. His preparation was immaculate and exerts of his lessons to the Men's Sunday School class are presented in **Exhibit 1**. His daughter, Fran would type the lessons for him. In addition, he was a charter member of the Greensburg Lions Club, a member of the Defenders of Bataan and Corregidor and a member of the American Legion and Veterans of Foreign Wars.

**Omar & Maxine - Most likely taken for a photo
In the Greensburg Methodist Church Directory**

Omar was recognized Tuesday, August 13, 1985, when the The Bronze Star Medal was awarded for "Meritorious Achievement," 7 December 1941 to 10 May 1942. He was presented this Certificate with appropriate medal in October, 1985. In the picture below his is the epitome of strength. A copy of the Official Certificate is Presented in **Exhibit 2.**

Omar Shuffett, 503 Milby St., Greensburg, holds the Bronze Star and accompanying certificate he was awarded in August--40 years after World War II ended. Shuffett was captured twice by the Japanese during the war and spent three and one-half years in prisoner of war camps. R-H photo by Bobby Watson.

Omar was recognized various times by the citizenry of Greensburg and Green County. One of most memorable times was when U. S. Marine Major J. S. "Deke" DiSimone researched Omar's war record and prepared a commemorative ceremony replete with a display of his awards and decorations. A copy of these framed medals is displayed below. Pictures of this ceremony are shown here. Bill Taylor, Greensburg Mayor, made the following comment just prior to the ceremony:

One of the things that sticks in my mind is that most of the soldiers were home and they were going to have a parade because Omar Shuffett was coming home. I was in my teens and I can remember the soldiers drilling in front of the courthouse, getting ready for the parade. One of the biggest parades we ever had in Greensburg was to honor one person, Omar Shuffett.

The ceremony contained numerous laudatory comments, but the pictures presented below, tell the story of a still strong man at the age 87. View the penetrating eyes, the erect posture, the immaculate dress, demonstrating the superb quality of a national hero.

He is in the company of an outstanding young Marine Major, two other veterans of World War II with great records, and an almost magical physician, Doctor Kenneth DeSimone, father of "Deke". The two veterans to the right of Omar are Johnny Matney and Morris Price. A bit of their background is below.

He is in the company of an outstanding young Marine Major, two other veterans of World War II with great records and an almost magical physician, Doctor Kenneth DeSimone, father of "Deke".

Major DeSimone had a distinguished career himself. He was commissioned a 2nd Lieutenant in 1986 and the Marine Corp provided him the opportunity to serve in the armor and military police fields throughout his career.

He retired in 2014 from the Marine Corp as a Colonel. His service included being deployed to nearly 40 countries around the world. He is a veteran of the wars in Iraq and Afghanistan.

In 2005 he was the Second Marine Expedition Force senior advisor to the Iraqi Border Police in the Anbar and Najaf Provinces. In 2011 he was the Second Marine Division, Provincial Police Advisor Team officer in charge and the senior advisor to the Afghan National Police Chief in the Helmand Province.

Johnny Matney served with distinction with Darby's Rangers,

a forerunner to the elite Army Rangers. He also served with the 1st Special Service Force, a unit which landed at Anzio. His unit was nicknamed "The Black Devils", coined by a comment found in the personal diary of a German Officer. They would often perform their duties behind enemy lines, hand-to-hand combat. Johnny was wounded twice, and after the war he returned to his home in Exie, Kentucky where he farmed and hunted to feed his family. Johnny Matney died at the age of 90, on Wednesday, September 25, 2013.

Morris Price served in World War II as well, and a display of his medals indicate a most dedicated and brave career with the U. S. Army. The author could not surface detailed military information on Morris. However, in viewing the medals encased and held by Mr. Price, it is easily ascertained that he provided quality service to his country. One can see The Purple Heart, 3rd Infantry Division and 5th U. S Army patches, Combat Infantryman's Badge. Several other medals earned for commitment and service for and with particular organizations are unidentifiable due to the clarify of the photo.

World War II heroes who have been honored in the past two years with research into their war records by Major Deke DeSimone, left, are second from left, Johnny Matney, Morris Price and Omar Shuffett. At right is Dr. Kenneth DeSimone, the host for all three awards ceremonies.

Omar accepting a display of his earned medals from Major "Deke" DiSimone

Medals awarded SSGT Shuffett were (1) Bronze Star, (2) Purple Heart, (3) Army Good Conduct Medal (4) American Defense Service Medal, (5) Asiatic-Pacific Campaign Medal, (6) World War II Victory Medal, (7) Philippine Defense Medal, (8) Philippine Liberation Medal, (9) Philippine Independence Medal/Ribbon, (10) Presidential Unit Citation w/two oak leaf clusters, (11) World War II Honorable Service Pin.

He was honored with an additional award by the State of Kentucky, when Governor Louis Nunn declared him to be a *Kentucky Colonel*.

Omar's medals and Staff Sergeant rank are displayed in a framed box

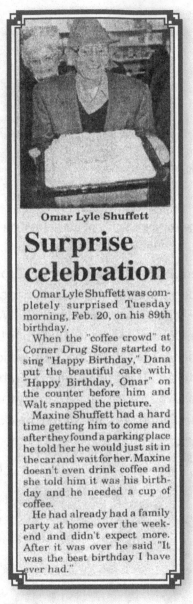

Omar Lyle Shuffett

Surprise celebration

Omar Lyle Shuffett was completely surprised Tuesday morning, Feb. 20, on his 89th birthday.

When the "coffee crowd" at Corner Drug Store started to sing "Happy Birthday," Dana put the beautiful cake with "Happy Birthday, Omar" on the counter before him and Walt snapped the picture.

Maxine Shuffett had a hard time getting him to come and after they found a parking place he told her he would just sit in the car and wait for her. Maxine doesn't even drink coffee and she told him it was his birthday and he needed a cup of coffee.

He had already had a family party at home over the weekend and didn't expect more. After it was over he said "It was the best birthday I have ever had."

<u>One other time for celebration was on Omar's 89th birthday when he was given a surprise party at the Corner Drug Store on Wednesday, February 28, 2001.</u>

I have always possessed a leaning toward the military and fortunately I was able to have a good Army active and Reserve career. But this is not about me. It is about a man in our community who was very quiet, well-mannered and "ran under the radar" so to speak. Yet, he had a most different and difficult military experience.

Omar Lyle Shuffett is one of the most dedicated and revered Green Countians that have served in the United States military in the defense of our great country. The total number of Green Countians that have served over time is quite large and most, after having served their military obligation returned to their hometown and began life all over again.

American Legion Post #124 recognizes the war casualties from Green County. In records from the Post, WW I thru the Vietnam War, a total of 94 of Green County's finest have given their lives while serving their country during wartime. The American Post is named the for Morris Rod Lowe. Lowe was the first to volunteer for service in WW II from Green County and the first to be killed in action (KIA). Corporal Lowe lost his life on December 2, 1942 and was awarded The Purple Heart posthumously.

All too often people serving their country in wartime will die via enemy action. The list of combat deaths for Green County from WW I through the Vietnam War total 66. Most of the fatalities occurred in WW II as this was obviously the largest war of our nation to date. A breakdown of casualties is as follows: WW I - 15, WW II - 46 and Vietnam - 5.

Corporal Morris Rod Lowe

Homage - Omar Lyle
Shuffett-Prisoner of War

A story of Torture, Suffering and Humiliation

Omar Lyle Shuffett was inducted into the U. S. Army Air Corps on September 28, 1940, and assigned to Chanute Field, Illinois where he was given his basic training. He was also trained as an airplane mechanic.

After receiving his initial basic training, Omar was deployed to Clark Air Field in the Philippine Islands, and was assigned to the 2nd Observation Squadron.

He was there for about six months and to then was sent to Nichols Field (near Manila). On December 8, 1941, just eight hours after the Japanese attack on Pearl Harbor, (which was Sunday, December 7, 1941 in the US, due to the crossing of the international date line) the Japanese attacked Clark Field with bombers and fighter planes resulting in the destruction of almost all of the aircraft and taking complete operational control of the air field. Omar was at Nichols Field when the attack initially occurred.

Some two weeks later, 43,000 Japanese troops invaded the islands. Even though the US had 130,000 troops to defend the islands, they were not well trained, did not have sufficient arms and armament, and therefore, could not forestall the eminent capture of the islands. The US troops were forced to retreat to a small thumb of land on the west coast of Manila Bay, the peninsula of Bataan.

The Rainbow War Plan, a defensive strategy for U. S. interests in the Pacific that was drawn up in the 1930's and later refined by the War Department, required that the defending force withdraw into the mountains of the Bataan Peninsula and await better-trained and better-equipped American reinforcements.

The Allied Commander of troops in the Philippines at the time of the attack was General Douglas MacArthur, a hero of esteemed quality. Recalled to active duty in July 1941, MacArthur conducted a valiant delaying action against the Japanese in the Philippines after war erupted in December 1941. Understanding the gravity of the situation, President Franklin D. Roosevelt, directed the general to surrender the islands.

He further ordered MacArthur to leave the Philippines and transition to Australia in March 1942 to command the Allied Forces in the Southwest Pacific Theater until a suitable time for his return to the Philippines. President Roosevelt supposedly remarked, relative to his decision to order General MacArthur to leave the islands, "I can see no valid reason for the American Forces to surrender a four-star general to our enemy....."

President Roosevelt told General MacArthur "Go to the southern part of Manila, be careful and not cross enemy lines and your wife and children will be waiting for you." MacArthur, his family and command staff, exited the Philippines via PT boats on Wednesday, March 11, 1942 and made their way to Mindanao. Mindanao is the second largest island of the Philippines at the southern end of the archipelago; it is mountainous and volcanic but considered the agricultural basin of the Philippines, where eight out of the top 10 export agro-commodities are derived.

Upon leaving the Philippines, General Mac Arthur commented, "I came through and I shall return". On Friday, October 20, 1944, he returned to the Philippines and waded ashore at the island of Leyte. He later that day made a radio broadcast where he related, "People of the Philippines, I have returned."

Although several Generals were stationed in the Philippines, Johnathan "Skinny" Wainwright was the ranking officer. It was Lieutenant General Wainwright who ultimately surrendered the Philippine Armed Forces to the Japanese on Wednesday, May 6, 1942.

Years later, on Sunday, September 2, 1945, General MacArthur was designed by the Presidet Harry S. Truman to sign for the United States on the USS Missouri the surrender documents from the Empire of Japan. (Missouri coincidentally was the home state of President Truman). Truman would officially name the day the

Japanese signed the official surrender--September 2, 1945-- as V-J Day, (Victory over Japan).

When Gen. MacArthur was asked who he wanted to accompany him at the surrender table, he supposedly remarked, "I want "Skinny." This would be a fitting tribute to Wainwright who spent four years in Japanese prison after the surrender of the Philippines, taking the place of MacArthur, should he have been the one captured.

Incidentally, only six years later, General MacArthur, serving as Supreme Commander of the United States forces sent to aid South Korea, was relieved of his command by President Harry Truman, on Wednesday, April 11, 1951, because he made public statements that contradicted the administration's policy. The General returned to the United States where he received a hero's welcome and spoke the memorable phrase, "Old soldiers never die, they just fade away."

Although a lot of soldiers didn't like General MacArthur, SSGT Omar Shuffett wasn't among them. "I like him", he offered, "and thought he was a great man."

More than 76,000 Americans and Filipinos under the American command laid down their arms, resulting in the largest single defeat in American history. The sick, starving and bedraggled prisoners of war were rounded up by their Japanese captors and made to walk 66 miles to a railhead for the trip to prison camps, a baneful walk under a boiling sun that turned into one of the most notorious treks in the annal of war, the Bataan Death March.

Thus began a tale of horror lasing for the next 3 years and 4 months.

The 31st Infantry Regiment was formed Thursday, April 13, 1916. In 1942, the 31st was a part of USAFFE's (United States Army Forces Far East) during World War II. The 31st Infantry is somewhat unique in that it has spent most of its life on non-American soil.

Omar was attached to the 31st Infantry Regiment. At this time he was a Specialist 2nd Class and pulled duty on the defensive positions

A Sergeant of the 31ˢᵗ, on detail at Camp John Hays became the campaign's first fatality. The 31ˢᵗ covered the withdrawal of the American and Philippine forces in the Bataan Peninsula. Despite starvation, disease, no supplies, obsolete weapons and often inoperative ammunition, the peninsula's defenders fought the Japanese to a standstill for four months, upsetting Japan's timetable for Asia's conquest. Captain Earl R. Short buried the colors and the cherished Shanghai owl to keep them out of enemy hands.

The Shanghai Bowl was a very important symbol of the lineage of the 31ˢᵗ Infantry Regiment. The large silver punch bowl and it's 65 matching cups were made in 1932 by a Shanghai silversmith from silver purchased by monetary contributions of the Officers of the 31ˢᵗ.

The Regimental colors and the Shanghai Bowl were recovered by none other than Captain Short after his release from a POW camp. Short returned to Corregidor Island at the direction of Major General Marshall in September 1945 to recover the buried colors and bowl. He pinpointed the area (some three years later) within a yard and a half of where he remembered burying them.

The Shanghai Bowl today is displayed in the headquarters of the Regiment's only remaining Battalion, the 4ᵗʰ Battalion, 31ˢᵗ Infantry Regiment, Fort Drum, New York.

Corregidor fell and the Bataan Death March which began in Mariveles Bataan, on the southern tip of the peninsula, on Thursday, April 9, 1942.

The horror story begins for Omar immediately after he was captured and became a part of the infamous march. He was initially captured on Thursday, April 9, 1942.

On a May night shortly after capture, Omar and others were taken on a freighter to Manila where they were marched through the city. The Filipinos were made to watch. They were then taken to Billibid Prison in Manila, where their sleeping assignment were drawn with chalk on the bare floor, marking off their respective sleeping place.

The prisoners were then forced marched north from Bataan

to San Fernando, located in Central Luzon and 41 miles north of Manila. They were then taken in cramped and unsanitary boxcars further north to Capas, a landlocked municipality in province of Tarlac, Central Luzon From there they walked and additional seven miles to Camp O'Donnell, a former United States military base located in Capas, Seventy-six thousand military, Filipino and American, were captured and some 54,000 thousand survived the march of 66 miles. Twenty-nine percent did not.

Omar told his family later, "At the beginning of my capture, I had concluded that I probably wouldn't live to the end of the march and was viewing escape as my only option. When the march was near clumps of bamboo and the shells from Corregidor providing a distraction, I saw chance to escape."

Omar further recalled, "I don't know if anyone saw me escape. I ran and found an American motor launch on the ocean as it was picking up survivors. I caught the motor launch, and it took me to Corregidor. This was our second day of capture. I and one other fellow made the escape only to be re-captured two weeks later."

While on Corregidor, which is located at the entrance to Manila Bay just south of Bataan, Omar was assigned to the 4th Marines under a Captain Schoffner and his duty was to man a .30 caliber machine gun. He was supposed to be a beach guard, but never made it to the beach. After recapture on Corregidor, he was held for about 10 days and searched daily.

During the deadly march, Omar related he saw between 60 and 70 men killed, however, he saw no beheading. Somewhere after the attack he contacted malaria. He and his fellow prisoners were taken to Camp O'Donnell first, and then on cars to the city of Cabanatuan, and marched to Cabanatuan Prison #1. He and his fellow prisoners were made to watch four soldiers in dress uniforms face a firing squad; they were first forced to dig their own graves.

He was later taken to Cabanatuan Prison #2 where the Japanese selected those who were able to work in the mines. They were then taken to Bilibid Prison prior to being loaded on ships to Japan. The trip to Japan took about 30 days. Some 300-400 men were held in the hold of the ship (name unknown). On each side of the hold was a bucket to be used as a toilet. Enroute, the ship was anchored off Formosa for 2 days, waiting for storm to pass. While in transit, an American submarine tried, unsuccessfully, to sink the ship carrying the prisoners of war. The ship landed at Yokahama, Japan on Thursday, November 26, 1942-- Thanksgiving Day in America.

The most grievous infraction of the Geneva Convention regarding the treatment of Prisoners of War was the announced policy by the Japanese that they would treat the soldiers captured in the Philippines as captives rather than as prisoners of war. They carried this out by under-feeding them, over-marching them, under clothing them, beating them, and executing them at the slightest provocation. As a result of not having proper food and the related vicious treatment, prisoners died at the rate of 30 to 50 per day.

The Japanese would not give Red Cross access to the prison camps. The Philippine Red Cross had money and food stocks to give to the prisoners, but they were refused access to Cabanatuan five times.

Upon arrival in Japan, Omar and other prisoners were taken to Tokyo on a train, then by subway to Osaka Prison where he was in two different prisons and forced to work in the steel mills. He was later under bombardment while at Osaka. He contacted a severe case of lice and had to beat his clothes in a stream to get himself of the vermin. He was interned at Osaka Prison for almost three years; it was an Imperial Japanese Navy installation located in Kamakura, outside Yokohama.

Not knowing whether the Japanese could speak English, Omar once remarked, "If the slant eyed SOB doesn't kill us, he'll starve us to death." For that, he was bashed in the face and are and couldn't see out of one eye. An English doctor grabbed him and got him away. He also developed blood poisoning in one arm as a result of the beating.

He was then taken to the Ohama nickel mine where he unloaded ships. When working in the hold of the ship, he would eat what he could steal, rice or soybeans, which he would procure by punching a hole in the bag so the food substance could fall out. He would then tie his underwear around his ankle to bind the bottom of his trousers so that when he put the rice down his trousers, it would not fall out.

Since he was considered strong enough, he was sent to work in the Osaka Steel Mills. During those three years his weight dropped significantly; as he was living on a starvation diet. When prisoners were too ill to work, some were never seen or heard from again. Omar said later, "I often worked when I was sick because I knew what would happen if I gave up."

While working at the steel mill, he and one other captive stole some fish from the Japanese kitchen. When his captors discovered the theft, they questioned the suspected soldiers and searched them.

When Omar denied any knowledge of the stolen fish, the Japanese, with their horrible interrogation tactics, rammed a rope down his throat. When they discovered the evidence of fish in the stomach, he was told he would be beheaded. The next morning, he was led to the place of execution, but for some reason the order was rescinded. He believed that it was only because he was working in the mills that he was spared.

The beheading having been avoided, Omar fell into a working environment with other prisoners. After the steel mills were destroyed by American bombers, Omar was transferred to the northern port of Honshu Island and was placed at work on a freighter hauling soybeans from China. He was on this freighter when the word came of the Japanese surrender.

From the steel mills, Omar was sent to the northern part of Japan. By supplementing his meager rations with soybeans, he began picking up weight

During this time he heard from his brothers only once. Ray, Avery and Vernon sent him a small package that contained food and badly needed vitamins. Omar was allowed to see the box, which was routed through the Red Cross, but when he reached for the package, a guard knocked him down with his rifle butt, the blows of which fractured his skull and dislocated his teeth.

At this point at 33 years of age, he had enough horrible experiences to last a lifetime. It is said that he believed that the U. S. could never be severe enough in our treatment of the Japanese to repay them for the atrocities committed against American soldiers.

Note that the return address that Omar's last name is spelled incorrectly as "Shoffett". His rank is stated as *"Pfc. Staff Sergeant"*, which in reality are two different U. S. Army ranks. The rank of Staff Sergent is hard to explain as Omar was captured by the Japanese in April, 1942, a mere two years after being inducted into the U. S. Military. How the Japanese determined the rank of Staff Sergeant is not clear. A Pfc rank can normally be attained with a year or so after entering the military. The rank of Staff Sergeant, since Omar was a Pfc. when he was captured, normally requires six years "time in grade" to be awarded another promotion.

Only twice did he find Japanese with a fellow feeling. One was a Christian Japanese who told Omar she was sorry for the ill treatment he was receiving. Another was an old Japanese woman who worked in the steel mills. In return for a favor and assistance to her in completing her job, she hid bits of food and told him where to find them.

Omar Shuffett ran the gauntlet of prisoner of war camps. (a) Bilidid Prison in Manilla, May 1942, (b) Cabanuatuan # 1, June & July 1942, (c) Cabanuatuan #2 -August, September & October 1942, both in Philippines (d) Yodogawa Bunsho, on the shoreline of Osaka, November 1942 to June 1945, and Oyeama June to August 1945. A camp roster is shown in **Exhibit** 3.

One note of history on Cabanutuan Prison, located thirty miles inside enemy lines and heavily guarded; In January 1945, some five months prior to Omar's arrival, the U. S. Army's Sixth Rangers, under the command of Lt. Colonel Henry Mucci executed a rescue mission for American and allied service men interned in the prison at Cabanutuan. In preparation in training for the mission, Mucci asked for volunteers to quote," die fighting rather than let harm come to those prisoners." Every single Ranger volunteered.

The results of the raid were some 530-1000 Japanese killed, 552

Allied prisoners of war were rescued, including American service men. This raid instituted the greatest rescue attempt of American military personnel in history. Research did not surface any rescue efforts beyond January 1945 from Japanese prison camps.

Omar talked about his two comrades in prison, with him in Yodogawa Bunsho prison--- Red Wilkinson and Harry Monozi. The roster shows Wilkinson as prisoner #143. Monozi is not specifically identified. (The name Monozi is Italian and is described as being derived from the Italian word "*Manzo,* meaning "steer", which is further derived from families who raised steers." Maybe we have the incorrect spelling). A review of the roster shows two Italian surnames with the like spelling, #134 and #307 Marchetti. A camp drawing is shown **Exhibit 4**. This appears to be a very large prison, housing 310 prisoners if reporting on Exhibit 3 is correct.

In August 1943, the Japanese authorities (as authenticated by the Japanese writing on the right top and side of the post card) sent a post card to Velma Strong, Omar's baby sister, two years younger than Omar, (born on Tuesday, April 28, 1914), Velma Pearl Shuffett, was now married to James T. Strong.

There is a postcard from Omar, addressed to and received in Greensburg, on Thursday, August 26, 1943, but was forwarded to Springfield, Kentucky (i. e. Economy Store might have contained the U. S. Post Office.) The contents /writing/ are not the dictated words by Omar. It is widely known that these comments were standard for communication as established by the Japanese authorities. One can readily understand this when reading the comment, "Please see that everything is taken care of." This comment just doesn't seem to fit with American correspondence language. Presented as **Exhibit 5** and some explanations are as follows: (a) The To Line: *Sce Des Prisoners de guerre* is of French origin with definitions as follows: *Sce*; this, *Des*: of, or from or by, Prisoniers: prisoners, *de*:of, *Guere*: war. Therefore, a loose translation would be "This prisoner of war."

Finally, Omar was in Osaka prison when the first atomic bomb fell on Hiroshima. Omar heard the Japanese guards talking about it. The guards began to leave the prison and one morning all were gone. U. S. was planes began to fly over and drop sacks of flour with a note stating, "Food is on it's way. Get on the train in 1-2 days."

Omar was released from captivity and sent to Yokohama on Monday, September 10, 1945 where he along with other released prisoners met with General Douglas MacArthur in a welcoming ceremony. The ex-prisoners were there to help the allied powers identify and collect statements regarding their conditions during their detainment. These documents would assist higher authorities bring cause for atrocities to the world stage.

He completed some 19 affidavits giving names, addresses, dates and crimes for each Japanese so charged. After his short time in Yokohama, he returned to the United States and was sent to White Sulphur Springs, Arkansas and Memphis, Tennessee for treatment of his injuries

Omar arrived back in the United States and was admitted to Letterman Hospital. On Tuesday, October 16, 1945, one day after arrived, the hospital sent a Western Union telegram stating words from Omar, *"Arrived Letterman Hospital Crissy Annez Ward 58 wonderful to be baack feeling fine see you soon."*

In reviewing this statement, the author tries to understand the meaning of the words *"feeling fine".* So many things surfaced that one is overwhelmed by the comment in lieu the previous tortures he had endured in the camps. A copy of this telegram is presented as **Exhibit 6.**

Quotes by Omar are quite moving. A must read for purchasers of this book. They are attached as **Exhibit 7.**

Staff Sergeant Omar Lyle Shuffett was honorably discharged on Sunday, November 17, 1946. His military separation and discharge form is provided as **Exhibit 8** and the official discharge citation is provided in **Exhibit 9.**

Omar was given a short furlough to Green County to visit with his family after which he returned to Sulphur Springs for treatment of the wounds he had received without proper attention over the long years.

Exerts from Omar's Letters to Velma

February 1940 - December 1945

Author's comment: The exerts from these letters are presented just as written including spelling and punctuation. The statements are not in ant certain order; they simply bring to light Omar's primary feelings. The author feels that so many of Omar's letters should be included as they truly display his affection for his family.

1st Letter
Chanute Field, Illinois - Sunday, February 11, 1940

Dearest Velma: Sorry to be so long in writing, but I've been in the hospital here for about twelve days; just the flu I guess. Anyway I'm out now and feeling fine. How is little Jim? Sure hope he is well.

Do you still plan to go to school in Louisville sometime this year? Let me know what you're going to do.

If you see Ray or Ester tell them I got their present and sure appreciated it.

I wish that I could have been stationed in Louisville & I will be in two or three years, just as soon as I rank high enough to get the help I need.

My name came up for foreign service before Xmas. I don't mind telling you-unless things change that I've got to go to the Philippines Islands (next to Japan); but I wish you wouldn't tell any of the folks around home. I'll just be gone two years, that's as long as anyone has out of the U.S. States unless of course we get in war.

How is "big Jim" I've been wondering if he is well. I'll have to be on duty in a few minutes, so I'll have to close for this time -- write real soon and tell me everything.

As ever, yours, Omar

2nd Letter
Chanute Field, Illinois - Wednesday, October 9, 1940

Dearest Little Sister: 8:40 p.m. At last I think I'm settled down for a few months, I have been working hard for the past ten days, had to study all my high school mathematics, and pass a hard test. Just got through yesterday & passed. The ones that passed will get to go to school for the next six months. at the end of the six months I will be getting $84.00 per month and expenses, so I think I've been lucky to pass and get in school.

Chanute Field is about one hundred miles from Chicago, and just a few miles from Champaign. There's about 16,000 enlisted here, but not many students; because they won't spend money sending one to school unless they are sure of them making the grade.

There's nothing here but planes and schools. after we finish school here we will be transferred to some other field. I'm going to try to get in Bowman field Louisville, but they're sending about 80% of the men here to foreign posting.

How is everybody at home have you heard from Delpha; and if so, is she married?

I miss "Little Jim" so much. how is he doing in school tell him to be sure and write when you do, I'll be expecting to get letters from you both soon.

How have you been Little Sister. I do hope you will take good care of yourself. I don't think I could take it if anything was wrong with you. Have you had an x-ray yet? I'm sure you will be OK. Guess you're planning to work most of the winter. I don't think you should unless you feel better.

Maybe you can read this - it's hard to write, and think of everything, among all this going, when they're off duty.

As ever, yours Omar S.

3rd Letter
Chanute Field, Illinois - Saturday, Novembe 16, 1940
(Written on stationery from)
Air Corps Technical School Chanute Field Rantoul, Illinois

Dearest Sister: I didn't mean to wait so long to write but thought I should wait util I was stationed somewhere so that I would give you my address. I have been in school about one month and have had to work awful hard because I had been out of school so long, but I made very good grades on my monthly exams. Averaged 88 on seven subjects and I believe I can do better. About 40% of the men fail here and most of them are college men.

This is the largest air corp school in the world except for pilots. it would cost anyone about $2,000 to take this course if they wasn't in the air corps. When they have finished this course they are sent to Flying Cadets station to train them.

I have never done anything that I like as well as this work, so you can see instead of wanting out, I think I'm lucky to be here. How is Jim, hope he is well, guess he will be having plenty of work to do especially after the tobacco market opens. Tell little Jim I want to see him awfully bad, and I'm expecting a letter from him this time.

Would like to see all of you, but I won't have much chance before I finish this course in school. after I finish it I'm sent to some airport out of the U.S. or in case war breaks out, I'll be home for a few days.

I got permission to speak to the Commanding Officer and ask to be sent to Louisville as soon as I finish school here. of course he couldn't promise me yet but I think I will have a good chance.

I haven't had a chance to write to anyone but you, I hope to soon; however, you might tell them they can write me anyway, Just in case they don't know, and I'll be glad to hear from any of the family.

Tell Little Jim I'm going to send him a present when I get paid. I've never been paid yet but I guess I will be soon. I'm in much better health than I was when I left home, you would hardly know me-I'll send you a picture of myself sometime soon. Guess I should close for this time. Excuse pencil and writing. I'll be expecting you to write as soon as possible. let me know about everything.

As ever yours, Omar

4th Letter
Chanute Field, Illinois - Wednesday 18, 1940

Dearest Velma: I wonder how you're feeling since you started working, I hope you will take care of yourself and not work to much. How is Big Jim and Little Jim. I sure wish I could see all of you Xmas, but I just won't have money to go anywhere, and I have a chance to pick up a little extra cash by working here, during the seven days we are supposed to be of.

I got to sign a pat payroll yesterday for Xmas - the first money I've had since I enlisted; so I'm sending a money order of $15.00 to give Avery to put on that note - tell him I'll send more in a few days; also I will send a list of fines that I want him to collect from the town & apply on same. Will send you more money the 1st of Feb.

We don't get much money here in school only $21.00 per month and we have to pay our laundry which is $3.50 out of that. But I have a rating comming up in Feb. & I'll get more, and about May or June if I keep my grades up I will get $84.00 per month so it won't be that long.

I don't know if I'll ever get a commission as a pilot on account of being one year to old, but I can get commercial license. In case of war I'm planning to get some help through some officers in three or four years when I've earned it.

I'm studying math. + airplane mechanic at present. I'm sending you & Big Jim & Little Jim a little Xmas. gift, of course its small but you will understand. I wish you would tell me how tobacco is selling this year and if it's helping business. I never get a ky, paper here.

I'm awfully busy today so I'll close for now. lots of luck during the holidays

As ever, Yours, Omar

5th Letter
Fort McDowell - Angel Island, California - Friday, May 30, 1941

Dearest Velma: Sorry I've been so long about writing but I guess you know that regardless of how often I write I do think an awful lot of my people and especially you, Jim & little Jim.

I've been traveling cross country and have had lots of work to do, otherwise; I would have written you before now. I am staying here at San Francisco until the 5th of June at which time I will sail for P. I. on the U. S. Washington and join my squadron in Manila. This is a beautiful place here I hate to leave, the people are friendly here in San Francisco its just like being at home and the climate just suits me.

I spend most of my time watching the big ships come and go. I had a picture of myself made today am sending to you just so you can see how well & what good health I'm in.

I don't know how long I'll be out of the states, you know how things are as well as I, but I hope you'll take awful good care of yourself for me, you know how much I want to find you looking well & happy when I come back even if it is three or fours years.

I may not tell you when things are bad, but you can depend on me to be a credit to the Army no matter what happens.

Is Vernon running for County Atty. Again? - I hope he don't run anymore because it's so much worry for him - I believe more than it's worth.

I am sending a money order for $20.00 for you to give Avery, will you please tell him to give five of it to Freeman Faulkner for store bill and the rest, for the note - tell him also that I just getting part of the money due me, and when I get stationed and draw all that due I think I'll have enough to finish paying the note - anyway - I'll send some every month now until it's paid.

How is my little boy? tell him just how much he means to his uncle and don't let im forget about me please while I'm away.

Yours, Omar

6th Letter
Second Observation Squadron (C&D) Air Corps
Clark Field, Pampanga, P I.
Monday, September 1, 1941

Dearest Velma: As usual I'm late about writing, but was a long tiresome trip over here, and I wanted to get stationed before writing, so you would know where to write me also. I surely hope all the folks are well, and especially yourself. I haven't been very well much of the time since I got over here, was in the hospital for about a month, but am getting back my strength fast considering the change of climate and about three million kinds of fever we have here in the tropics.

I know exactly how to take care of myself anywhere, so you must never worry any about me. I left San Francisco June 6th and arrived in Manila, P. I. June 25th; also stayed one day at Honolulu.

The trip was quite an experience for me, especially the first two days at sea, you could guess what was wrong I suppose; anyway, I was plenty sick, and being sea sick is like being air sick, when you have experiences both you'll know that up until that time you have never been bad off. We have two main airports here - one is at Manila, and the other is Clark Field about 70 mi inland from Manila, where I am stationed.

We are in mountain country at Clark Field and it is very nice. You would be supprised if you see Manila. some parts of it are so beautiful, I'll send you some picture of interesting things here later. Most of the natives which consists of several different tribes live in grass covered huts; east of our camp we have a tribe of pygmie negros, just like you would find in Africa.

I have been in the villages at times, and the smell reminds me of some of those long Green Co. polecats.

Have you heard from Delpha lately? if so be sure and tell me how she is and tell me of all the rest, if they're well, happy, what they're doing etc. and tell my little boy how much I miss him.

You'll find enclosed a money order for $10.00 to give Avery, and there will be more on the way by the time this reaches you. We don't get paid in American money here and it's a little trouble getting it changed.

I don't know how long it will take to reach you, but you can let me know and answer as soon as possible please. Don't ask anything about the Army when you write, our mail is all checked - you'll understand - write me and use the address on the stationery. Give all the folks my regards and tell them where I'm located.

Write real soon, As always, Omar

The next two letters are from the American Red Cross, Louisville Chapter, in response to Velma's request to determine Omar's status

1st Letter-Tuesday, January 27, 1942

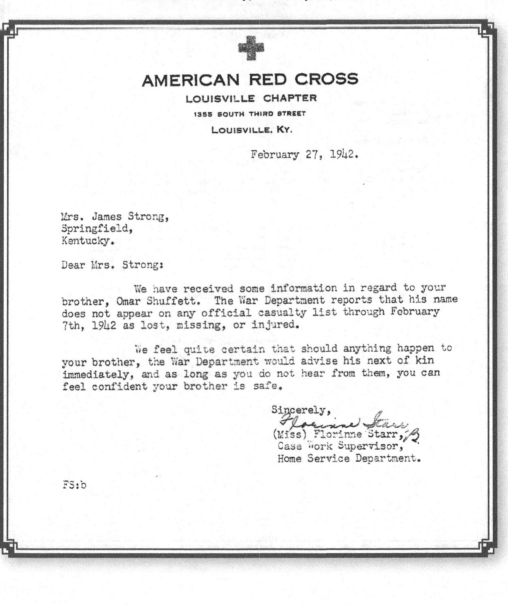

AMERICAN RED CROSS

LOUISVILLE CHAPTER
1355 SOUTH THIRD STREET
LOUISVILLE, KY.

February 27, 1942.

Mrs. James Strong,
Springfield,
Kentucky.

Dear Mrs. Strong:

      We have received some information in regard to your brother, Omar Shuffett. The War Department reports that his name does not appear on any official casualty list through February 7th, 1942 as lost, missing, or injured.

      We feel quite certain that should anything happen to your brother, the War Department would advise his next of kin immediately, and as long as you do not hear from them, you can feel confident your brother is safe.

                    Sincerely,

                    (Miss) Florinne Starr,
                    Case Work Supervisor,
                    Home Service Department.

FS:b

243

2ⁿᵈ **Letter - Tuesday, August 11, 1942**

AMERICAN RED CROSS

LOUISVILLE CHAPTER

1355 SOUTH THIRD STREET

LOUISVILLE. KY.

August 11, 1942.

Mrs. James Strong,
Springfield,
Kentucky.

Dear Mrs. Strong:

There is very little information or assistance we can give you
in obtaining word of your brother, Private Omar Shuffett, whose last address
is Clark Field, Phillipine Islands. The families of the boys who were listed
as being in the Phillipines at the time of Japanese occupation have been
notified of their status being reported "Missing". There has been no official list of prisoners.

If you will check with the person who was listed as the next of
kin, I am sure that they will tell you that they have received official notice
from the War Department. We have been assured that the Japanese Government
will allow someone from the International Red Cross to go into the occupied
territories and official lists would eventually be sent to the United States.

We hope this arrangement will be carried out shortly, and that
the families will be notified of the present whereabouts of their relatives.

Yours very truly,

Florinne Starr

(Miss) Florinne Starr,
Case Work Supervisor,
Home Service Department.

FS:b

The next communication relative to Omar's status is displayed in the following two notes. Judging from the previous handwriting displayed in Omar's letters, this does not appear to be his script in the first note.

The first note displayed evidently comes from Osaka, Japan and has Japanese characters and portraying a date of November 5, 1943. At this point Omar had been a POW since April 1942, a period of 20 months. The first note also has a different outlying marks.

The second note is undated but, appears to be written after the first note. It carries the Number 309, which seems to be unrelated to any Japanese prison facility. However, the Japanese characters in the lower right hand corner are the same on both notes indicating the addressee of Velma Strong.

Note #1

YODAGAWA BUNSHO
OSAKA JAPAN
Nov. 5, 1943.

DEAR SISTER —

HOPE YOU AND ALL THE FOLKS ARE WELL. I AM WELL AND HOPE I CAN BE WITH YOU AGAIN SOON.

TAKE GOOD CARE OF LITTLE JIM, AND TELL HIM I AM ALL RIGHT AND HOW MUCH I MISS HIM.

WISHING YOU A MERRY CHRISTMAS AND A HAPPY NEW YEAR.

AS EVER, YOUR BROTHER.
OMAR L. SHUFFETT

（大阪俘虜収容所）

大阪 党内納

Note #2

To-
Mrs. James Strong
Greensburg, Ky.

From-
309
Omar Lyle Shuffett
P.F.C.

Dearest Velma:

am wondering why I haven't heard from home for so long. Hoping and praying that all are well, and that soon we can be together again. I am ~~being~~ in very good health, and will take the best care of myself possible.

Please tell all the family to write more often. Remember me to little Jim, tell him I think of him every day and hope to see him soon. Take good care of the Jim's, and yourself.

Your Brother,
Omar Lyle Shuffett

（大阪俘虜收容所）

Mrs. James Strong

Greensburg

Kentucky

United States of America

7th **Letter**
Kennedy G. H. - Memphis, Tenn.
Sunday, December 2, 1945

Dearest Velma: Hope you have gained a few lbs. since I last saw you, if you know what I mean. How is Jim, Little Jim & Brenda?

I've been here for about ten days, it's an awful large place, but not near as nice a Ashford G. H.; well, anyway I am expecting a furlough soon. I want to be with some of the family X'mas. You know its been a long time since I've spent Xmas at home my plate may have been broken, or something.

Please excuse me for not writing, I am not well - better I think - at least nothing to worry about.

I am expecting to see you soon, will let you know when, & if. Give my best to Jim, L. Jim and Brenda.

please write soon, As always, Omar

P.S. Do you know if I left any pictures at your house? I can't find some of them.

Undated Letter From
Moore General Hospital
Swannanoa, N. C.
Office Of The Chaplain

MOORE GENERAL HOSPITAL
SWANNANOA, N. C.
OFFICE OF THE CHAPLAIN

In reference to: Ward

S/Sgt. Omar Shuffett   408

Dear Mrs. Strong

    I wish to inform you that, your brother has been admitted to this hospital for observation or treatment and the patient's condition is not serious. In case of a serious change you will be notified by the authorities immediately. For medical information concerning the patient contact the Office of the Registrar at this hospital.

    You may be assured that the patient will receive the best of medical and nursing care and nothing will be left undone which may in any way contribute to the patient's comfort.

    The usual visiting hours are:
        Sundays: 2 P. M. to 9 P. M.
        Weekdays: 5:30 P. M. to 9 P. M.
However, I advise you wait until you hear from the patient, before making a trip here just now.

    In the meantime mail may be addressed to the patient at this hospital, ward 408 and I suggest that you write often as mail is always welcome to the patient.

Very sincerely yours,

Ellis U. Youngdahl

ELLIS U. YOUNGDAHL,
Chaplain, Lt. Col., U S A

8th Letter
Moore General Hospital
Ward 408 - Sqannanoa, N. C.
Monday, Match 25, 1946

As this is the last letter from Omar that the I have, I am repeating it in it's entirety.

Dearest Velma: Hows things with you? Jim, Brenda - and L. Jim? Sure hope you are in better health than when I last saw you. If not I'll have to take you out camping soon I guess, and see what I can do for you.

I arrived here March 21st, am O. K we do nothing but rest here, no games, no nothing. The climate will be good for me I'm sure; although, I think I'm about well anyway. Had planned to see you before now, but couldn't get a furlough. I'll be trying to get one again soon though, would like to see the Derby this year; maybe we can do something together this next time, if we are both well. I hope so.

This dump I'm in now is no damn good, just between us, and I'll be glad when I can get out. The treatment is O. K., and perhaps I should be thankful for it, and I know inside I really am; but I'm tired of taking orders - I would like to jam this place up Moores rear end, or whoever its named after. (bet you think I'm a bad boy) The nurse just brought me your letter. sure glad you're better, and you have seen Gene. I sure miss he and Wesley Hazel.

We were together all time at Memphis. I had a lot of nice friends there. not much news just wanted you to know I'm O.K. and I'll keep my chin up all the time. You all write soon please. Will include my present no good address, remember me to all the family.

Your little Bro, Omar

A Hospital Letter

Memphis, Tennessee - March 27, 1946

One very important element of Omar's life was his total unending love and a affection for his baby Sister, Velma Pearl who was born on Thursday, May 28,1914. When Omar was in recovery in Moore General Hospital in Memphis, Tennessee, a "Gray Lady" by the name of Mary Sue Jones with the Red Cross would see Omar often.

On March 27, 1946, she wrote a three-page letter to Velma describing Omar's condition and his comments. Some of her most potent comments relative to Omar and his condition are as follows:

"It was my privilege to have your brother Omar as a patient in the ward on which I was a Gray Lady. I learned to know you quite well just hearing him speak of you so often."

"He loved his "little sister" more than anything in the world. He said that many times during his time here. He related that he could not have pulled through his ordeal except for the thought of you."

"He is going to be blue and despondent for awhile until he gets adjusted. We must let him know that we are all behind him 100%."

"He is awful homesick to see his family. Omar is very proud and he loves all of you very much, so please tell all of them how much he is going to need their love and good will."

"He is going to have a long hard pull of it, Mrs. Strong, but he has an awful lot of willpower, so if we can keep his morale high, I feel surely he will win this victory."

"My husband became very fond of Omar and when I would come home, the first thing he would ask is, "How's Shuffett?"

"When I first saw Omar he was very blue and down in the dumps, but when he left he had a smile on his face."

"Surely the Lord had something very definite for Omar and I pray they everything that is good, is ahead of him."

"You can tell him I wrote to you, but don't tell him I discussed his physical condition. I don't think he would like that."

**Omar sitting at home after his return from captivity.
Notice the big arms on the sofa, the box radio and
the end table of the 1940 era.**

Omar Lyle Shuffett died at The Jane Todd Crawford Hospital in Greensburg, Kentucky at 10:14 PM on Saturday, June 16, 2001 at the age of 89. Ironically, it was Father's Day

He was survived by Maxine, his loving, faithful and devoted wife since 1946, a span of some 55 years. In addition, his daughters-- Carolyn McDaniel and Fran Stroud--and two grandchildren survived him, along with one sister, Delpha O'Hara of Detroit, Michigan.

Omar's death certificate was signed by Dr. William L. "Bouchie" Shuffett.

The nickname "Boochie" Is said to have been originated with a housekeeper who worked for Dr. Shuffett's parents and when she first saw him and picked him up, she called him "My Little Boochie".

Dr. Shuffett's parents were Avery, Omar's business partner and Cleo Kemp Shuffett, Maxine's (Omar's wife's sister). (This makes Fan and Carolyn and Boochie double first cousins.) Funeral was conducted at the Foster-Toler-Curry Funeral Home on June 18th. The Reverend Dale Curry officiated. He was interned in the Greensburg Municipal Cemetery. Active pallbearers were Boochie, Jim Strong, Mel Shuffett, James A. Shuffett, Paul Mills, Dick Mills and George Edwards.

Sadly, Maxine passed away on Thursday, July 18, 2002, at Audubon Hospital in Louisville, just thirteen months after Omar died. She was born on Saturday, August 18, 1917. She, likewise, is survived by her daughters and her grandchildren. In addition, she was survived by two brothers--George Kemp of Lebanon and James Kemp of Lexington. The funeral services were held at Foster-Toler-Curry Funeral Home on Friday, July 19th and her active pallbearers were "Boochie", George E. Kemp, Mel Shuffett and Bob Kress. She was interned in the Greensburg Cemetery with her lifetime partner.

Listing of Exhibits

Exhibit Number	Content
1	Quotes from Sunday School Lessons
2	Bronze Star Citation
3	Japanese Prison Roster
4	Hand drawn Map of Osaka Prison
5	Postcard from Yodogama Bunsho Prison
6	Telegram from Letterman Hospital
7	Quotes by Omar Shuffett
8	Official Military Separation & Discharge
9	Certificate of Discharge

Exhibit 1
Exerts from Omar's Sunday School Lessons

January 22, 1989
"Forgiveness: A Measure of Love"

It may seem a little unusual, but I think most everyone, forgiving and asking for forgiveness is sometimes pretty difficult. It was Alexander Pope , who wrote, "To err is human, to forgive, diving".

One of the main reasons that keeps most of us from practicing forgiveness or receiving it are: Pride, We are only human, No one is perfect or War experiences.

There are some persons who think they must do certain good deeds in order to earn forgiveness.

Throughout his ministry, Jesus emphasized that he was the savior for all people.

Our country and our social groups may be divided as some of those are as self-righteous as the Jews were. Rich, poor, black, white, etc. But more to the point, what is our attitude toward the poor and downtrodden?

February 26, 1989
"Becoming a believer"

On Jesus's last trip to Jerusalem, were all these people following him, just to get to see him, or were they looking for the "goal post", that is, "The meaning of Life". Some wanted to know if Jesus was the Messiah, some wanted to know more about the true meaning of life and some were just hoping to be healed.

Jesus went to Zacchaeus house for lunch. They must have had a very interesting talk. The scripture doesn't tell us anything about what they ate. However,

Zacchaeus did remark, "Behold Lord, the half of my goods, I gave to the poor and if I have defrauded anyone, I will restore it fourfold".

Collecting taxes by government has always been a major responsibility. Solomon taxed the people excessively which was a major factor in the downfall of the nation after his death.

October 15, 1989
Untitled

To begin, "A moment of silence for those in our church who have special needs".

In prayer he said, "Lord, we have come here this morning to worship you and to praise your name for sending your son, Jesus Christ into the world to show us your love in the fullest and most complete way". "Father, forgive us this morning for the mistakes that we make so often, and for the times when er have strayed away from you will, kind of like lost sheep".

Well, it's no trouble for most of us to identify the kingdom with cathedral churches and respectable congregations, but what about the forgotten street people, there should be some way to make them feel that the kingdom if for them also?

He told of the story where the Pharisees criticized because he ate and drank with the tax collectors and sinners. He told of how Jesus said, "I have not come to call the righteous, but sinners to repent".

Author's Comment

Having read the entire sermons from which the above is taken, it further defines Omar Lyle Shuffett to me that his presentation come straight from the heart, and he must have been a truly devoted Christian. Omar taught Sunday School for several years and his lessons are numerous.

sunday school lessons.docx

THE UNITED STATES OF AMERICA

TO ALL WHO SHALL SEE THESE PRESENTS, GREETING:

THIS IS TO CERTIFY THAT
THE PRESIDENT OF THE UNITED STATES OF AMERICA
AUTHORIZED BY EXECUTIVE ORDER, AUGUST 24, 1962
HAS AWARDED

THE BRONZE STAR MEDAL

TO

STAFF SERGEANT OMAR L. SHUFFETT

FOR

MERITORIOUS ACHIEVEMENT
7 DECEMBER 1941 TO 10 MAY 1942

GIVEN UNDER MY HAND IN THE CITY OF WASHINGTON
THIS   13TH   **DAY OF**   AUGUST   19 85

CHIEF OF STAFF

SECRETARY OF THE AIR FORCE

AF FORM 2227, JUL 70

Exhibit 2

Yodogawa Bunsho

1	Metta	63	Williams	125	Paulhus	187	Sigueros	249	Cole
2	McBride	64	Hays	126	Mayberry	188	Zahler	250	HILL
3	WM MILLER	65	Mullinax	127	J M Davis	189	Browse	251	V JOHNSTON
4	ED STEWART	66	HOLLINGSWORTH	128	Ragan	190	POLIDORE	252	Warren
5	Draper	67	G KING	129	Erwin	191	Ferrel	253	Barela
6	VLASAK	68	KOPLUR	130	DALY	192	Carr	254	Beam
7	Lundgren	69	CAVENAUGH	131	McKinney	193	W J Davis	255	RAY
8	Bunch	70	FLIPPEN	132	McCreanor	194	Love	256	Vance
9	Hirshfield	71	Montoya	133	Heiman	195	Drennen	257	CONLEY
10	Feldstein	72	L A Anderson	134	MASCOLO	196	Tackett	258	Gates
11	Underwood	73	Berger	135	DiPasquale	197	McNeil	259	Placko
12	CHIPS	74	Ball	136	Ahart	198	Ramsey	260	Jensen
13	Owen	75	Pickard	137	COLLINS	199	Crance	261	Sersain
14	Bemis	76	Shuffett	138	Lee	200	Messler	262	Gainey
15	Malouf	77	HYER	139	Sparks	201	Clark	263	Tootle
16	BAYNARD	78	Deal	140	Girard	202	HEARD	264	Broderick
17	Chavez	79	T E Smith	141	Chesselet	203	Naylor	265	Gannon
18	FERRARO	80	CARTER	142	Jurkovic	204	McArdle	266	CUILLSON
19	James	81	Hamlin	143	WILKINSON	205	Mullen	267	MILLER, D
20	Hawkins	82	Van Camp	144	Corrillo	206	ACKERMAN	268	MICKUCKI
21	Harrell	83	Mitchell	145	COKER	207	Schwabe	269	Klusendorf
22	Bulit	84	Tierney	146	SS HAYNES	208	T R ANDERSON	270	Brantley,
23	Phillips	85	Leach	147	Kukec	209	HARMON	271	MORTVEDT
24	Stackhouse	86	SERVOLATZ	148	HUNT	210	Jakubzak	272	TORTI
25	Griffin	87	BYRD	149	OEFFIER	211	SKIPPER	273	Cavallero
26	Kidd	88	Nuckles	150	McDonald	212	Finseth	274	Spizziro
27	O'Rorke	89	BLACK	151	PFEIFER	213	Hoover	275	Vanderwort
28	Blackman	90	Jeffries	152	Lorraine	214	MEAD	276	NAULT
29	Wm T Penrod	91	Daniel	153	Turner	215	CROW	277	STERNBERGH
30	Wm K Roberts	92	REEVES	154	WISELL	216	Tracer	278	Weber
31	Gabour	93	MOULTON	155	J E Wilson	217	SONTAG	279	Ozanich
32	Travis	94	Cooper	156	Bartz	218	Costello	280	VASAL
33	Naymick	95	CHAMBERS	157	WHEELER	219	Windham	281	McCloud
34	FISH	96	ANGUS	158	CRAWFORD	220	Olson	282	Bollin
35	Ziarko	97	Brownlee	159	Gibbs	221	WALLER	283	Otwell
36	Remy	98	Edmundson	160	Ringer	222	DOUGHERTY	284	Defibaugh
37	WOISHNIS	99	Hart	161	REVARK	223	Madison	285	Franklin
38	Forinash	100	Minor	162	McElhinney	224	Nelson	286	F G SMITH
39	FRAZIER	101	GIBSON	163	WOJAS	225	Wright	287	E H Anderson
40	Campbell	102	DALE	164	SLIVENICK	226	Ringo	288	Longoria
41	Chas L Wilson	103	W W Smith	165	Dreasher	227	COLLERT	289	Wagner
42	DELANY	104	Purlee	166	W K Smith	228	Clendenon	290	MANN
43	Kuretich	105	Bostic	167	Swor	229	Henson	291	ANDRUS
44	Denelegi	106	H H Smith	168	Manceaux	230	Dabrowski	292	MELVIN
45	CARLTON	107	Vaitkus	169	Gillihan	231	Harrington	293	Yung
46	Bob F Miller	108	POLLOCK	170	KARLSON	232	HANSON	294	Vassey
47	Duckworth	109	W W JACKSON	171	Bussell	233	CHILDS	295	Coffee
48	Don L Baker	110	MERRELL	172	WESTERN	234	BURNEY	296	Doane
49	Lay	111	B V KING	173	Stevenson	235	Frisch	297	Tidwell
50	A JOHNSON	112	Hamilton	174	Milburn	236	FREY	298	Booker
51	Lewis	113	GARLINGHOUSE	175	W H GILLETT	237	POST	299	Dronberger
52	Sherman	114	Davies	176	Stepper	238	Dow	300	Byall
53	HUDDLESTON	115	M O Johnson	177	W M Martin	239	Frederick	301	Zimmerman
54	LANE	116	Curby	178	R ROBERTS	240	Creighton	302	Stewart, EW
55	SHELDON	117	Buhler	179	Merianos	241	PRICE	303	Pupo
56	Torres	118	McAuliffe	180	Karpus	242	D KING	304	HALEAPLE
57	MAYNARD	119	Knox	181	LUCAS	243	Ely	305	Parker
58	MM GILLETTE	120	Tyson	182	Pomnietzky	244	Reed	306	Parrett
59	Peralta	121	Egner	183	Lower	245	Rardin	307	Marchetti
60	EMLAY	122	J Smith	184	Massey	246	Ennis	308	GIOIA
61	Blackater	123	T L PENROD	185	LANDON	247	Herle	309	Warden
62	Barnes	124	J B Miller			248	HELLIKER	310	Rodes

Exhibit 3

Prison Roster Comments

A. <u>Note that Omar is identified as Prisoner # 76.</u>
B. <u>Translation of Yododawa = Yodo River, Translation of Bunsho = Branch. (Therefore, Bushoe may have been an off shoot of the Yoda River)</u>
C. <u>In the prison drawing shown in Exhibit 4, a "canal" is projected on the extreme left side ofthe drawing. This could be the Bushoe or off shoot of the Yodo River. Just speculation, of course.</u>

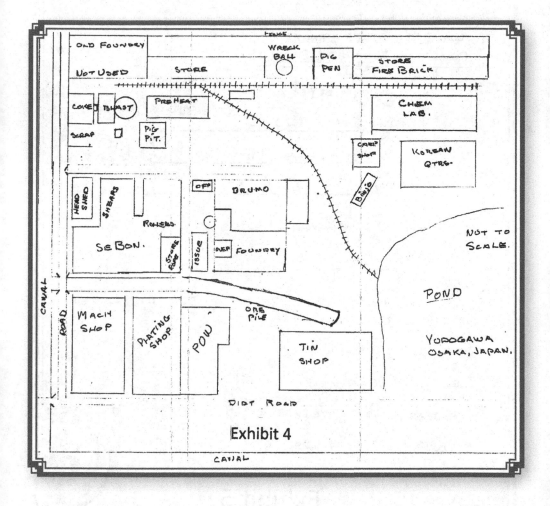

Exhibit 4

FROM:

Name. Omar L. Shoffett,

Nationality. American

Rank. Pfc. STAFF SERGEANT

Camp Osaka Yodogawa Bunsho

P.O.W. Camp.

To: See DES PRISONNIERS DE GUERRE

AUG 28 1943

Mrs. James Strong,

Greensburg, Kentucky. *Springfield*

U. S. A.

Ky.

% Economy Store,

IMPERIAL NIPPONESE ARMY.

I am interned in Osaka Yodogawa Bunsho Prisoner
of War Camp.

My health is usual.

I am working for pay.

Please see that everything is taken care of.

My love to you: Velma.

Exhibit 5

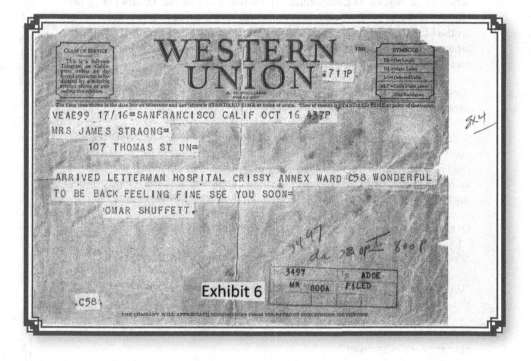

WESTERN UNION

CLASS OF SERVICE

This is a full-rate Telegram or Cablegram unless its deferred character is indicated by a suitable symbol above or preceding the address.

1201

A. N. WILLIAMS
PRESIDENT

SYMBOLS

DL = Day Letter

NL = Night Letter

LC = Deferred Cable

NLT = Cable Night Letter

Ship Radiogram

The filing time shown in the date line on telegrams and day letters is STANDARD TIME at point of origin. Time of receipt is STANDARD TIME at point of destination.

VEAE99 17/16=SANFRANCISCO CALIF OCT 16 437P

MRS JAMES STRAONG=

107 THOMAS ST UN=

ARRIVED LETTERMAN HOSPITAL CRISSY ANNEX WARD C58 WONDERFUL
TO BE BACK FEELING FINE SEE YOU SOON=

OMAR SHUFFETT.

Exhibit 6

3497

MR 800A

ADSE

FILED

C58

THE COMPANY WILL APPRECIATE SUGGESTIONS FROM ITS PATRONS CONCERNING ITS SERVICE

Exhibit 7
Quotes by SSGT Omar Shuffett

He commented about his fellow workers, "When they were unable to work, they were never seen nor heard of again. I often worked when I will ill, because I knew what would happen if I gave up."

When on Corregidor he commented, "The Artillery fire was so intense during the month that I was on Corregidor that there was hardly a tree or any vegetation left on the island by the time Gen. Jonathon Wainwright surrendered the island to the Japanese on the morning of May 10, 1942. We had been on half rations while I was there and we had very little ammunition left."

"I didn't know the island had been surrendered until I saw a company of Japanese coming up the hill."

"I don't think anyone can be proud about being one of those who lost in the war, even though we did hold out for five months. We lost most of our planes during the first week of the war, and then many of the Air Corps personnel were moved across the bay to the Bataan Peninsula where we served with the Infantry until April 9, 1942, when General King surrendered, Bataan to the Japanese."

Of his 89th birthday celebration, "It was the best birthday I have ever had."

"I'm grateful that I had the opportunity to play a tiny part in World War II."

"We held on to Bataan and Corregidor for five month and we left a lot of graves there. I just hope history shows we did the best we could."

"I didn't do anything special. I'm just a survivor and there's no need for you to recognize me in any way."

While in Osaka Steel Mills he commented, "If the slant eyed SOB's don't kill us, they will starve us to death."

"I don't know why I survived when so many of my friends didn't."

"If I told you what really occurred, no one would believe me. I know what Freedom means!!"

"The experience was horrible."

"Everyone, I'm sure, has heard many stories about Bataan and Corregidor. I'll just say that I ran the gauntlet of five prisons."

"I weighted 175 pounds prior to capture and weighted less than 80 when released."

"My family didn't know where I was for over a year."

"The japs did let me write a post card and they told me what to say, but I didn't care. I just wanted my family to know that I was alright."

When receiving the Bronze Star Medal, he remarked, "During the month of August when I received this award, a lot of people were made to remember the end of the most devastating war in our history. The news media's main focus seemed to be on Hiroshima, Japan, and the horrors of the first atomic bomb, but several American ex-prisoners of war, or as many of them whom intervening time has spared, were remembering other names and places."

"I was at Nicholas Field at Manila when the Japanese attacked on December 7, 1941. We lost most of our planes during the first week of the war, and then many of the Air Corps personnel were moved across the bay to the Bataan Peninsula where we served with the Infantry, until April 9, 1942, when General King surrendered Bataan to the Japanese. At the time Bataan was surrendered, the soldiers were out of food, water and ammunition."

"During the roundup of prisoners and the first two days of the Bataan Death March, several were able to escape. Some made it to the mountains and some over to Corregidor. I was one of those who got to Corregidor and was with the Fourth Marines until May 10, 1942."

"During the roundup of prisoners and first two days of the Bataan Death March several were able to escape."

"I didn't know the island had been surrendered until I saw a company of Japs coming up the hill."

"I don't think anyone can feel proud about being one of those who lost the war, even though we did hold out for five months. Looking back, after forty years and realizing that despite obsolete weapons and ammunitions, without air support, and a critical shortage of food and medical supplies, maybe we performed about as well as anyone would have reasonably expected."

"I knew the war was over when the Japanese guards began disappearing, fearing reprisal b the Americans. American planes began flying over the prison camp, dropping food in 55 gallon drums."

"I will always remember what it means to be free, and I will always remember my experience of coming home after those years in prison, without seeing a newspaper, hearing a radio, sleeping on a bed, or even having a knife or fork in my hands. It was sometimes a shocking traumatic experience, and it was not easy to readjust to life after such a long time in prison camps. I still think of it as a deeply personal matter, but it is something everyone has to do for themselves."
"I was very pleased to have the Bronze Star come to me, even though it has been a long time since the dramatic events of the war."

quotes of SSGT shuffett.docx

ENLISTED RECORD AND REPORT OF SEPARATION
HONORABLE DISCHARGE

1. LAST NAME - FIRST NAME - MIDDLE INITIAL		2. ARMY SERIAL NO.	3. GRADE	4. ARM OR SERVICE	5. COMPONENT
SHUFFETT OMAR L		15 046 357	S/Sgt 2 Sep 45	AAF	RA
6. ORGANIZATION		7. DATE OF SEPARATION	8. PLACE OF SEPARATION		
2nd Observation Squadron		17 Nov 1946	Moore Gen Hosp Swannanoa N C		

9. PERMANENT ADDRESS FOR MAILING PURPOSES	10. DATE OF BIRTH	11. PLACE OF BIRTH			
Greensburg Green Co Ky	20 Feb 1912	Greensburg Ky			

12. ADDRESS FROM WHICH EMPLOYMENT WILL BE SOUGHT	13. COLOR EYES	14. COLOR HAIR	15. HEIGHT	16. WEIGHT	17. NO. DEPEND.
Sea 9	Brown	Brown	5' 8½"	165 LBS.	0

18. RACE			19. MARITAL STATUS		20. U.S. CITIZEN		21. CIVILIAN OCCUPATION AND NO.
WHITE	NEGRO	OTHER(specify)	SINGLE	MARRIED OTHER (specify)	YES	NO	Auto Mechanic 5-81.010
X			X		X		

MILITARY HISTORY

22. DATE OF INDUCTION	23. DATE OF ENLISTMENT	24. DATE OF ENTRY INTO ACTIVE SERVICE	25. PLACE OF ENTRY INTO SERVICE
	28 Sep 1940	28 Sep 1940	Fort Knox Ky

SELECTIVE SERVICE DATA	26. REGISTERED YES NO	27. LOCAL S.S. BOARD NO.	28. COUNTY AND STATE	29. HOME ADDRESS AT TIME OF ENTRY INTO SERVICE
	X	None	None	Elizabethtown (Hardin Co) Ky

30. MILITARY OCCUPATIONAL SPECIALTY AND NO.	31. MILITARY QUALIFICATION AND DATE (i.e., infantry, aviation and marksmanship badges, etc.)
Airplane Mech 686	Marksman

32. BATTLES AND CAMPAIGNS

Philippine Islands

33. DECORATIONS AND CITATIONS Distinguished Unit Badge with 2 Oak Leaf Clusters
American Defense Ribbon with 1 Star   Asiatic-Pacific Ribbon with 1 Star
Philippine Defense Ribbon with 1 Star   World War II Victory Ribbon   Good Conduct Medal

34. WOUNDS RECEIVED IN ACTION
None

35. LATEST IMMUNIZATION DATES				36. SERVICE OUTSIDE CONTINENTAL U. S. AND RETURN		
SMALLPOX	TYPHOID	TETANUS	OTHER (specify)	DATE OF DEPARTURE	DESTINATION	DATE OF ARRIVAL
Not Available				6 May 41	APTO	24 May 41

37. TOTAL LENGTH OF SERVICE						38. HIGHEST GRADE HELD			
CONTINENTAL SERVICE			FOREIGN SERVICE						
YEARS	MONTHS	DAYS	YEARS	MONTHS	DAYS	S/Sgt	26 Sep 45	USA	15 Oct 45
1	8	10	4	5	10				

39. PRIOR SERVICE

None

40. REASON AND AUTHORITY FOR SEPARATION   Certificate of Disability for Discharge Section I AR 615-361
16 September 1946 Moore Gen Hosp Swannanoa N C

41. SERVICE SCHOOLS ATTENDED	42. EDUCATION (Years)		
	Grammar	High School	College
Air Corps Tech Sch Chanute Field Ill Airplane Mech	8	4	1/0

PAY DATA

43. LONGEVITY FOR PAY PURPOSES			44. MUSTERING OUT PAY		45. SOLDIER DEPOSITS	46. TRAVEL PAY	47. TOTAL AMOUNT, NAME OF DISBURSING OFFICER
YEARS	MONTHS	DAYS	TOTAL	THIS PAYMENT	None	$21.40	158 25
6	1	20	$300	$100			Lloyd Burton Maj FD 356.36
							Finance Officer

INSURANCE NOTICE

IMPORTANT   IF PREMIUM IS NOT PAID WHEN DUE OR WITHIN THIRTY-ONE DAYS THEREAFTER, INSURANCE WILL LAPSE. MAKE CHECKS OR MONEY ORDERS PAYABLE TO THE TREASURER OF THE U. S. AND FORWARD TO COLLECTIONS SUBDIVISION, VETERANS ADMINISTRATION, WASHINGTON 25, D. C.

48. KIND OF INSURANCE			49. HOW PAID	50. Effective Date of Allotment Discontinuance	51. Date of Next Premium Due (One month after 50)	52. PREMIUM DUE EACH MONTH	53. INTENTION OF VETERAN TO
Nat. Serv.	U.S. Govt.	None	Allotment Direct to V. A.	30 Nov 46	31 Dec 46		Continue Continue Only Discontinue
			X				

54. **55. REMARKS** (This space for completion of above items or entry of other items specified in W. D. Directives)
Lapel Button Issued
Soldier entitled to travel pay
ASR score (2 September 1945) 122
Separated from the service on the basis of a temporary service record
and affidavit from the soldier

56. SIGNATURE OF PERSON BEING SEPARATED	57. PERSONNEL OFFICER (Type name, grade and organization - signature)
Omar L. Shuffett	MARY E KELLY 1st Lt WAC *Mary E Kelly*

WD AGO FORM 53-55
1 November 1944
This form supersedes all previous editions of WD AGO Forms 53 and 55 for enlisted persons entitled to an Honorable Discharge, which will not be used after receipt of this revision.

Exhibit 8

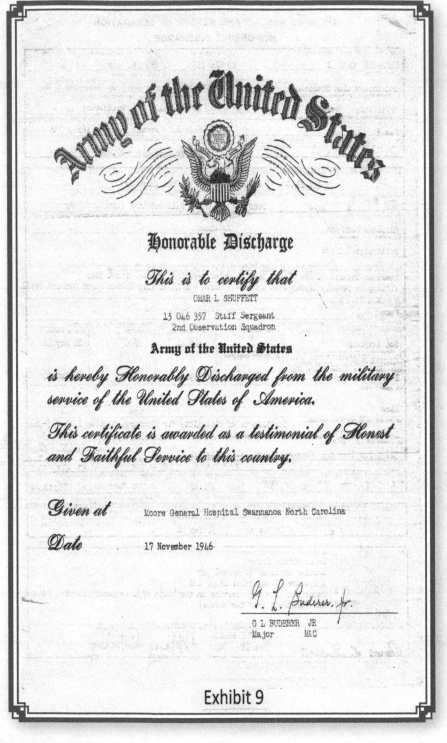

Army of the United States

Honorable Discharge

This is to certify that

OMAR L SHUFFETT

15 046 357 Staff Sergeant
2nd Observation Squadron

Army of the United States

is hereby Honorably Discharged from the military service of the United States of America.

This certificate is awarded as a testimonial of Honest and Faithful Service to this country.

Given at   Moore General Hospital Swannanoa North Carolina

Date   17 November 1946

G. L. Buderer, Jr.

G L BUDERER   JR
Major   MAC

Exhibit 9

Epilogue

There can be no other conclusion than to say, "Omar Lyle Shuffett was a great man" in all aspects of the word. It was my distinct pleasure to have known him when in my youth and a greater pleasure to bring his story to print in hopes that others, of all ages, will understand that it takes men like Omar Lyle Shuffett to keep the great country of ours safe!!

*   *   *

<u>**His devotion to country, family and church is unparalleled in the annuals of American history!!!**</u>

*   *   *

SECTION 9

PROMINENCE

The Story of The Woodson Lewis Family
The Store - The Family - The Man

Contents

Prominence

The Store - The Family - The Man

Glover's Station

Appendix 1 - Lineage - Major Events In The Woodson Lewis Family

Appendix 2 - Comments Related To The Lewis Family Lineage

Appendix 3 - Various Dates Of Relative Importance

A Most Important Event

Promince

As I originally thought about this story, I had every intention of writing about **"Woodson Lewis"**, the man and store as I knew it in the 1940's and 1950's. As I began to type and assemble data it became readily apparent that the time of my youth and the scope of presentation were more than what I originally perceived.

My thoughts continued to revert to the physical being of the Woodson Lewis Store on the corner of South Public Square and Highway 68 & 70 and all the Lewis family that worked there, all the people employed there and certainly all the customers that made this a once in a lifetime experience to view and enjoy enterprise at work at its best in this era. This building stands today much as it did when it was constructed in 1900. The majestic structure is nostalgic in presentation and makes one desirous to return to the hustling and bustling times of yore.

Entering this building one sees the original almost eight-foot glass doors with peeling paint, the oil-stained floors, the majestic ceiling heights, the show case that covers the entire front, which is accessed by tall windows that open inward to gain access

Then the decorative posts greet one at the bottom of the staircase with the decorate railing leading to the second floor where equally high ceiling greet you. As you ascend the stairs by going up four steps to a four-foot square landing, then turning left to ascend seventeen more steps which will take you to the second floor which in its heyday was where the furniture was displayed.

The upstairs metal ceiling has a small square design where the metal ceiling downstair has small squares resembling flowers. One might reflect that these ceiling are now outdated but they were quite popular in the 1940's and 1950's and prior.

The store had two elevators, one from the basement to the side building (white exterior) which was determined to be unusable about 1950. The other was (when in operation) is located in the left rear corner of the store. The steel shaft which held the elevator as it ascended can be viewed the back of the store. The wheel that supported the cable which was attached to the elevator is still in place on the second floor. Just another majestic sight of by gone days.

The basement, which could be entered from the alley, which is a continuation of 1ˢᵗ Alley, was primarily used for storing and displaying furniture.

Some readers may ask, why would you write about a department store when your stories are about your youthful memories. The reason is, that the Woodson Lewis stores of bygone days have been replaced by the Wal-Mart's, Lowe's etc. and that is due to such things as population growth, yearn for a larger line of commodities, more employment opportunity in larger cities, etc. and there's certainly nothing wrong with that and it's just called progress. However, this is a cherished memory of mine in the 1940's and 1950's when progress was measured differently and at a slower pace.

However, the most important element of this story is the unequaled contribution to the town of Greensburg, the County of Green and all surrounding communities by the family of Lewis. Ah yes, where do we start?

"Well, let's just start"!!

The Store - The Family - The Man

These three elements are so intertwined I may speak of Woodson Lewis in a personal sense in one paragraph and a store activity in another. It is not a matter of flowing the story, it's a matter of providing those moments to a future generation in saying, "that's how it was in those days" and all these activities are intertwined.

The Man referred to in the sub-title is Woodson Lewis Jr. who initially took over the management of the Woodson Lewis store in 1930 after his father Woodson Lewis, Senior succumb to an illness and died, Junior successfully operated the business until the closing in the mid 1990's.

Mr. Wood, as he was known to many of us possessed a demeanor that was unequaled in our community. His day-to-day manner was that he was always considerate of others, always smiling and extremely gracious in his every conversation. He was constantly in motion, greeting, assisting customers and seemed to be everywhere at once within the confines of the Woodson Lewis store.

To relate how Woodson Lewis Jr. and the Woodson Lewis family became an integral part of our community. A more detailed composition of the Lewis family is presented in Appendix 1.

Mr. Wood's immediate family consisted of wife Geraldine, one son William "Weazy" Lewis and two daughters, Mrs. Anne (Lewis) now Griffith and Mrs. Ruthie Brummal (Lewis) now Derrick.

Mr. Wood (Woodson Lewis Jr.) married the love of his life, Mary Geraldine (Miller) Lewis of Abington, Illinois on August 24, 1930. They were married and moved to Greensburg. Geraldine readily found a place in the Woodson Lewis store. Geraldine was a natural fit for the Woodson Lewis store and all customers, visitors, friends, included all the people of Greensburg, Green County and surrounding communities. She was a homemaker and businesswoman all combined into one fine friendly lady. She was born in Cherokee, Iowa October 15, 1909. She was educated at Iowa State University in Ames, Iowa and Lombard College, Galesburg,

Illinois and was a schoolteacher in Abington, Illinois public schools at the time of her marriage.

As she had majored in Home Economics, she became a vital part of the piece goods and pattern department of the store. In addition to working in the store and raising a family she maintained an active interest in the community and the Barrett Memorial Presbyterian Church. She was a active participant in the Mary Barrett Auxiliary of the church and an avid bridge player.

Geraldine (aka Mrs. Wood) died on July 4, 1993 at the Homewood Health Care Center in Glasgow, Ky. Until a few weeks before her death she continued to reside in the family home at 210 North Main Street.

In addition to Geraldine, there were dedicated employees over the span of time the store was operational. I would be hard pressed to define them all, but three people come immediately to the forefront who worked for Mr. Wood are Joe Pal Taylor, over 50 years. Leon Christie and Harry Gilkerson were also long serving employees. The name and continuous appearance of Miss Ruth Lingle Lewis whose office (if an open desk behind a brown stained wooden railing defines an office?) would find her daily facing the public, always portraying a pleasant "Hello" and further defining the always public serving attitude of "Woodson Lewis Store." Mr. Wood's office had no walls, just a railing was behind Miss Ruth. The railings forming quasi office space are still in place and vendors of Glovers Station Antique Mall currently display quilts, etc. over the railing displaying their goods.

The Woodson Lewis family in the 1940's and 1950's was a very prominent family in Greensburg. If one didn't know them personally, they were certainly known by name and sight as they worked in the store six days per week. Mr. Wood, as he was called was the most humble, successful businessman I have ever known. Mr. Wood is occasionally referred to as Woodson Lewis Jr. and in his obituary, he is referred to as Woodson Lewis II.

After the store closed around five pm, he could often be seen tending to the flowers in his front yard. If a passerby, either on foot or in an auto would callout or blow the horn, Mr. Wood would always return the greeting with a wave and a smile. I can never remember not seeing this gentleman without a smile on his face.

The stately home of Woodson Lewis, Jr. is located on a key corner site at the main entrance to Greensburg from the north. This house was built by Alex Marshall and completed in 1904 for Woodson Lewis Sr. An architect designed the house using plans by Lewis's wife.

The Woodson Lewis house of today is the best of a very few local examples of Neo-Colonial architecture, a style originating in the 1880's that attempted to recreate the charms of early American buildings. The "T" shaped, two-story house is also unusually well preserved. The wooden exterior detail includes narrow weatherboarding, typical of the style, a dentiled cornice, oversized keystones over the first-floor windows, Palladian windows in two dormers, and two-columned porches. Woodson Lewis, Sr. died August 13, 1931 and ownership of the property passed to Woodson Lewis, Jr. The home is still standing on North Main Street.

The first home of Woodson Lewis, Sr. was a two-story wooden construction, on the same location as the present home, accented by a front porch with the roof being supported by four square wooden columns. When moved to South Second Street, renovations include: (1) Center window was 5removed from the second floor. (2) The two first floor doors were converted to windows and a central door was added. The original home was moved to South Second Street sometime in 1902, when preliminary work and construction began on the present structure. Newspaper accounts of the moving of the old residence and construction of the new residence are listed below. The following is an EXACT translation from the related newspaper articles!!

August 11, 1899   Woodson Lewis had a well drilled at his place this week by Mr. Paxton and water was reached at a depth of 30 feet.

May 16, 1902	Rock and lumber is being placed on the ground for the new resident to be built for Lewis on the site of his present home. The new building will be a handsome modern structure and will replace a notable old landmark.
June13, 1902	Some of the rooms in the Cowherd Hotel were decorated by O. A. Fulton this week, and Woodson Lewis will soon move in to reside while his new residence is being built.
August 1, 1902	Alex Robinson as experienced considerable trouble in moving the Woodson Lewis residence to make room for the new edifice, but has it nearly out of the way now, and will soon begin the rock work for the foundation.
September 12, 1902	Alex Robinson has the old Woodson Lewis residence nearly on its foundation. He found house moving no easy job and has learned a lot throughout the hardest of teacher's experience.
September 19, 1902	The work of laying of the foundation for Woodson Lewis new residence has been commenced.
January 1, 1903	Mrs. Mary E. Shreve has rented the former residence of Woodson Lewis which was moved to the lot near the Academy.

January 26, 1903   Work is progressing nicely on the Woodson
                          Lewis residence.

The following is a series of photos depicting the Woodson Lewis
residence from 1902 through 2010.

<u>Pictured here are Woodson Lewis Sr. standing.</u>
<u>Woodson Lewis, Jr. in basket</u>
<u>Archibald Lewis in black hat on left</u>
<u>William Lewis standing next to Woodson Lewis, Sr.</u>
<u>Woodson Lewis, Jr. mother on right</u>

Original Lewis house, moved in 1902
from North Main Street to South Second Street
Greensburg, KY

**The new Woodson Lewis home as originally constructed in 1904.
One of the children sitting on the steps are sisters
Minnie Brummal & Hortense Lewis**

The two young ladies in the are sisters Minnie Brummal
and Hortense Lewis. Circa 1912

Photo taken in the winter, revealing the snow
covered ground and icy trees.
Date of photo unknown

The Woodson Lewis home 2010

Mr. Wood was a small man in terms of masculine build, standing about 5' 6" tall, but his intellect and presence was that of a giant. The

**The stately home of Ruth "Ruthie" Brummal (Lewis) Derrick
April 2022**

Mayor of Greensburg, Mr. Bill Taylor, remarked at the time of Mr. Wood's death, "There was an air of greatness about the little man who stood so tall and straight, lived in the big house on the corner and to all of us was about all there was to the Woodson Lewis store." While serving in the army, he qualified for West Point via academic testing at Fort Sam Houston, Texas. He entered West Point in 1919 and graduated as a Second Lieutenant, U S Army in 1923.

He served five years in the military relative to his obligation for a West Point education. Thereafter, he chose not to pursue a military career and returned to Greensburg to work in the family business. One might wonder why he would give up a promising military career to return to hometown and be totally emerged in the family business. It was easy to determine that he was part of a very proud family that loved Greensburg and he viewed that as being very important in what he could do the city.

In 1928 Mr. Wood returned to Greensburg to head the mercantile company his grandfather had founded in 1828. He introduced a philosophy that households could purchase furniture from Woodson Lewis' store with little money down (sometimes nothing) and a promise to pay later. Enough of the promises were kept so that the practice continued into a time when helping young people get a start in housekeeping almost became a lost art.

I distinctly remember that a management style of Mr. Wood would be that after the customer had purchased their furniture, he would tell the couple, "Go pick out a couple of lamps or go pick out a couple of end tables to go with your new furniture." I have witnessed this thoughtfulness many times, as my dad was the Railway Express Agent in Greensburg, he would deliver new furniture from the train to the store and often we would overhear this conservation with the customer and Mr. Wood when the offer of free merchandise would be expressed.

Cadet Woodson Lewis at West Point
circa 1920

In addition to managing a successful business, he was quite involved in public service such as (1) Serving on the Town of Greenburg Board of Trustees 1930, (2) Elected Town Clerk in October 1939, and was re-elected four times to serve, (3) Appointed to the Greensburg Town Council in 1948, (4) Served as the Chairman of the Board of Trustees for the Town of Greenburg 1950 to 1952. His leadership as Chairman of Trustees led to the Kentucky Legislative made Greensburg a fifth-class city and he automatically became a member of Greensburg's City Council.

From 1957 thru 1977, he served as the President of The Peoples Bank and Trust Company. From 1977 thru 2007 he served as a director of the bank. At the time of his retirement, bank officials paid tribute to Mr. Wood as loyal and faithful and noted that during his tenure with the bank the institution's assets grew from $300 thousand to $21 Million. At the time of his death, he was Director Emeritus of the Bank.

His other public service included (1) A founder of the Industrial Foundation, (2) A charter member and past president of the Greensburg Rotary Club, (3) Served as a member of the Draft Board during World War II, (4) Served in World War I, (5) A member of the American Legion and (6) Served as Elder of the Greensburg Presbyterian Church.

Mr. Wood was born October 31, 1897 in Green County, the son of the late Woodson Lewis, Sr, and Willis Taylor Lewis and died August 14, 1984 in the McDowell Wing of Jane Todd Crawford Hospital at the age of 86. Foster and Jones Funeral Home was in charge of the arrangements. Funeral services were held on August 15, 1984 at the Greensburg Presbyterian Church with the Rev. James E. Evans officiating.

His Pallbearers were Charles Derrick, Mitch Lewis, Lyn Griffiths, Tom Griffiths, Mike Griffiths and Garland Russell.

The Honorary Pallbearers were H. H. Durham, Coleman Paxton, Jim Durham, Harry Gilkerson, Sam Moore II, Morris Butler, J. B. Henderson, Don Mitchell and Leo Christi. This group of gentlemen was derived from local business associates and loyal employees. Mr. Wood was interned in the Greensburg City Cemetery.

Yes, this is a story about people and events that occurred in my youth, but it's more than that. It's a tribute to a great American, who served with distinction as a great father, compassionate business owner, community minded citizen.

Well, what happens now? The building that housed the Woodson Lewis Store from 1900 until October 11, 1991, when the property was transferred to a group of local investors and was subsequently transferred to Historic Greensburg, Inc. on October 18, 1991, thus recorded in Deed Book 167, Page 302. The building continues to serve the community with distinction now as "Glover's Station Antique Mall." Well, let's talk about Glover's Station!!!!

Glover's Station

Before there was a Glover's Station, there was a Green County. The county center was named Glover's Station in 1780 and once the county name became Green, the county seat was named Greensburg. Green County was formed in 1792 from portions of Lincoln and Nelson counties. Green was the sixteenth county in order of formation. The first post office arrived in 1807 and was variously known as "Greensburg" and "Greensburg Court House" during the early 19th century. The county is named for Revolutionary War Hero General Nathanael Greene, but the reason the final "e" is missing is unknown.

The Woodson Lewis store originally began business in 1928. The county center was named **"Glover's Station"** in 1780 after its founder John Glover.

The current owner of record A small point of clarification here: The name **"Glover's"** is derived from the founder's name and **"Station"** at this time in history was defined as "a single-family log home that was at least one and one-half stories high with "gun ports" constructed in the walls and thick wooden doors and shutters that could be barred from the inside."

Appendix I

LINEAGE - MAJOR EVENTS IN WOODSON LEWIS' FAMILY

<u>"It is not the author's intent to display a factual history of the Lewis family, but merely to present a flow of events, descendents, marriages, etc. that led to the success, grace and importance of this family and their impact on the city of Greensburg and Green County."</u>

Year	Name	Event
1803	William Lewis	Born 23 July 1803-Pittsylvania County, Virginia. Died March 31,1890.
1828	William Lewis	(1) Came to Green County Associated with firm of Allen, Brawner & Carlile (WL Store). (2) Purchased Allen, Brawner & Carlile.
1834	William Lewis	Married Polly Grove 20 August 1834. Polly born 1 April 1816, died 5 July 1835. William & Polly has one daughter, Mary G. Lewis, married J. C. Buchanan 21 October 1852.
1835	Mary G. Lewis	Daughter of William & Polly, born 26 June 1835. Died 17 December 1898.
1840	William Lewis	Married Ann West Carlisle,11 March 1840. Ann West born 10 August 1823, died 6 March 1909. Nine children were born to this union.

| 1841 | John William Lewis | (1) | (Son) Born 14 October 1841. Married Elizabeth Phillips 20 June 1877. died 20 December 1913. (No information on Elizabeth Phillips) One daughter Mary Lewis Magnet |

| 1843 | Archibald Lewis | (2) | (Son) Born 5 June 1843, died 31 October 1922. |

| 1845 | Elizabeth P. Lewis | (3) | (Daughter) Born 25 October 1945, died 2 April 1927. Married Frank Baldwin 28 August 1879.To this union two children were born. William Lewis Baldwin. Born 15 June 1881. Edith Baldwin Conway. Born 29 May 1883. |

| 1848 | Thomas E. Lewis | (4) | (Son) Born 18 February 1848, died 21 November 1882. Married Sallie P Hawkins on 27 July 1880. |

| 1850 | Henry Carlile Lewis | (5) | (Son) Born 13 April 1850, died 15 November 1900. Married Mary Hicks. To this union two children were born. Mary Carlile Lewis. Born 28 January 1897. Catherine Lewis. Born 23 January 1899. |

| 1853 | Ann Mariah Lewis | (6) | (Daughter) Born 1 April 1853. Married Levi Taylor. To this union two children were born. Henry S. Tyler & Ann Carlile. |

| 1856 | Charles Woodson Lewis | **(7)** | Born 11 January 1853. Died 13 August 1931. Burial in Greensburg Cemetery. Married Willia Taylor. To this union four children were born. William T. Lewis, Woodson Lewis, Minnie Brummal and Hortense Lewis. |

This is the first time the Brummal name
Has entered into the Lewis lineage.

(a) (Son) William T. Lewis. Born in
1895. Married Ruth Lingle 23 Oct
1923. William killed in car wreck
in 1926. One son was born to this
union.

(b) (Son) Woodson Lewis, Jr. born
August 31, 1897. Married
Geraldine Miller. Woodson Jr. died
August 14, 1984. Geraldine died
July, 1993.

(c) Minnie Brummal

(d) Hortense Lewis Married to
William T. Chaudon (daughter of
Charles Woodson Lewis)

1861	Hortense Lewis	(8)	Daughter of William Lewis & Ann West Carlile
	James Carlile Lewis	(9)	Born 28 January 1863. Died 4 July 1929/To this union two children were born. Matilda Francis & James Carlile Lewis, born 13 January 1901 who married Mary Francis Beale
1861	Morgan's Raiders		Raided and ransacked store and rode away with piece goods streaming in the wind. No one was shot or injured as far as my research shows.
	Woodson Lewis, Sr.		Son, of William Lewis, came in business with his father.

1863	James Carlisle Lewis	(Son) Born 1863 Son of Woodson Lewis Sr.
1868	Minnie M. Taylor,	Daughter of Josiah Taylor, who was, in his day, one of the most successful oil men of Green County, married John Y. Taylor. One child "Willie" was born from this union, who afterwards became the wife of Woodson Lewis and "after a few years of happy sweet life, "shedding her light wherever she could" was called to the home above, where she would welcome her mother, Minnie".

Mrs. Lewis ("Willie") and Woodson Lewis left four children.

1. William Lewis died 31 May 1889
2. Woodson Lewis, Jr. 1897
3. Minnie Brummal Lewis
4. Hortense Lewis

Memo: Mrs. Taylor's brothers were John M. Brummal of Columbia and Joe H. Brummal of Greensburg. From this point forward the name "Brummal" began to appear in the Lewis family tree.

1878	William Lewis	(1) Began to acquire additional property.
1889	William Lewis	(2) Died 31 May,1889.

1897	Woodson Lewis, (Jr)	Born October 31,1897 to Woodson Lewis Sr. and Willia Taylor Lewis. Died 14 August 1984. His father was Woodson Lewis. His Mother Willia Elizabeth Lewis. Spouse Geraldine Miller Lewis.
1901	Minnie Brummal Lewls	Born 1901. First married to Robert Pendelton then Married Jack Allen Sanders June 2, 1933. Died May 20, 1938. No children were born to this union. A more detailed version of this marriage may be seen in the chapter entitled "Jack Allen Sanders".
1902	Hortense Lewis	Married W. P. Chaudoan Hortense died 1939. To this union two children were born. William Lewis Chadoan & George Woodson Chadoan.
1904	Willia (Taylor) Lewis	Died 4 July,1904.
1919	Woodson Lewis, Jr.	Entered West Point 1919. Graduated 1923.
1922	Minnie M. (Taylor) Lewis	Married Mr. John Y. Taylor, to which union was born, Willie Elizabeth Taylor. Willie became the wife of Woodson Lewis. Mrs. Lewis left four children, William Lewis, Woodson Lewis Jr., Minnie Brummal Lewis and Hortense Lewis, ages ranging from two to eight years of age. Mrs. Taylor was the daughter of Mr. Josiah Taylor, who was in his day, operated one of the most successful oil businesses in Green County. Born 22 November 1848. Died 13 January,1922.

1926	William T. Lewis	Born 1895. Died October 1926. Married Ruth Lingle. To this union two children were born. Woodson Lewis lll and Elizabeth Condor Lewis.
1927		Hortense Elizabeth Lewis, born July 20,1927 Married William Chadoan. To this union, two children were born. William Lewis Chadoan & George Woodson Chadoan.
1930		Lewis Jr. married Mary Geraldine Miller 24 August 1930. Three children were born to this union. Woodson takes over the management of the store.
1931	Anne C. Lewis, daughter	Born 13 June 1931. Died September 23, 2003. Married Victor Griffiths 1955 and to this union five children were born.

(1) Elizabeth Brummal Griffiths married Jim Murphy (Reside in Crestwood, Ky)
(2) Leonard Victor Griffiths Died 22 October 2019.
(3) William Michael Griffiths
(4) Thomas Walter Griffiths married Allison Griffiths (Resides in Greensburg)
(5) Ann Carlile married John Fugua (Resides in Cincinnati)

| 1934 | (Son) William "Weasie" Lewis, | born Jan 15, 1934. Died Jan 10, 1993. Married Wanda Keltner, June 1958. To this union, two children were born. |

Gail West Lewis (born 1960) Married James Mitchell Bragg Oct 1991.

Woodson Mitchell Lewis - born 1962. Wife named Susie plus one daughter was born to this union.

1935   (Daughter) Ruth ("Ruthie") Brummal Lewis, born1935.

Married George Erwin Derrick in 1960. (Derrick, a retired Colonel, US Army) died July 9, 2008. To this union two children were born, Mary Brummal Derrick, born 1963. Died 1987. Charles Erwin Derrick born 19 January 1961.

1955   Anne Lewis Griffith,   born 13 June 1931, did 23 Sept 2003

1958   William "Weasie"   Married Wanda Keltner, June 1958. To
        Lewis   this union two children were born. Daughter, West Lewis married James Mitchell Bragg in October 1991. Son, Woodson Mitchell Lewis Gail West Lewis. She changed her name to Gail West and married Bragg.

1962   Woodson Mitchell Lewis. Born 1962.

1964   Woodson Mitchell Lewis. Married Susie Hall.

1984   Woodson Lewis Jr. died 14 Aug 1984

1987   Mary Brummal Derrick died 1987.

1993   William "Weasie" Lewis, died 10 January 1993.

1993   Geraldine (Miller) Lewis died 4 July 1993.

2003   Anne Lewis Griffith died 23 September 2003

<u>Memo</u>

The research that produced the above was from various sources. All was of public record. This presentation of dates and people in the Lewis family is not intended to be a through documented lineage but merely a rough cut as to the pertinent dates and people they will fit the story as presented. My thanks to Ruthie Brummal (Lewis) Derrick who has been of great assistance in aligning the lineage.

Appendix 2

COMMENTS RELATED TO THE LEWIS FAMILY LINEAGE

1828

William Lewis, came to Green County from Pennsylvania County, Virginia and was first associated with the firm Allen, Brawner and Carille. Mr. Lewis purchased this firm and continued to operate the business under his own name. All commodities associated with a general store were sold including clothing, yard goods, hardware, furniture and appliances. Initially the firm also carried grocery items, wagons and buggies, and even Chevrolet automobiles. The firm was then located in a building occupying the site of the present Corner Drug Store.

William Lewis was later joined by his brother, Thomas Lewis, and the firm was then known as William Lewis and Brother.

1861

During the Civil Warm Morgan's Raiders visited Greensburg, ransacked the store and destroyed property. Then the vandals tied bolts of calico to the horns of their saddles and let the material unwind in the dirt behind them as they were leaving town.

1878

In the years following the war, Mr. William Lewis started acquiring property on the south side of the square, and celebrated the fiftieth anniversary during the administration of Rutherford B. Hayes

1890

Mr. William Lewis died May 31, 1890 and was succeeded by his son Woodson Lewis, Sr. who named the firm Woodson Lewis.

1900

During the proprietorship of Woodson Lewis, Sr. a disastrous fire (April 20, 1900) started in an adjacent building and quickly spread to other buildings, completely destroying some buildings and damaged the Woodson Lewis store. Salvaged merchandise was subsequently sold from a temporary location on the north side of the square.

Woodson Lewis Sr. began construction of a new brick building, still standing at the present time. The brick was made on the Lewis farm on Buckner's Hill. The building was constructed in the fashion of that day, i.e. being an iron-front building. The walls of the building are 16" thick and have never leaked or cracked. The most imposing commercial structure on the public square is the Woodson Lewis Furniture Company building. The façade features a metal parapet-cornice and a metal storefront, both manufactured in Evansville, Indiana.

The façade also includes stone lintels over the windows. The long side heights and decorative brick panels at the third story. The Woodson Lewis Company annex was constructed sometime between 1908 and 1919. The two-story frame structure was sheathed with tin pressed to resemble stonework. The plate glass storefront and tin pilasters and cornice are original to the building.

Appendix 3

VARIOUS DATES OF RELATIVE IMPORTANCE

1919

Woodson Lewis Jr. entered West Point.

1923

Woodson Lewis Jr. graduated West Point and served five years in the US Military.

1924

Wednesday, August 13,1924 the old homestead of Woodson Lewis, Sr, about a mile northwest of town was in flames. The entire structure was destroyed. John Crumption, who was residing in the house seceded in saving most of his household effects but lost his crop of some 60 bushels of wheat.

1926

William Lewis died in 1926.

1928

Woodson Lewis Jr. left the military and returned to Greensburg to manage Woodson Lewis store.

1931

The stock of goods at Woodson Lewis was sold Monday September 10, 1931 to Mrs. Robert W. Pendleton for $23,000. The store will continue to be operated under the name of Woodson Lewis.

1931

After the death of Charles Woodson Lewis, Sr., Woodson Lewis, Jr. bought the store and operated it until his death on August 14, 1984.

1991

Building sold to a group of local businessmen on October 11, 1991. See Lewis Store History for other transactions

1847-1996

Fifty-six articles about Woodson Lewis store, etc. appeared in seven different newspapers.

The store and its activities, new products, sales, promotions etc. were publicized in such newspapers as The Courier-Journal (April 27, 1847), The Baltimore Sun (April 30, 1847), Greensburg Times (several news item from April 21, 1886 thru February 23, 1888), Adair News (September 18, 1901 plus six other times), Green County Record (Numerous articles) Record - Herald, numerous articles From 1847 thru 1938. Greensburg Record - Herald, numerous articles from 1966 thru 1996. The Green County Record, Record-Herald and Greensburg Record - Herald are the same newspaper, the names have just changed over the years.

A Most Important Event

There are many important events in the life of the Lewis family and some of them have produced here in the previous paragraphs. On March 6, 1996, I would say was the last most important talked about and attended event in this modern age was the auctioning of the inventory and fixtures by the Durrett Realty Company. The building was absolutely jam packed with would be purchasers and some just wanted to attend this historic event. Auctioneers Todd Durrett and Mike Bottoms did an excellent job in keeping the bidding organized in the crowded building.

Finis Durrett relayed numerous events of the past and particularly recalled an event where he came to the store one day with his dad and Mr. Wood quietly and seemingly unnoticed except for a small wink slipped a pocketknife in his pocket as a gift. This was the kind of man Mr. Wood was.

His business practice, as previously noted was to benefit every customer.

On this sale day, the highest item sold was an attractive roll top desk which brought $1,500. An old gasoline engine brought $300. An elaborate set of scales went for $170 and a sweeper, brand name National purchased in 1904 cost $37 now bid in at $360.

The large antique 300 pound National Cash Register which sold for $2,500 in 19623 brought only $600.

A hand made porch swing with a woven seat. Bidding was fast and quickly sold for $300 to an antique dealer who reportedly planned to double his money.

Over the years, Woodson Lewis store has sold from dry goods, groceries, machinery, seed, lime, fertilizer, hardware, furniture, automobiles, and most likely other items as well.

At the auction, Mitch Lewis, grandson of Woodson and Geraldine Lewis noted that the business was not permanently closing and was being relocated to Buckner's Hill, which incidentally was the location of where the bricks were made for the original building on the Lewis farm in 1900.

Well, after the auction, what's next? As we have come from the 1940's and 50's (well, really from 1803), it seems that a pretty good span of history has been covered. Will we remember it? Probably not. Oh, we'll hear bits and pieces from stories of the past, but as those of us born in the 1930's die off, the younger generation will only have publications like this one to really understand "Mr. Wood" and who he was. People will look at the Woodson Lewis sign on the side of the building and wonder, "Who was Woodson Lewis?" as the business is now Glovers Station Mall.

The Woodson Lewis Store History
A chronological listing of the Woodson Lewis Lot and
Store History from 1796 through 2021 is listed below

LOT 7, EARLY HISTORY

1796 Aug 9 DB 1 p100	Jacob White deeded ¼ of Lot 7 by Trustees
1800 Sep 2 DB 2 p201	Jacob White to Richard Morrow
1801 Jun 16 DB 2 p279	Richard Morrow to Thomas Marshall
1812 Jan 11 DB 6 p261	Thomas Marshall to Edward Bullock
1818 Jun 16 DB 8 p319	Edward Bullock to Thomas S. T. Moss and Thomas Hargrove
1819 Jun 3 DB 9 p100	Thomas Hargrove ½ interest to Edward Bullock
1821 Jun DB 10 p156	Thomas S. T. Moss mortgages his property
1822 Jun 17 DB 10 p 268-270	Property is sold to pay mortgage debt, Thomas S. T. Moss to William Gray Mentions tavern house on property operated by Moss

LEWIS STORE HISTORY

1828 Brief History	William Lewis purchased firm of Allen, Brawner, and Carlile at the corner of Cross (Court) Street and the square, later location of Corner Drug Store
Date unknown	Thomas Lewis, brother of William, joins the firm
1847 Apr 18 newspaper	Fire destroyed W. Barnett's storehouse occupied by W. Lewis store
1874 about His obituary	Thomas A. Lewis retired from the business
1878 Brief History	Business at present location by this year (unverified by me, but all the written history of the business says this)
1884 Nov 13	Thomas A. Lewis died

1886 Jun 23 RH	Lewis & Lewis, business name in store ad Howell & Allen store also ran an ad
1890 Mar 31	William Lewis died
1890 Apr 22	Will of William Lewis recorded with the courts, estate divided, no mention of store
1893 Apr 11 DB 35 p517	**Woodson Lewis bought corner lot and store from B. W. Penick and his wife and M. M. Taylor for $1,850.** Mentions property was owned by Thomas S. T. Moss, then Josiah Brummal, then to Penick.
1896 Jan 17 RH	Woodson Lewis and Howell, Allen & Co established the Greensburg Buggy Co. The carriage sale room was built on the same lot that Goff Motors was built years later, on North Main Street.
1896 Nov 20 RH	Howell, Allen & Co. have closeout sale *(on corner lot in photo A)* R. L. Durham passed law exam to become an attorney *(next door in photo B)*
1899 Jan 6 RH	J. M. Howell bought Dr. O. H. Shively's drug store in the southwest corner of the square *(next door in photo B)* *(Note the two 1800s photos of the corner building that shows signs for these businesses. The photo with the Woodson Lewis sign (Photo B) had to have been taken Jan 1899-Apr 1900 when the building burned.)*
	*Considering all available information including newspaper clippings, deeds, maps, and photos, I would say Woodson Lewis moved into the corner building after Howell, Allen & Co. left. BUT WHEN? ***IF we assume that Howell, Allen & Co. stayed in that building until they closed in 1896, then Woodson Lewis would have moved there sometime between December 1896 and March 1900 when that building burned.** ***IF, however, Howell, Allen & Co. moved from the corner building at some earlier point, then we cannot closely estimate a date for Woodson Lewis moving his store there.**
1900 Apr 20 RH	Fire destroyed the Woodson Lewis store on the corner and other buildings
1900 Dec RH	The rebuilt store was completed on the same lot
1901 Mar RH	James C. Lewis, brother, locates in Greensburg and joins the business Name becomes Woodson Lewis & Brother
1905 May 22 RH	James C. Lewis left the business
1922 Feb 24 RH	First ad for Woodson Lewis & Son

1931 Aug 13	Woodson Lewis Sr. died
1931 Sep 10 RH article	Mrs. Robert Pendleton buys stock Store will operate under Woodson Lewis name
1931 Sep 14	Will of Woodson Lewis Sr. recorded with the courts, estate divided in equal parts among heirs. Stipulates that Woodson Lewis Jr. is to operate the store as long as he wishes.
1932 Dec 7 DB 64 p441	All Woodson Lewis Sr. properties officially deeded to his heirs. His grandchildren, Woodson Lewis III and Elizabeth Conder Lewis, received the store property.
1938 Aug 1 RH	Had a sale of goods, furniture, etc. to settle partnership, Woodson Lewis Jr. becomes surviving partner in business.
1980 Nov 6	Woodson Lewis III died
1980 Nov 11	Will of Woodson Lewis III recorded with the courts, estate to his wife Norma Jean.
1984 Mar 21 DB 148 p161	Widow of Woodson Lewis III, Norma Jean Lewis, deeds the half interest in the store property she inherited from her husband to her son, William Woodson Lewis.
1984 Aug 14	Woodson Lewis Jr. died William "Weasie" Lewis became president of the business.
1991 Sep 18 RH	The store building was put up for sale by Lewis heirs. The business will move to the one-story adjoining building when sold by William "Weasie" Lewis.
1991 Oct 11 DB 167 p295	Property purchased from William Wood Lewis and Conder Lewis Tucker by this group: Sam Moore, Garth Bobrowski, Joe Miller, Bill Rogers, Joe DeSpain, Howard Moore, Rod Moore, Jim Frank
1991 Oct 18 DB 167 p302	Property transferred from group to Historic Greensburg, Inc.
1992 Nov RH	Glover's Station Antique Mall opened in the Lewis building
1996 Mar RH	Lewis auction of inventory and fixtures, Woodson Lewis business has moved to Buckner Hill
2021 PVA office	Property still owned by Historic Greensburg, Inc. 121 South Public Square 100x110\WOODSON LEWIS STORE

Pictures of the Woodson Lewis Family homes
and businesses are listed below:

Storefront of current structure plus Annex

Storefront of original Woodson Lewis Store

People in the picture above are from left to right: Unknown, Unknow, Pilson Smith (A), H.L. "Pal Joe" Taylor (B) Bram Penick, Two Little Boys - Lawrence Hagan, Otis Moss (C), Baby, Mary Lewis, man beside baby - Henry Lewis, Woodson Lewis, Man in Window Upstairs, Judge Hamilton. Next doorway, Jim Anderson, Dr. Omar Shively. The boy in the straw hat, <u>Joe Perry (D).</u> Next doorway, Jim Howell.

During the proprietorship of Woodson Lewis, Sr., a disastrous fire started in an adjacent drug store and quickly spread to include the other buildings on the south side of the Square, destroying them.

From the Lewis Store, some of the merchandise was salvaged and the goods were subsequently sold from a temporary location on the south side of the square.

<u>Memo:</u>

Spelling and punctation is presented as printed in the publication of the picture. Identify and a little history of the people (noted above as A, B, C, D)

(A) Pilson Smith, was later County Judge of Green County, elected in 1941 and served 12 years. (B) "Pal Joe" Taylor is most likely "Joe Pal" Taylor, who worked for Woodson Lewis, Jr. for over fifty years. (C) Otis Moss, operated a US mail route in the 1940's. The author remembers Mr. Moss, who with other mail carriers, A. T. "Tom" Wright included would their mail on a long table in back of the US Post Office which at that time was located on the corner of 1st Alley and Court Street. Mr. Moss had a home in Happyville as well as a camp in the county where he employed a full time cook and would invite gentlemen of Greensburg to spend a night at his cabin, eating excellent meals prepared by his cook and listening to hound dogs chase racoons throughout the night. (D) Joe Perry' home is still standing and as of this writing contains the offices of Durrett Realty Company on the corner of Main Street and Columbia Avenue.

Epilogue

Writing a story about "The Man" - "Mr. Wood", and his family has brought the author a lot of pleasure.

✣

A TRIBUTE TO GREENSBURG'S TALENTED ARTISTS

Pansy Phillips & Mildred Colvin

It would be extremely impolite to exit "Memories" without recognizing two of Greensburg's finest artists. Both have won numerous awards and are highly regarded professionals in the world or art.

Mrs. Pansy Phillips - Artist Extrodinare

This picture has relevance to me in that the three structures that form what I refer to as one of the biggest streets in Greensburg for businesses. The painting above was produced in 1990 by Pansy Phillips, a noted Greensburg artist. The businesses are depicted here have a strong family presence to the author in that my father operated the Railway Express Agency at the Depot. The Depot was built in 1913, provided passenger service until 1952 with freight service continued until 1980. Wagon in front was purchased by my father when the depot closed and we took it to or farm in the Thurlow community, where we placed in a pasture and used it to hold baled hay to feed the cattle. The wood finally rotted, and the metal remaining was given to the junk yard.

The building in the background on the far left is the Double-Cola Bottling Company which produced a variety of cold drinks, including "Double-Cola", the preferred soft drink of the 1940's and 1950's. Otherwise referred to as "Big Dub." Ski was also a big favorite "pop" produced from the Double Cola Bottling Plant.

The Bottling Company began its operation in March 1926. Soft drink products of the bottling company were Ward's Orange Crush, Lemon-Crush, Lime-Crush and Cocoa-Crush. The current building was constructed and manned in 1939. The building's new equipment included a bottle washer capable of washing 2000 bottles per hour. Mr. Gabe Taylor acquired the business prior to 1937.

The building to the right rear is the American Needlecraft which employed some 60 plus people in its heyday (98% women). The factory produced high quality pillows, comforters, bedspreads, etc. The company was once contracted to produce ranging in size from one foot square to six feet tall, cloth bananas, dice, apples and other fruit for the movie Top Banana, a musical. My mother, Morton (Blakeman) Wright was the plant manager for a number of years. The Needlecraft opening in 1944 by Mrs. R. L. Durham and moved to the present building in 1944. Ownership changed hands in 1964 to a Mr. L. F. M Schultz and Mr. Herman Swartz, natives of New York City. AM moved out of the building about 1967.

The street, barely shown to the right is Henry Street where mom, dad and I resided from 1942 until 1954. Mr. Gabe, Isobel and Jean Allen Taylor were our neighbors on Henry Street and Mr. Gabe was most gracious to young lads wanting a summer job, as he was to me. He employed me for one summer in 1952 and I rode with a Mr. Armon Vaught delivering soft drinks to Columbia, Ky and surrounding communities. In 1956, Mr. Gabe Taylor announced his retirement and Mr. "Jodie" DeSpain became the President. The Greensburg Bottling Company ceased operation 1n 2004.

An additional exquisite painting by Pansy. This painting belonged to Omar & Maxine Shuffett And is now in the possession of Fran & George Stround (Daughter & Son-In-Law of the Shuffetts)

Pansy is a most extraordinary, multi-talented person. Having had the privilege to know Pansy, it is an understatement to say, "She was an outstanding Greensburg resident.

She was a most extraordinary, multi-talented person. She was an artist, founder of the local art club, mentor to many fledging artist, local historian, former teacher (art, elocution and general education), defense worker during World War II and a master of life.

Her life's experiences had taken her first to the Pacific Coast where she worked for Lockheed Aircraft in the building of P-38 bombers, then to the Atlantic Coast where she went to capture the land and seascape on canvas.

Following her graduation from Greensburg High School in 1928, she enrolled for the summer at the Conservatory of Music and Expression in Louisville. She returned to Greensburg where she taught art and expression, coached high school plays and performed in local talent and variety shows. She then journeyed to Bowling Green, Ky. where she attained a teaching certificate through her studies at Western Kentucky Teachers College and returned home to teach, first at Webb, and then in Greensburg. Pansy described the end of her teaching career as, "Trying to cram unwanted learning into heads totally satisfied that they had already arrived was total frustration."

Her later public work experience including as a referral agent for W. P. A., her job as a ticket seller at the Franklin Theatre, and a shopkeeper where her work as an artist and that of friends was sold. In 1950 she began to teach art, and this turned into the Greensburg Art Club. She related her drawing began when she was old enough to hold a pencil but that she lacked the "will and determination" to be a great artist.

She was active in church and community activities. She taught a Sunday School class for 35 years at the Greensburg Methodist Church, served on church boards and as church historian and was a member of the United Methodist Women. She was a charter member of the Green County Historical Society, founder and member of the Art Club, Friend of the Library, Friend of Horse Cave Theatre and a member of several committees that prepared Greensburg's All Kentucky City presentation.

In her book, *The Land Beyond the Mountains*, noted Kentucky writer, the late Janice Holt Giles included this dedicatory statement to Pansy, "But here's the joy, my friend and I are one."

Thank you Pansy, for having been among us and left your knowledge and color presentation for us to enjoy for generations to come.

Mrs. Mildred Colvin - Artist Extrodinare

This painting was produced by Mrs. Mildred Colvin, another most talented resident artist of Greensburg, Ky.

This picture portrays the L&N Depot in the center, the footbridge to downtown Greensburg on the far left under the big tree and The American Needlecraft on the right. The street in the center is Depot Street.

Mildred was a professional in the true sense of the word. In addition, she was a most gracious lady, friendly and outgoing. Mildred began seriously painting in 1959, and for many years sold her work through Colvin's Art Gallery which she had established on Columbia Highway.

She was best known for her works that concentrated on the scenes and people of Kentucky. She was proficient in landscapes, street scenes, still life, portraits, character studies and seascapes.

She worked in various media, through oils and watercolors were her specialties. She was a charter member of the Kentucky Watercolor Society and became a charter member of that organization in 2002 when she won the People's Choice Award for her painting, "Shelling on Sanibel."

She won numerous awards throughout her career, and featured in shows in Greensburg, Campbellsville, Columbia,

Louisville, Lexington and numerous other venues. Appearances in such magazines as "Kentucky Bankers Magazine" where one of her paintings appeared on the cover in August 1984, let to other opportunities. She was commissioned to do 48 paintings for banks in Central Kentucky. She was a longtime member of the Greensburg Art Club.

A true artist whose work will bring joy to owners of her art for ages.

A most beautiful presentation of flower by Mildred. This painting is now in possession of Fran & George Stroud (Daughter and Son-In-Law of the Shuffetts)

SECTION 11

FAMILY PHOTOS OF THE AUTHOR AND FAMILY - 1940'S & 1950'S

Dad & Mom (A.T. "Tom" & Morton Wright) Circa 1953

Dad standing by burley tobacco stalks on tobacco sticks. Tobacco plant 6' tall.

Dad standing by hay field circa1953   Mom sitting in back year circa 1954

Cattle grazing in pasture
on our farm   Mom in side yard
summer 1954

Dad in Illinois 1933

Christmas tree 1953

Bennie Lieux (boarder)
foot bridge 1952

W. T. Boyd Residence -
Henry Street 1952

<u>**Old Courthouse on Square in Greensburg 1952**</u>

<u>**Sophomore boys class - Greensburg High School 1951**</u>
<u>**Author on third row from bottom right side (white "T" shirt)**</u>
<u>**Greensburg's "Greensburg's Minnesota Fats" in Chapter**</u>
<u>**1 is David Blakeman Front row fifth from left.**</u>

Greensburg Basketball Team 1953
Front Row: L to R: William Earl Hendersn, Leo Wright,
Larry Gumm, J. R. Bishop, Billy Gumm
Back Row: L to R: O'Connell Milby, Milton
Williams, T. G. Bardin, James Lobb and
Willlis Leslie Elwood "Red" Jefferies

Leo playing basketball 1952   First Grade Class 1942 digging Victory
                                      Garden (Leo - left with "hoe")

The 1954 class of Greensburg High School had their 30 year class reunion last week at the TGT clubhouse in Gabe. Those attending the reunion were left to right: Charles Bale, Kenneth E. Harris, William Lewis Warren, Betty Lou (Pickett) Von Reitzenstein, Maxie Squires, Bobby Bale, Kenneth McAfee, David Lobb, Eyvonne (Jones) Lobb, Royal Mays (partially hidden), Doris Ann (Acree) Patterson, Annabelle (Akin) Henderson, William Earl Henderson, Fanola (Cox) Upton, Hobart H. Judd, Margie (English) Simpson, Leo Wright, James W. Lobb, Anne (Fitzgerald) Cobb, Arnold J. Shaikun and Roxy (Gilkeson) Anderson. Not pictured: Martha A. (Posey) Strader. R-H photo by Tom Stone.

<u>Senior Class of 1954 - class reunion 1984</u>

Interesting isn't it, how we are all
intertwined in a small town!!!!!

These pictures were not taken in the 1950's but
hold a special place in author's heart

Top Photo

In September 1961, along with some 2500 other Army Reservists belonging to Kentucky's own 100th Training Division were called to active duty with the mission to reopen Fort Chaffee, an army post just outside Fort Smith, Arkansas for the purpose of conducting basic training, advanced individual training and to operate various military related schools.

As a member of the 100th Division, I made my way to Fort Chaffee and soon thereafter purchased a house trailer and moved it to Fort Smith to serve as our living quarters and then brought my family to Fort Smith where we rented a space to park our trailer at 2700 South 56th Street along with two other families, one of them was another soldier stationed at Ft. Chaffee and the other was the wife of soldier currently serving in Korea.

As I was pulling into the driveway upon my return home from work one cold winter day late in 1961, I spied my two lovely children all bundled up to ward off the cold, Angela age four on the left and Susan age two on the right waiting for me on the front stoop. Now the photography may not be the best, but it was a great sight for me. I was warmly welcomed with tender hugs and kisses and have cherished this grainy photo ever since. Love you girls!!!!!!!

Bottom Photo

Fast forward from 1961 to 2016, this beautiful young lady is my great granddaughter Mya Shea Bell, age five. She is dutifully placing rose pedals on the aisle awaiting the wedding procession of my grandson Woody Back and his beautiful bride to be Amanda. Young man in background is unknown as well as gentleman seated to the right.

As always, Mya was exceptionally proficient in her duties and received a rousing round of applause from the wedding attendees upon completion of her duties. I love you Mya Shea!!!!!!

ONE FINAL TRIBUTE TO MY BEAUTIFUL WIFE WHO IS GONE FROM US IN BODY ONLY AND FOREVER REMAINS IN OUR THOUGHTS AND PRAYERS

A Summer For "J"

Summer emerges slowly after winter and spring
And when it arrives, it's such a wonderful thing
Now I know you like trees and sun
Then a walk in the summer is surely a lot of fun
The sky above is usually bule
With a soft warm breeze and lazy cloud or two
If you go to a park you can watch the squirrels
As they run for the food and go 'round in swirls
Families bring food baskets of tasty treats
While they watch the children perform acrobatic feats
A frisbie will be tossed and soar through the air
And young'uns will chase it as if they didn't have a care
Now an Otters game is a pleasant place to go
To relax in the shade and just watch the show
Players throw and bat and slide and scream
But they're just tryin' to win for the ole' home team
Swimming is good and really make you work
Then you swallow water and cough and you feel like a jerk
You can also sit in the sun and read
But the skin will burn if the lotion you don't heed
The rain will come and freshen the air
And the coolness will make you feel as if climbing the stair
After the rain you see a colorful arc in the sky
And J & I will hold hands as we slowly stroll by
There ae many many things that you can do
But you suddenly look around and summer's all through
Now fall and winter will have their space
But the summer will come again and brown your beautiful face

a summer for j.docx   leo wright

Penned by Leo Wright

-----To **Joyce**, The sunshine has warmed your skin. The gentle wind has dried your tears. The gales of hope and love has kept you safe from harm. The rain has cooled you from the heat of the day. And until we meet again, may God protect and keep you. All my love!!!!! (Leo Wright - 2017)

<u>Goodbye everyone and thank you</u>
<u>for reading "Memories"</u>

Printed in the United States
by Baker & Taylor Publisher Services

Printed in the United States
by Baker & Taylor Publisher Services